MW01518712

Old Church Slavic Reader

OLD CHURCH SLAVIC READER

Francis J. Whitfield

Edited by

Henning Andersen & Michael S. Flier

Commentary by Michael S. Flier

Berkeley Slavic Specialties
2004

Published in the United States by

Berkeley Slavic Specialties
P.O. Box 3034
Oakland, California 94609-0034

http://www.berkslav.com

ISBN: 1-57201-065-7

Dedicated to
the students of Slavic 210
and to
Celina Whitfield

PREFACE

Francis J. Whitfield designed his *Old Church Slavic Reader* as a convenient one-year graduate-level introduction to the phonology, morphology, syntax, and lexicon of Old Church Slavic (hereafter OCS), the oldest written form of Slavic. He first issued the *Reader* in the fall of 1962 for Slavic 210, the introductory OCS course required of all entering graduate students in Slavic languages and literatures at the University of California, Berkeley. Rendered in Whitfield's distinctive hand-printed letters, the *Reader* contained the basic elements of OCS grammar together with reading selections from the OCS canon and a glossary. The schematic grammar was intended to serve as an outline, with direct references to the two modern OCS textbooks Whitfield valued most highly, *Altkirchenslavische Grammatik* (2 vols. in 1) by Paul Diels (Heidelberg, 1932, 1963 [2nd ed.]) and *Manuel du vieux slave* (2 vols.) by André Vaillant (Paris, 1948).

While acknowledging the significance of OCS for comparative Slavic linguistics and for the development of the various Slavic literary languages, Whitfield emphasized the study of OCS as a language in its own right. In his view, students of Slavic needed to gain mastery of OCS as a coherent linguistic system in theory and as an imperfectly transmitted medium in scribal practice. Comparison of the theoretical ideal with the language actually encountered in texts provided students with a rich philological experience that would serve them well in all future encounters with the Slavic text, whether in a linguistic or a literary setting. The numerous references to Vaillant's *Manuel* and Diels' *Grammatik* demonstrated the importance of knowing French and German for future research.

It is our purpose here to make Whitfield's *Reader* available to a wider audience of readers who wish to take advantage of his particular insights into the structure of OCS. Because it was intended as a guide and not a textbook, we have provided brief commentary on the use of the grammar, letting the book and the references speak for themselves. A corrected and augmented version of the *Reader* was produced around 1968 in typewritten form and included Whitfield's textual annotations. The present work is based on this improved and expanded version.

The publication of the *Reader* has been a collaborative effort and we wish to acknowledge here the contributions of those who have participated. At Harvard, Michael Flier edited and formatted the grammar and prepared four appendices, the first providing a prose exposition of the phonology, the second demonstrating the operation of the actualization rules, the third and fourth offering sample nominal and verbal paradigms, respectively. Michael Flier's assistant, Giorgio DiMauro, rendered the Greek texts into machine-readable format. At UCLA, Henning Andersen and his assistants, Katya Pertsov and Mel Strom, converted into digital form the OCS texts, the Greek, Latin, French, and Old High German parallels, Whitfield's notes to the texts, and the glossary, and did the final formatting. We are especially grateful to Gareth Perkins, who helped Whitfield revise and reproduce the 1968 version, for supplying the graphics illustrating the Old Church Slavic manuscripts and for printing the current edition.

No student who took Frank Whitfield's course in OCS will ever forget his inspirational teaching, his meticulous analysis of the data, and his magisterial command of OCS and its relationship to the other Slavic languages. It is with great pleasure that we dedicate this new edition to all of the many students fortunate enough to have taken Berkeley's Slavic 210 from the master himself and to Celina Whitfield, Frank's devoted wife and companion, who provided support and good humor all along the way.

Henning Andersen   *Michael S. Flier*
Los Angeles, Calif.   Cambridge, Mass.

CONTENTS

INTRODUCTION

Old Church Slavic (also Old Church Slavonic) is the name given to the language underlying the oldest written Slavic texts. Its emergence and subsequent history is bound up with the spread of Christianity among the Slavs and the role of the Byzantine church and state exerting their political and cultural influence in central and eastern Europe.

In 862, the Byzantine emperor Michael III received a request from Prince Rostislav of Great Moravia to send a teacher qualified to transmit Christian teachings to the Slavs in their own language. The emperor entrusted the task to the patriarchal librarian and scholar Constantine the Philosopher and his older brother Methodius, both because of their erudition and because they were natives of Thessaloniki, and thus bilingual in Greek and Slavic.

On the basis of their spoken Slavic dialect, the brothers were able to fashion Old Church Slavic (OCS) into a liturgical language, suitable for rendering primarily Greek texts vital to Christian worship and instruction and comprehensible to the Slavs of Moravia. They devised a new alphabet (glagolitic) and set about translating the Gospels, the Psalms, and other relevant Christian texts into OCS. Models of Greek syntax and lexical formation proved indispensable in fashioning previously nonexistent Slavic terms and constructions for this earliest written form of Slavic.

Arriving in Great Moravia around 863, they began to train followers for the priesthood. After some forty months, they made their way to Rome via Pannonia, where they attracted more pupils. They arrived in Rome in 867 in hopes of having their followers ordained as priests by the pope. The pontiff received them warmly and permitted the celebration of the Slavic mass in Saint Peter's Cathedral. While still in Rome, Constantine fell ill and on his deathbed took monastic vows under the name Cyril (869).

Following initial successes in Great Moravia and Pannonia, the persecuted followers of Methodius brought the Church Slavonic tradition to Bohemia and to the Balkans (Croatia, Serbia, Macedonia, and Bulgaria). From there it spread to the East Slavs in Rus' in the late tenth and eleventh centuries.

From the perspective of linguistics and philology, OCS is the Slavic language closest to reconstructed Late Common Slavic and is thus indispensable for research in Slavic historical linguistics. In its later redactions it is the primary form of expression for medieval Slavic culture and therefore significant as well for its influence on the formation of many of the Slavic literary languages .

Francis Whitfield's *Old Church Slavic Reader* was designed for classroom use. It is an admirably succinct description of the basic phonology and morphology of OCS combined with excerpts from the major OCS texts, notes to the texts, and a glossary. It is presented here with a minimum of commentary and exemplification. Sample actualizations and inflectional paradigms are provided in appendices at the end of the volume.

For more detailed treatment of the cultural, historical, and linguistic aspects of OCS, one should consult the extensive bibliographies in Jos Schaeken and Henrik Birnbaum, *Das altkirchenslavische Wort: Bildung – Bedeutung – Herleitung.* Altkirchenslavische Studien, I (Munich, 1997) and *Die altkirchenslavische Schriftkultur: Geschichte – Laute und Schriftzeichen – Sprachdenkmäler (mit Textproben, Glossar und Flexionsmustern).* Altkirchenslavische Studien, II (Munich, 1999).

MAJOR OLD CHURCH SLAVIC MONUMENTS

A. Glagolitic

1. **Codex Zographensis** (*Zog.*), in the M. E. Saltykov-Ščedrin Public Library, St Petersburg: 303 parchment folios, containing an incomplete tetraevangelion (Matt. 3.11 through John, with lacunae) and, in cyrillic, a synaxarion and a fragment of a menologion. Ff. 41–57 (Matt. 16.20–24.20) are a late insertion, probably of the late eleventh or early twelfth century. The manuscript derives its name from the Bulgarian Zographos Monastery, on Mt Athos, where it was seen in 1843 by Anton Mihanović, then Austrian consul in Constantinople. In 1860 it was presented by the monks of the monastery to Emperor Alexander II of Russia, who gave it to the St Petersburg Public Library.

> V. Jagić, *Quattuor evangeliorum codex glagoliticus olim Zographensis nunc Petropolitanus,* Berlin, 1879.

> L. Moszyński, *Ze studiów nad rękopisem Kodeksu Zografskiego* (Komitet Słowianoznawstwa Polskiej Akademii Nauk, *Monografie Slawistyczne, 3*), Wrocław–Warszawa–Kraków, 1961.

> L. Moszyński, *Język Kodeksu Zografskiego,* v. 1: *Imię nazywające (rzeczownik);* v. 2: *Imię określające i zastępcze (przymiotnik, liczebnik, zaimek).* Wrocław–Warszawa–Kraków–Gdańsk–Łódź, 1975, 1990.

2. **Codex Marianus** (*Mar.*), in the Lenin Public Library, Moscow, and (two folios only, Matt. 5.23–6.16) the National Library, Vienna: a tetraevangelion of 173 parchment folios, beginning at Matt. 5.23 and ending at John 21.17. Fol. 134 (John 1.1–23) is a late, cyrillic replacement, and Fol. 167 (John 18.13–29) has been lost. It is named after the Monastery of the Virgin Mary on Mt Athos, where it was discovered. The Vienna folios were originally taken by Mihanović and passed through the hands of Fr. Miklosich and A. Leskien. The bulk of the manuscript was taken by the Russian Slavist V. I. Grigorovič, after whose death in 1876 it became the property of the Moscow Public and Rumjancev Museum.

> V. Jagić, *Quattuor evangeliorum versionis palaeo-slovenicae codex Marianus glagoliticus,* Berlin and St Petersburg, 1883.

3. **Codex Assemanianus** (*Assem.*), in the Vatican Library: an aprakos-evangelion and synaxarion of 158 parchment folios. It was bought in Jerusalem, in 1736, by the Jesuit orientalist and papal librarian J. A. Assemani, through whose nephew, Archbishop S. E. Assemani, it passed into the Vatican collection.

> F. Rački, *Assemanov ili Vatikanski evangelistar*, Zagreb, 1865.

> I. Črnčić, *Assemanovo izbornô evangjelie*, Rome, 1878.

> J. Vajs and J. Kurz, *Evangeliarium Assemani*, I. Prague, 1929; II. Prague, 1955.

> V. Ivanova-Mavrodina and A. Džurova, *Asemanievoto evangelie. Starobŭlgarski glagoličeski pametnik ot X vek*. I: *Faksimilno izdanie*. II: *Xudožestveno-istoričesko proučvane*. Sofia, 1981.

4. **Psalterium Sinaiticum** (*Ps. Sin.*), in the Monastery of St Catherine, on Mt Sinai: a psalter of 177 parchment folios, containing Psalms 1 through 137 (Septuagint numeration). It was first edited by L. Geitler, in 1883.

> S. N. Sever'janov, *Sinajskaja psaltyr'. Glagoličeskij pamjatnik XI veka* (Pamjatniki staroslavianskogo jazyka, IV), Petrograd, 1922.

> M. Altbauer, *Psalterium Sinaiticum, an 11th century glagolitic manuscript from St Catherine's Monastery, Mt Sinai* [photographic reproduction], Skopje, 1971.

5. **Euchologium Sinaiticum** (*Euch. Sin.*), in the Monastery of St Catherine, on Mt Sinai (105 folios), the M. E. Saltykov-Ščedrin Public Library, St Petersburg (3 folios), and the Library of the Academy of Sciences, St Petersburg (1 folio): part of a compilation of prayers for various occasions (the Sinai ms., also called 'Geitler ms.', after L. Geitler, who first edited it, in 1882) and fragments of liturgical text (the 'Krylov fragment'—one folio, in the Library of the Academy of Sciences, and the 'Uspenskij fragments'—two folios, in the St Petersburg Public Library). The third folio in the St Petersburg Public Library, sometimes called the 'Kondakov fragment', was originally the tenth folio of the 'Geitler ms.'

J. Frček, *Euchologium Sinaiticum, texte slave avec sources grecques et traduction française* (*Patrologia Orientalis*, XXIV, 5, and XXV, 3), Paris, 1933, 1939.

R. Nahtigal, *Euchologium Sinaiticum, starocerkveno-slovanski glagolski spomenik* (Akademija znanosti in umetnosti v Ljubljani, Filozofsko-filološko-historični razred, *Dela*, I–II), Ljubljana, 1941–1942.

St. Słoński, *Index verborum do Euchologium Sinaiticum*, Warsaw, 1934.

6. Glagolita Clozianus (*Cloz.*), in the Museo Civico, Trent (12 folios), and the Ferdinandeum, Innsbruck (2 folios): contains homiletic texts. The manuscript derives its name from Count Paris Cloz, in whose library the Trent folios were discovered by B. Kopitar, who published an edition of them in 1836. The Innsbruck fragments were later discovered, and edited in 1860, by Fr. Miklosich.

V. Vondrák, *Glagolita Clozův*, Prague, 1893.

A. Dostál, *Clozianus codex palaeoslovenicus glagoliticus, Tridentinus et Oenipontanus*, Prague, 1959.

7. Kiev Missal (*KM*), in the collection of the Ukrainian Academy of Sciences, Kiev: 7 parchment folios containing Roman Mass prayers, given to the Kiev Theological Academy by Archmandrite Antonin Kapustin; first published in 1877 by I. I. Sreznevskij.

V. Jagić, "Glagolitica. Würdigung neuentdeckter Fragmente" (*Denkschriften der Kaiserlichen Akademie der Wissenschaften in Wien, Philosophisch-Historische Klasse*, XXXVIII, 2, pp. 44–58), Vienna, 1890.

C. Mohlberg, *Il messale glagolitico di Kiew (sec. IX) ed il suo prototypo romano del sec. VI–VII* (*Atti della Pontificia Accademia Romana di archeologia*, II), Rome, 1928.

J. Hamm, *Das glagolitische Missale von Kiew* (Oesterreichische Akademie der Wissenschaften, Philosophisch-Historische Klasse; *Schriften der Balkankommission, Linguistische Abteilung*, XXVI), Vienna, 1979.

V. V. Nimčuk, *Kyjivs'ki hlaholyčni lystky, najdavniša pam"jatka slov"jans'koji pysemnosti*, Kiev, 1983.

Kievskie glagoličeskie listki X v. iz Central'noj naučnoj biblioteki AN SSSR v Kieve [photographic reproduction], Kiev, 1983.

J. Schaeken, *Die Kiever Blätter* (Studies in Slavic and General Linguistics, 9), Amsterdam, 1987.

B. Cyrillic

1. **Sava Gospel** (*Sav.*), in the Drevnexranilišče Centrarxiva, Moscow: 129 parchment folios of an aprakos-evangelion, comprising ff. 25–151 (with two folios numbered 139) and Fol. 164 in a manuscript of 166 folios (the remaining material is of later date). The name of Sava, apparently the scribe, appears on 49r and 54r.

> V. Ščepkin, *Savvina kniga* (Pamiatniki staroslavjanskogo jazyka, I, 2), St Petersburg, 1903.

> N. M. Karinskij, "Perečen' važnejšix netočnostej poslednjago izdanija Savvinoj knigi", *Izvestija Otdelenija russkogo jazyka i slovesnosti Imperatorskoj Akademii nauk*, XIX, 3, pp. 206–216. St Petersburg, 1914.

> O. A. Knjazevskaja, *Savvina kniga. Drevneslavjanskaja rukopis' XI, XI–XII i konca XIII veka.* Moscow, 1999.

2. **Codex Suprasliensis** (*Supr.*), in the Lyceum Library, Ljubljana (118 folios), the Saltykov-Ščedrin Public Library, St Petersburg (16 folios), and the Zamojski Library, Warsaw (151 folios). The parchment manuscript, a fragment of a menologion for the month of March, containing hagiographic and homiletic material, was discovered in 1824 in the Basilian cloister in Supraśl, near Białystok, where it had probably been brought by monks from Mt Athos. The discoverer, Canon Michał Bobrowski, professor at the University of Wilno, sent the manuscript to Kopitar, who failed to return the first sixteen quaternions (now in Ljubljana). Quaternions 17–18 were apparently stolen and, in 1856, were acquired by the Petersburg Imperial Library. The remainder of the manuscript was acquired by the Zamojski Library in 1868. The first edition of the codex was published by Miklosich in 1851.

> S. N. Sever'janov, *Suprasl'skaja rukopis'* (Pamjatniki staroslavjanskogo jazyka, II, 1), St Petersburg, 1904.

K. H. Meyer, *Altkirchenslavisch-griechisches Wörterbuch des Codex Suprasliensis.* Glückstadt-Hamburg, 1935.

J. Zaimov and M. *Kapaldo, Suprasŭlski ili Retkov sbornik.* 1–2. Sofia, 1982–1983.

Note: For an up-to-date survey of all OCS texts, major and minor, and a complete bibliography, see Schaeken and Birnbaum 1999, especially pp. 87–135, 251–89.

GRAMMAR

ALPHABETS

Glagolitic

1	ⰰ	a	200	ⱄ	s
2	ⰱ	b	300	ⱅ	t
3	ⰲ	v	400	ⱆ	u
4	ⰳ	g	500	ⱇ	f
5	ⰴ	d	600	ⱈ	x
6	ⰵ	e	700	ⱉ	ω
7	ⰶ	ž	800	ⱋ	ψ
8	ⰷ	ʒ	900	ⱌ	c
9	ⰸ	z	1000	ⱍ	č
10	ⰹ ⰺ	ι ı	-	ⱎ	š
20	ⰻ	i	-	ⱏ	ъ
30	ⰼ	ⰼ	-	ⱐ	ь
40	ⰽ	k	-	ⱑ	ě
50	ⰾ	l	-	ⱓ	ü
60	ⰿ	m	-	ⱔ ⱕ ⱗ	ę N 𝒩
70	ⱀ	n	-	ⱘ	ǫ
80	ⱁ	o	-	ⱙ	ǫ̈
90	ⱂ	p	-	ⱚ	θ
100	ⱃ	r	-	ⱛ	υ

Cyrillic

1	а	a	300	т	t
-	б	b	400	оу, ȣ	u
2	в	v	500	ф	f
3	г	g	600	х	x
4	д	d	700	ѱ	ps
5	є	e	800	ѡ	ω
-	ж	ž	900	ц	c
6	ѕ, ꙃ	з	90	ч	č
7	з	z	-	ш	š
8	н	i	-	щ	ψ
9	ѳ	θ	-	ъ	ъ
10	і	ı	-	ы	y
20	к	k	-	ь	ь
30	л	l	-	ѣ	ě
40	м	m	-	ю	ü
50	н	n	-	ꙗ	ä
60	ѯ	ks	-	ѥ	ë
70	о	o	900	ꙙ	N
80	п	p	-	ѧ	ę
90	ҁ	ϙ	-	ѫ	Q
100	р	r	-	ѭ	ǫ̈
200	с	s	400	ѵ	υ

PHONOLOGY

WORD: one or more syllables.

SYLLABLE: final element [vowel] (+ preceding consonant or consonant cluster).

VOWEL: element necessarily present in final position in syllable. ˛

Back = V^B	u	o	a	ъ	y		o
Front = V^F	ü	e	ě	ь	i	ę	ǫ̈

CONSONANT: element that cannot occupy final position in syllable.

	1	2	3	4	5
Neutral = C^N	s		p t		
	z		b d		
				m n	l r
				v	
Velar = C^V		k x			
		g			
Semi-soft = C^{SS}			c		
			ʒ		
Soft = C^S	š		č ʮ		
	ž		ӕ		
				ń	ľ ŕ

14

SYLLABLE TYPES

V	-	any vowel but ъ, ь, y
CV	-	*not* C^N + ü, ᶐ̈
	-	*not* C^V + V^F
	-	*not* C^{SS} + V^B other than *a*
	-	*not* C^S + V^B (except in composition)
CC(C)V	-	no geminates
	-	obstruents follow only sibilants
	-	sibilant agrees in voice with following obstruent

ACTUALIZATION

$$\mathbf{V} \begin{cases} V^B & u & o & a & ъ & y & ᶐ \\ V^F & ü & e & ě & ь & i & ę & ᶐ̈ \end{cases}$$

j

$$\mathbf{C} \begin{cases} C^N & s & z & & t & d & n & l & r & p & b & m & v \\ C^S & š & ž & č & ɥ & ʀ & ń & ľ & ŕ & pľ & bľ & mľ & vľ \\ C^V & x & g & k \\ C^{SS} & ʒ & c \end{cases}$$

$$\begin{cases} C^N & & st & zd & sn & zn & sl & tr & dr & str \\ C^S & ɥ & ɥ & ʀ & šń & žń & šľ & ɥŕ & ʀŕ & ɥŕ & šv \\ C^V & sk & & & & & & & & & xv \\ C^{SS} & sc & & & & & & & & & sv \end{cases}$$

1. $[C^S\_\_, C^{SS}\_\_, j\_\_, Ci\_\_, ji\_\_]$ $V^B \downarrow V^F; ě_2 \downarrow i$
   a. $onC \downarrow ᶐ̈C$
   b. $y_2 \downarrow ę$
   c. $[C^{SS}\_\_]$ $a \downarrow a$
   d. $[Vj\_\_, \#j\_\_]$ ъ, ь $\downarrow i$
2. $[\_\_]$ $j \downarrow \varnothing$

3. $[\_V^F]$ $C^V \downarrow C^S$

    a. $[\_\check{e}_2, \_i_2]$ $C^V \downarrow C^{SS}$; $x \downarrow s$

4. $[\_e]$ $C^{SS} \downarrow C^S$

5. $[\_j]$ $C \downarrow C^S$

6. $[\_V]$ $Ci \downarrow C^S$; $ji \downarrow \varnothing$

7. $[\_t]$ x, gs, ks, z, t, st, $d \downarrow s$; p, b, $v \downarrow \varnothing$

8. $[\_]$ gtV, $ktV \downarrow \psi V^F$

9. $[\_s]$ s, z, t, d, p, $b \downarrow \varnothing$

10. $[\_V^B]$ gs, $ks \downarrow x$

11. $[\_V^F]$ gs, $ks \downarrow \check{s}$

12. $[\_C]$ $or \downarrow ra$; $ol \downarrow la$; $er \downarrow r\check{e}$; $el \downarrow l\check{e}$;
                                ьr $\downarrow$ rь; ьl $\downarrow$ lь; ьr $\downarrow$ rь; ьl $\downarrow$ lь;
                                ьm, im, ьn, in $\downarrow$ ę

13. $[\_m]$ $d \downarrow \varnothing$

    a. $[\_]$ sedm $\downarrow$ sedm

14. $[C^N\_C, C^V\_C]$ on $\downarrow$ Q

Finally, after applying the relevant numbered rules, delete all consonants following the vowel farthest to the right in the resulting form.

NOUN DECLENSION 1

Masculine			Notes: V[aillant] pp. 87–94 (§§57–60), D[iels] pp. 153–60 (§§62–63)
Sg			
N	-ъ		
G	-a	-u	V90–92 (58–59), D154 (62.2)
D	-u	-ovi	V90–94 (58–59), D155 (62.3) 159 (63.2)
A	-ъ	-a	V86 (53), D155 (62.4)
I	-omь	-ъmь	V89–90 (57), 92 (58.12), D154 (162.1) 158 (63.1)
L	-ě$_2$	-u	V90–93 (58-9), D156 (62.6)
V	-e ~ -u	-u	V91 (58), D159 (63.3) 156 (62.5)
Pl			
NV	-i$_2$	-ove, -ovi	V93 (59.70) 92 (58.12), D156 (62.10) 159 (63.4)
G	-ъ	-ovъ	V90–92 (58) 93 (59.8), D156 (62.11) 159 (63.5)
D	-omъ	-ъmъ	V89–90 (57.9–10), D159 (63.1)
A	-y$_2$		
I	-y	-ъmi	V93 (59.5), D157 (62.13) 159 (63.5)
L	-ě$_2$хъ	-охъ	V91 93 (58–59), D157 (62.12)
Du			
NAV	-a	-y	V91 (58), D156 (62.7)
GL	-u	-ovu	V91 (58), D156 (62.8)
DI	-oma	-ъma	V91(58), D156 (62.9)

Neuter			V95–96 (61), D168–69 (70) 172–73 (72.3)
Sg			
NAV	-o		
Pl			
NAV	-a		
Du			
NAV	-ě$_2$		
	Sg D	-ovi	V96 (61.5), D172 (72.2)
	Sg I	-ъmь	V96 (61.6), D169 (70.1) 172 (72.1), D173 (73.1)
	Sg V	-e	V96 (61.9)
	Pl D	-ъmъ	V96 (61.3), D169 (70.1) 173 (73.1)
	Pl I	-ъmi	V96 (61.8), D173 (73.2)
	Du DI	-ъma	V96 (61.7), D169 (70.2) 172 (72.3)

NOUN DECLENSION 2

Sg			Pl		Du	
N	-a, -i		NAV	-y₂	NAV	-ě₂
G	-y₂		G	-ъ	GL	-u
D	-ě₂		D	-amъ	DI	-ama
A,	-ǫ					
I	-oǫ̈ -ǫ -omь		I	-ami		
L	-ě₂		L	-axъ		
V	-o					

Notes:		
General		V96–99 (62–63), D175–77 (77–80)
Sg N	-i	V98–99 (63), D176 (79), 177 (80.2)
Sg I	-ǫ	V98 (62.5), D175 (77.1), 176 (78.2)
Sg I	-omь	V98 (62.6), D183 (84.25)

NOUN DECLENSION 3

Sg			Pl			Du	
	masc.	*fem.*		*masc.*	*fem.*		
N	-ь		NV	-ije	-i	NAV	-i
G	-i		G	-iji		GL	-iju
D	-i		D	-emъ, ьmъ		DI	-ьma
A	-ь		A	-i			
I	-emь -ьmь	-ijǫ	I	- ьmi			
L	-i		L	-exъ, -ьxъ			
V	-i						

Notes: V99–104 (64–67), D178 (81)

NOUN DECLENSION 4

Consonant-stem endings:

Sg		Pl		Du	
N	-y, -ę, -i	N	-e (masc)	GL	-u
G	-e	G	-ъ		
L	-e	I	-y		

	Type	Notes
Masculine		
- (e)n- stems	kam-en-, dьn-	V105–6 (69), D163–64 (65)
-t- stems	lakъt-, desęt-	V106–7 (70) 157 (102), D164 (65.14) 217–18 (102.5–7)
-jan-, -ěn- stems	riml´ěn-in-	V107 (71.2), D164–66 (66)
-tel-j- stems	dělatel-j-	V107–8 (71.3), D166–67 (67)
-ar-j- stems	mytar-j-	V108 (71.4–6), D167 (68)
Neuter		
-es- stems	neb-es-	V108–9 (72) 110–12 (73), D169–72 (71)
-en- stems	im-en-	V109 (72.2), D173–74 (74)
-ęt- stems	otroč-ęt-	V109 (72.3), D174 (75)
Feminine		
-er- stems	mat-er-, dъẙ-er-	V112–13 (74.2–3), D178 (82)
-ъv- stems	crьk-ъv-	V112–15 (74.4–8), D179–80 (83)

Sg	*masc.*		*neut.*	*fem.*	*masc.*		*neut.*	*fem.*
	DEFINITE ADJECTIVAL DECLENSION				**PRONOMINAL DECLENSION**			
N	-y (i)		-oe	-aě	-ъ		-o	-a
G		-a(a)go -aego		-y₂ę		-ogo		-oę
D		-u(u)mu -uemu		-ě₂i		-omu		-oi
A	N or G		-oe	-Qǫ	N or G		-o	-Q
I		-y(i)mь		-Qǫ		-ě₂mь		-Qǫ
L		-ě₂(ě)mь		-ě₂i		-omь		-oi
		-ě₂emь						
Pl								
N	-i₂ji		-aě	-y₂ę	-i₂		-a	-y₂
G		-y(i)xъ				-ě₂xъ		
D		-y(i)mь				-ě₂mь		
A	-y₂ę		-aě	-y₂ę	-y₂		-a	-y₂
I		-y(i)mi				-ě₂mi		
L		-y(i)xъ				-ě₂xъ		
Du								
NA	-aě		-ě₂i	-ě₂i	-a		-ě₂	-ě₂
GL		-uü				-oü		
DI		-y(i)ma				-ě₂ma		

Notes: Adjectives: V119–37, D188–202. Pronouns: V138–54, D203–14

azъ V147–49, D213
čii V138, D207
čьto V139, 142–43, D210
dъva V138, D215
dъvoe V138, D220
edinъ V138, D215
elikъ V153, D212
čkъ V150, D206
i(že) V138 145–46, D207
inakъ V150, D206
inъ V138, D206
kakъ V150, D206
kolikъ V153, D212
kyi V143–44, D210
kъto V138 142–43, D209
kъdo V138 142, D206
moi V138, D207

mъnogъ V154, D212
našь V138, D207
něčьto V142, D210
někakъ V150, D206
někyi V144, D210
někъto V142, D209
ničьtože V142, D210
nikakъže V150, D206
nikyiže V144, D210
nikъtože V142, D209
oba V138, D215
oboe V139, D220
onъ V138. D206
ovъ V138, D206
samъ V138, D206
sebe V147–49, D213
selikъ V153, D212

sicь V139–51, D208
sikъ V151, D206
svoi V138, D207
sь V139–41, D208
sьe V141, D208
takъ V150, D206
tolikъ V153–54, D212
troe V139, D220
tuь V154, D212
tvoi V138, D207
ty V147–48, D213
tъ V140, D206
tъже V141, D206
vašь V138, D207
vьsakъ V151, D206
vьsь V150, D208

CONJUGATION

1. STEMS: The many forms of the verb are conveniently described as being constructed on one or the other of two stems:

FIRST STEM	SECOND STEM
Non-past	Aorist
Imperative	(Imperfect — only if the second stem
Imperfect	ends in -a- or -ě-)
Present Active Participle	Infinitive
Present Passive Participle	Supine
	Past Active Participle
	Past Passive Participle
	Perfect Active Participle
	Verbal Substantive

There is a limited number of regular correspondences between the forms of the two stems. It is therefore possible to establish, for most verbs, a single base from which the two stems may be derived by use of the following table:

				Examples	
Base suffix	1st stem suffix	2nd stem suffix	Base	1st stem	2nd stem
—	—	—	nes-	nes-	nes-
			moli-	moli-	moli-
-ě-	-i-	-ě-	mьně-	mьn-i-	mьn-ě-
-j-	-j-	—	umě-j-	umě-j-	umě-
			bor-j-	bor-j-	bor-
-a-	-j-	-a-	glagol-a-	glagol-j-	glagol-a-
-ova-	-uj-	-ova-	věr-ova-	věr-uj-	věr-ova-
-nǫ-	-n-	-nǫ-	dvig-nǫ-	dvig-n-	dvig-nǫ-

1.1 Other correspondences than those illustrated above are exhibited by the stems of the following verbs or their compounds:

ber-	bьra-	V309 (219), D266 (129)
dad-	da-	V312–13 (222), D277, 280 (134)
der-	dьra-	V309 (219), D266 (129)
dъm-	[dǫ-]	V303 (214), D246 (121.1.2)
ěd-	ě(xa)-	V304 (214), D279, 281 (134)
isk(j)-	iska-	V309 (218), D269 (130.5)

kov-	kova-	V308 (218), D266–67 (129)
lęg-	leg-	V302 (214), D250 (121.9)
met(j)-, metaj-	meta-	V307–8 (218), D269 (130.5)
osnov-	osnova-	V308–9 (218), D266–67 (129)
per-	pьra-	V309–10 (219), D266 (129)
plěv-	plě-	V303 (214), D246 (121.1.1), 248 (121.2.3)
plov-	plu-	V307 (217), D247 (121.1.4)
-rętj-	-rět-	V302–3 (214), D252 (122)
rov-, ŕev-	ru-, ŕü-	V307 (217), D247 (121.1.4)
rьv-	rьva-	V308 (218), D266–67 (129)
sęd-	sěd-	V302 (214), D250 (121.9)
slov-	slu-	V307 (217), D247 (121.1.4)
stan-	sta-	V288 (204), D278, 281 (134)
[-sъp-	-su-]	V303 (214)
sъs-	sъsa-	V308 (218), D266–67 (129)
-trov-	-tru-	V307 (217), D247 (121.1.4)
tьk-	tьka-	V308 (218), D266–67 (129)
věd-	vědě- (-věda-)	V314–16 (224), D278, 280–81 (134)
zov-	zъva-	V310 (219), D266–67 (129)
žen-	gъna-	V310 (219), D266–67 (129)
žid- (žьd-)	žьda-	V310 (219), D266–67 (129)
živ-	ži-	V303 (214), D250 (121.8)

2. NON-PAST: First stem (+ link) + personal ending.

2.1 *Link*: If the stem does not end in -i-, it is linked to all endings that begin with a consonant. Before -n- (3 pl) the link is -o-; elsewhere it is -e-.

2.2 *Personal endings*:

	Sg	Pl	Du
1	-ǫ	-mъ	-vě
2	-ši	-te	-ta
3	-tъ	-ntъ	-te

2.2.1 *Notes on personal endings*:

3 sg:	-tь	V227 (147.3), D227 (108.2)
	-Ø	V228–28 (147.3), D227–28 (108.3)
1 pl:	-my	V228 (147.5), D228 (108.6)
	-mĭ	D228 (108.5)
3 pl:	-Ø	V229 (147.7), D227–28 (108.3)
	-ǫtъ ~ -ętъ	V271 (189.3), 47 (26.c.1), D107 (30)
3 du:	-te ~ -ta ~	V228 (147.4), D228 (108.7)
	-tě	

2.3 *Assimilation and contraction*:

-ae- ~ -aa- ~ -a-	
-ěe- ~ -ea- ~ -ě-	V229 (148), 54 (31.5),
	D112–14 (35, 36.2)
-ue- ~ -uu- ~ -u-	

2.4 *Exceptions*:

by- (irr)	V311–12 (221), 227 (147.3), D276 (134), 279 (134.1–2)
dad- da-	V312–13 (222), D277 (134)
dovьlě-	V263 (180.6), D278 (134). 281 (134.20)
ěd-	V313–14 (223), D267–67 (134)
imě-j-	V316–17 (225), D278 (134), 281 (134.18)
věd- vědě-	V314–16 (224), 227–28 (147.3), D278 (134), 280 (134.12–13)
xot-ě-	V262–63 (180.3–5), D278 (134), 281 (134.19)

3. IMPERATIVE: First stem (+ link) + personal ending.

3.1 *Link*: If the stem does not end in -i-, it is linked to all endings that begin with a consonant or Ø. Before a consonant the link is -ě$_2$-; before Ø it is -i$_2$-.

3.2 *Personal endings*:

	Sg	Pl	Du
1	(-mь)	-mъ	-vě
2	-Ø	-te	-ta
3	-Ø	(-ǫ)	(-te)

3.3 *Notes:*

-i- ~ -ĕ-	V230–31 (149), D231 (110.1)
1 sg, 3 pl, 3 du	V231–33 (150), D231 (110.3)
Periphrases	V232–23 (150–51)
1 pl -my	V228 (147.5), D228 (108.6)

3.4 *Exceptions:*

by- (irr)	stem: bǫd	V231–32 (150), D276 (134)
dad- da-		V312–13 (222), D277 (134), 280 (134.9)
ĕd-		V313–14 (223), D277 (134)
ĕd- ĕ(xa)-		V304 (214), D281 (134.26)
pek-	stem: pьk-	V301 (213), D248 (121.4)
rek-	stem: rьk-	V301 (213), D248 (121.4)
tek-	stem: tьk-	V301 (213), D248 (121.4)
vĕd- vĕdĕ-		V314–16 (224), D278 (134), 280 (134.14)
vid-ĕ-		V317 (226.1), 262 (180.2), D262 (126.1)
xot-ĕ-		V262–63 (180.3–5), D278 (134)
žeg-	stem: žьg-	V300 (213), D248 (121.4)

4. IMPERFECT: Stem (+ link 1) + -ax- (+ link 2) + personal ending.

4.1 *Stem:* The stem is the first stem of the verb unless the second ends in -a- or -ĕ-.

4.2 *Link 1:* If the stem does not end in -a- or -ĕ-, it is joined to the formant -ax- with the link -ĕ-.

4.3 *Link 2:* The formant -ax- is joined to the endings beginning in Ø or consonant with the link -e-.

4.4 *Personal endings:*

	Sg	Pl	Du
1	-ъ	-omъ	-ovĕ
2	-Ø	-te	-ta
3	-Ø	-ǫ	-te

4.5 *Notes:*

V242–46 (158–59), 228 (147.4), D234–38 (113), 228 (108.7)

4.6 *Exceptions*:

by- (irr)		V311–12 (221), 224 (158.5), D279 (134.3)
dad- da-	stem: dad-	V312–13 (222), D277 (134)
ĕd- ĕ(xa)-	stem: ĕd-	V304 (214), D279 (134)
met(j)- metaj- meta-	stem: metj- meta-	V307–8 (218), D236 (113.2)
stan- sta-	stem: stan-	V288 (204), D281 (134.22)
zov- zъva-	stem: zъva-, zov-	V310 (219), D236 (113.2)
žen- gъna-	stem: žen-	V310 (219), D236 (113.2)
žid- (žьd-) žьda-	stem: žьda-, žid-, žьd-	V310 (219), D236 (113.2)

5. PRESENT ACTIVE PARTICIPLE: First stem (+ link) + -ntj + adjectival endings *except* in the definite N sg masc.

5.1 *Link:* If the stem does not end in -i-, it is linked to the formant -ntj-. In the indefinite N sg masc (and the definite N sg masc, which is constructed thereon) and in the indefinite N sg neut, the link is -y_2-; elsewhere it is -o-.

5.2 *Endings:* These are the regular adjectival endings, except for the following:

Indefinite:		Definite:	
N sg masc	-Ø	N sg masc	-i (added to the indefinite form)
N sg neut	-Ø	N sg fem	-ija
N sg fem	-i	N pl masc	-ei (also regular -$i_2$ji)
N pl masc	-e		

5.3 *Notes:*

V126–28 (83), 246–47 (160), 251 (165), D232–34 (111)

5.4 *Exceptions:*

by- (irr)	V310–12 (221), 251 (165), D276 (134)
gor-ĕ-	V262 (180.1), 317 (226.2), D262 (126.3)
imĕ-j-	V316–17 (225), D281 (134.18)
vĕd- vĕdĕ-	V315 (224), D281 (134.15)

6. PRESENT PASSIVE PARTICIPLE: First stem (+ link) + -m- + regular adjectival endings.

6.1 *Link:* If the stem does not end in -i-, it is joined to the formant -m- with the link -o-.

6.2 *Notes:*

V247–48 (161), D234 (112)	

6.3 *Exceptions:*

pita-j-		
pitě-j-		V265–66 (184.4), 309 (218.9), D264 (127.4)
věd-	vědě-	V315 (224.5), 247 (161), D281 (134.16)
viдě-		V247 (161), D262 (126.2)

7. PRODUCTIVE AORIST: Stem (+ link) + -x- + personal ending.

7.1 *Stem:* The stem is the second stem of the verb, with the following modifications:

If the second stem ends in –CnQ-, the aorist stem is regularly without -nQ-.

If the *base* ends in -ьr-, the aorist stem ends in -rě-.

7.2 *Link:* If the stem ends in a consonant other than m, n, l, r, it is linked to the formant -x-. In the 2, 3 sg the link is -e-; elsewhere it is -o-.

7.3 *Personal endings:*

	Sg	Pl	Du
1	-ъ	-omъ	-ově
2	-Ø	-te	-ta
3	-Ø	-ę	-te

7.4 *Notes:*

General	V234 (152), 240–42 (157), D239–40 (114)
2, 3 sg -tъ	V234–36 (154), D227 (108.3)
3 du -te ~ ta ~ -tě	V228 (147.4), D228 (108.7)
1 pl -omy	V228–29 (147.5), D228 (108.6)

7.5 Exceptions:

(-pьr-)	V305 (215), D249 (121.4)
tьr-j-	V284 (201), D249 (121.4)
živ- ži-	V303 (214), D249 (121.4), 250 (121.8)
by- (irr.)	V312 (221), D279 (134.4), 276 (134)
dad- da-	V313 (222), D280 (134.10), 277 (134)
ěd-	V313–14 (223), D280 (134.8)
verbs in -Cnǫ-	V288–91 (205), D259 (125.2)

8. S-AORIST: Ablauted second stem + -s- + personal ending.

8.1 *Ablaut:* e > ě, o > a, ь > i, (but rь > rě)

8.2 *Personal endings:* as for productive aorist, 7.3.

8.3 *Notes:* The s-aorist may be found with verbs that have second stem ending -m- or -n-. The suffix -tъ is usually added to the 2, 3 sg forms (e.g. proklьn-: proklętъ).

S-aorist forms, except in the 2, 3 sg, may also be found with the following verbs or their compounds:

bl′üd-	čьt-	-lęk-	rek-	tręs-	vrьz-
bod-	ěd-	męt-	sěk-	ved-	žeg-
cvьt-	greb-	nes-	tek-	vlěk-	

See V234 (153.1), 236–38 (155), D238–40 (114.2)

9. SIMPLE AORIST: Stem (+ link) + personal ending.

9.1 *Stem:* The stem is the second stem of the verb, but without the -nǫ- if the stem ends in -Cnǫ-.

9.2 *Link:* The link -e- appears before Ø or consonant.

9.3 *Personal endings:* as for imperfect (4.4)

9.4 *Notes:* The simple aorist may be found with verbs that have a second stem ending in -Cnǫ- and with the following verbs or their compounds. See V238–40 (156), D238 (114.1).

ěd- ě(xa)- (simple aorist stem -ěd-; see V304 (214), D281 (134.26)	
id-	
krad-	[-pas-]
-lěz-	-rǫt-j- -rět-
lęg- leg-	sęd- sěd-
mog-	tręs- [?]
pad-	vrьg-

10. INFINITIVE: Stem + -ti. SUPINE: Stem + -tъ.

10.1 *Stem:* The stem is the second stem of the verb, but, if the *base* ends in -ьr-, -ьr- is replaced by –rě-.

10.2 *Notes:*

General	V252 (167–68), D243 (119–20)
Inflected infinitive	V348 (250.3), 288 (204)

10.3 *Exceptions*:

cvьt-	stem:	cvit-	V298 (211), D247 (121.2)
-črьp-		-črěp-	V299 (212), D247 (121.2)
čьt-		čit-	V298 (211), D247 (121.2)
id-		i-	V303–4 (214), D278 (134)
strig-		strьg- [strig-]	V301 (213), D248 (121.2–3)
tek-		tek-, tik- [?]	V301 (213)
tlьk-		tlěk-	V301–2 (213), D247 (121.2)
vrьg-		vrěg-	V300 (213), D247 (121.2)
-vrьz-		-vrěz-	V296 (210), D247 (121.2)

11. PERFECT ACTIVE PARTICIPLE: Stem + l + regular indefinite adjectival endings.

11.1 *Stem:* The stem is the second stem of the verb, but without a final -d- or -t-, and regularly without -nq- if the stem ends in -Cnq-.

11.2 *Notes*: V250–51 (164), D242 (116).

11.3 *Exceptions*:

brĕg-	stem:	brьg-	V299 (213.2), D247 (121.2)
id-		šь-	V303 (214), D278–79 (134)
vlĕk-		vlьk-	V300 (213.3), D248 (121.2)
verbs in -Cnǫ-			V288–91 (205), D259 (125.2)

12. PAST ACTIVE PARTICIPLE: Stem (+ link) + -ъš- + adjectival endings *except* in the definite N sg masc.

12.1 *Stem:* The stem is the second stem of the verb, but regularly without -nǫ- if the second stem ends in -Cnǫ-.

12.2 *Link:* If the stem ends in any vowel but -i-, or if it ends in -i- and the base ends in -i-j-, it is joined to the formant -ъš- with the link -v-.

12.3 *Endings:* as for present active participle (5.2).

12.4 *Notes:* V248–49 (162), D115 (241–42).

13. PAST PASSIVE PARTICIPLE AND VERBAL SUBSTANTIVE

13.1 *N-form:* Stem (+ link) + -n- (to which the PPP adds regular adjectival endings; the VS adds -ij- and neuter endings of the first noun declension).

13.11 *Stem:* The stem is the second stem of the verb; but second stems in -Cnǫ- drop -nǫ-, and second stems in -Vnǫ- replace it with -nov-.

13.12 *Link:* If the stem ends in a consonant or -i-, it is joined to the formant -n- with the link -e-.

13.2 *T-form:* Second stem + -t- (to which PPP and VS add as above –13.1).

13.21 *Occurrence of the t-form:* The t-form is regularly found only with verbs whose *bases* end in -ьr- or a nasal consonant, and with the following verbs or their compounds:

by- (irr)	V312 (221), D255 (123.7)
li-j-	V281 (198), D255 (123.7), 273 (131.6)
otvrьz-	V296 (210), D250 (121.6–7)
pi-j-	V281 (198), D255 (123.7)
[plov- plu-]	V307 (217)
slov- slu-	V307 (217), D247 (121.1.4)

[-sъp- -su-]	V303 (214)
věz-	V296 (210), D250 (121.6)
vi-j-	V280 (198), D255 (123.6)
živ- ži-	V303 (214), D250 (121.8)

13.3 *Notes*: V249–50 (163), 251–52 (166), D242–43 (117–18).

13.4 *Exceptions*: The following verbs or their compounds have exceptional formations. Unless otherwise noted, the stem common to PPP and VS is not attested for all the verbs.

bi-j-	bijen- (VS also bitij-)	V280 (198), D255 (123.6–7)
blagoslovi-	blagosloven-	V259 (176), D132 (49.7)
-čez-nǫ-	[-čeznoven-, -čezen-]	V290 (205)
drъz-nǫ-	drъznoven-	V289 (205), D259 (125.2)
dъm- [dǫ-]	dъmen-	V303 (214), D246 (121.1.2), 250 (121.1.6)
dъx-nǫ-	dъxnoven-, dъšen-	V289 (205), D259 (125.2)
id-	VS šьstij-, -šьstvij-, -itij-	V303 (214), D281 (134.25)
klik-nǫ-	kliknoven-	V288 (205), D259 (125.2)
kol-j-	kolen-, klan-	V283 (201), D252 (123.1)
kos-nǫ-	kosnoven-	V289 (205), D259 (125.2)
kry-j-	krъven-	V282 (199), D255 (123.6–7)
my-j-	mъven-	V282 (199), D255 (123.6–7)
mьr-	VS -mrъtij-, -mrъtvij-	V305 (215), 251 (166.2)
obu-j-	obuven-	V282–83 (200), D255 (123.6), 256 (123.8)
plъz-nǫ-	VS plъzenij-, [plъznovenij-]	V289 (205)
poči-j-	VS [počьvenij-]	V281 (198)
poj- pě-	VS pěnij-, pětij-; PPP pět-	V284 (201), D255 (123.6), 256 (123.7)
ri-nǫ-	rinoven-, rьven-	V288 (204), D258 (125)
ry-j-	[rъven-]	V282 (199)
sě-a-	sě(a)n, sět-	V278–79 (195), D272 (131.4)

-sěk-nǫ-	-sěčen-; VS -sěknovenij- [-sěknoven-]	V292 (206), D260 (125.2)
-stignǫ	-stižen- [-stignoven-]	D290 (205)
ši-j-	šьven-	V281 (198), D255 (123.6), 256 (123.8)
-trov- -tru-	troven-	V307 (217), D247 (121.4), 250 (121.7)
tъk-nǫ-	tъčen-, [VS also tъknovenij-]	V290 (205)
vlěk-	vlěčen-,vlьčen-	V300 (213), D248 (121.2.2)
vъskrъs-nǫ-	vъskrъsnoven- vъskrъsen-	V289 (205), D259 (125.2)
zaby-	zabъven- VS also zabytij-	V282 (199), 312 (221), D255 (123.6–7)
žeg-	žežen-, žьžen-	V300 (213), D248 (121.2,5)
žьr-j-	VS žrъtj-, žьrenij-	V283 (201), 250 (121.6–7)

14. CONDITIONAL AUXILIARY:

	Sg		Pl		Du	
1	bimь	byxъ	bimъ bіxomъ	byxomъ	byxově
2	bi	by	biste	byste	—
3	bi	by	bǫ bišę	byšę	—

14.1 *Notes:* V255–56 (172), 312 (221), D280 (134.5), 276 (134)

TEXTS

Assemanianus, Zographensis, Marianus: Luke 1

ASSEMANIANUS	ZOGRAPHENSIS

ASSEMANIANUS

1. Poneže ubo mnoʒı našɴ| čınıtı
pověstь · o i|zvěstьnъiiхъ vъ
nas ·| veψeхъ ·

2. ěkože prědašɴ na|mъ ·
Въıvъšei isprьva · sa|movidьci i
slugъı slovesi ·|
3. İzvoli sɴ i mъně xuždъšu · po|
vъsěхъ vъ istinǫ · po rɴdu| pısatı
tebě · slavьnъı O te|ofıle ·
4. Da razuměešı o niхъ|že naučilъ
esı slovesexъ utv|rьždcnic ·

5. Въı͞ѕ vъ dьni iroda| c͞rě
iüdeiska · ierei eterь| imenemъ
zaxaria · ω'ͭ| efımerię avıanɴ · i|
žena emu oͭ dъψerь aronь ·| imɴ
ei elısavetь ·
6. bě|šete že oba pravedъ|na
prědъ b͞mъ · xodɴψa| vъ
zapovědexъ vьsěхъ · İ
opra|vdaniiхъ g͞niхъ bes poroka ·|

7. i ne bě ima čɴda · poneže bě
e|lısaveθь neplodъı · ͐ i oba|
zamatorěvъša vъ dьnexъ| svoiхъ
běsta ·

ZOGRAPHENSIS

1. Po ńeže ubo. mnozi načɴšɴ.|
čıniti pověstь. ŏ ızvě|stъnъιхъ vъ
nasъ veštexъ|*

2. ěkože prědašɴ namъ. bъιvъ|šei
ıskoni samovidьci.| ı slugъı
slovesi ·
3. ızvo|li sɴ ı mьně хoždьšü.
ı|s prьva po vsěхъ. vъ ısti|nǫ po
rɴdu. psati tebě.| slavьnъı t'eofile.
4. da ra|zuměeši. ŏ ńiхъže
ɴаu|čilъ ̣sɴ ěsi slovesexъ.|
utvrьždenьe.

5. bъıstъ| vъ dьni ıroda c͞rě.
ıüdeıska.| ıerei eterь ımenemь
zaxarič.| ŏtъ dьnevъппıę črědъı
ăvi|ăńɴ. ı žena ego ŏtъ dъšterъ
ă|rońь. ımɴ eı. elisavetь.|
6. Běăšete že ŏba pravьdъna|
prědъ b͞mь. xodɴšta vъ zapo|
vědьхъ vsěхъ. ı opravьda|пιιхъ
g͞niхъ. bes poroka.|

7. ı ne bě ıma čɴda. po ńeže bě|
elisavetь neplodъı. ı oba|
zamatorěvъša vъ dьnexъ| svoiхъ
běăšete.

---

* The Assemanianus text omits the most frequent diacritic of the original, the
macron, which has no apparent function.

MARIANUS

1. Poneže ubo mьnoʒi načNSN|
činiti pověstь o ızvě|stovanъıxъ
vъ nasъ ve|štexъ.

2. ěkože prědašN na|mъ bъıvъšei
iskoni samovidьci| ı slugъı
slovese.

3. ızvoli sN i| mьně xoždъšü is
prьva po vьsěxъ.| vъ ıstinꝍ po
rNdꝍ pisati tebě.| slavъnъı teofile.

4. da razu|měeši o nixъže naučilъ
sN esi| slovesexъ utvrъždenie •:•

5. Bъı|stъ vъ dьni iroda cěsěrě
iüde|iska. ıerei edinъ imenemъ
za|xarič. otъ efiměrię avieNN.| ı
žena ego ᵒtъ dъšterъ arѡnь.| ı
imN ei elisavetь.

6. běašete že| oba pravedъna
prědъ bm̄ъ. xodN|šta vъ
zapovědexъ vъsěxъ. ı
o|pravъdaniixъ gn̄i[i]xъ* bes
poroka.

7. i ne bě ima čNda. poneže bě
eli|savetь neplodъı. ı oba
za|matorěvъša vь dьnexъ svo|ixъ
běašete.

1. Ἐπειδήπερ πολλοὶ ἐπεχείρησαν
ἀνατάξασθαι διήγησιν περὶ τῶν
πεπληροφορημένων ἐν ἡμῖν
πραγμάτων,

2. καθὼς παρέδοσαν ἡμῖν οἱ ἀπ'
ἀρχῆς αὐτόπται καὶ ὑπηρέται
γενόμενοι τοῦ λόγου,

3. ἔδοξε κἀμοὶ παρηκολουθηκότι
ἄνωθεν πᾶσιν ἀκριβῶς καθεξῆς σοι
γράψαι, κράτιστε Θεόφιλε,

4. ἵνα ἐπιγνῷς περὶ ὧν κατηχήθης
λόγων τὴν ἀσφάλειαν.

5. Ἐγένετο ἐν ταῖς ἡμέραις, Ἡρῴδου
βασιλέως τῆς Ἰουδαίας ἱερεύς τις
ὀνόματι Ζαχαρίας ἐξ ἐφημερίας Ἀβιά,
καὶ γυνὴ αὐτῷ ἐκ τῶν θυγατέρων Ἀα-
ρών καὶ τὸ ὄνομα αὐτῆς Ἐλισάβετ.

6. ἦσαν δὲ δίκαιοι ἀμφότεροι
ἐναντίον τοῦ θεοῦ, πορευόμενοι ἐν
πάσαις ταῖς ἐντολαῖς καὶ
δικαιώμασιν τοῦ κυρίου ἄμεμπτοι.

7. καὶ οὐκ ἦν αὐτοῖς τέκνον, καθότι
ἦν ἡ Ἐλισάβετ στεῖρα, καὶ ἀμφότεροι
προβεβηκότες ἐν ταῖς ἡμέραις αὐτῶν
ἦσαν.

Mar. 6 (и́) в подл. выскобл. но слѣды видны. (J = Jagić) Gk. 5 γυνη
αυτω] η γυνη αυτου °αυτης] αυτη 6 δικαιοι αμφοτεροι] α. δ.

ASSEMANIANUS	ZOGRAPHENSIS

8. Вⷮы̄ˢ že služɴ|ѱu emo vъ čınu
črědъi svo|eę prědъ b͞mъ •

8. bъistъ že| služɴštü mu. vъ čınu
črě|dъi svoeę prědъ b͞mь.

9. po obъıčаʿü ie|reiskumu • klüčı
sɴ emu poka|ditı • vъšedъšu že vъ
cr̄kvъ| g͞nǫ •

9. po o|bъıčaü erě͡ıskumu.
klüči| sɴ emu pokaditi.
vъšьdъ|šü vъ cr'kovь g͞nǫ.

10. İ vse množьstvo lüdıi •| bě
m|͡tvǫ děę vъně vъ godъ
tı|mıana •

10. ı̇ vьse| množьstvo l'üdıi bě.
mo||litvǫ děę. vьně vъ godъ|
tьmiěna.

11. Avı že sɴ emu an͞ɪɪ̈ɪъ| g͞nь •
stoę o desnǫǫ̈ olʿtarě
ka|dılъnaago •

11. ăvi že sɴ emu| an͞ɪɪ̈ɪъ g͞nь.
stoę o desnǫǫ̈ ŏ|l'tarě kadilьnaăgo.

12. ʿİ sъmɴte sɴ zaxa|rıě viděvъ •
i̇ sṫraxъ napade| na nь •

12. ı sъmɴ|te sɴ zaxarıě viděvь.
i̇ stṙa|xъ ɪɪapadc ɪɪa ńь.

13. Reče že kь nemu an͞ɪɪ̈ɪъ g͞nь •|
ne boı sɴ zaxarie • Zane uslъıša|na
bъı̄ˢ m|͡tva tvoě • ı žena tvo|ě
elısaveѳь • rodıtъ s͞nъ
tebě •| i narečeši imɴ emu
ioanъ •

13. reče že kъ ńe|mu an͞ɪɪ̈ɪъ g͞nь.
ne boı sɴ zaxarıě.| za ńe
uslъıšana bъistъ| molitva tvoě.
i̇ žena tvoě| elisavьtь. rodıtъ s͞nъ
tebě.| ı narečeši ı̇mɴ ěmu
ı̇oan'nъ.|

14. İ bǫ|detъ radostь tebě velıě •
İ| mnoȝi o rodьstvě ego
vъzdra|duǫtъ sɴ •

14. i̇ bǫdetъ tebě radostь
i̇| veselьe. ı̇ mnoȝi o roždь|stvě
ego vъzdraduǫtъ sɴ.|

15. Bǫdetъ| bo velı prědъ b͞mъ •
İ| vına i̇ sıkera ne imatъ| pıtı •
i d̄xmъ s͞tmъ| isplъnitъ sɴ • Eѱe i
črě|va m͡tre svoeę •

15. bǫdetъ bo velıı prědъ b͞mь.|
i̇ vina i̇ tvorena kvasa. ne ıma|tъ
piti. ı̇ d̄xa s͞ta ı̇splъ|nitъ sɴ. ěšte že
i̇ črěva m͡re| svoeę.

MARIANUS

8. bъistъ že slu|žъněstu emu. vъ
činu črědъı| svoeę prědъ bm̃ъ.

9. po obъı|čaü iereiskumu. klǔči
sn| emu pokaditi vъšedъšü vъ|
crk̃vъ gn̄ǫ.

10. ι vъse mъnožъstvo| lüdii bě
molitvǫ děę vьně| vъ godъ
temběna .

11. ěvi že sn emu anᷤr̃ъ| gn̄ъ stoę o
desnǫǫ̈ oltarě kadilъna| ego.

12. ι sъmnte sn zaxariě viděvъ. ι|
straxъ napade na nь.

13. reče že kъ nemu| anᷤr̃лъ. ne
boi sn zaxarie. zane uslъı|šana
bъistъ molitva tvoě. ι žena|
tvoě elisavetь roditь sn̄ъ tebě.
ι| narečeši imn emu
ioanъ.

14. ι bǫdetъ te|bě radostь i
veselie. ι mъnoзi o roždь|stvě ego
vъzdraduǫtъ sn.

15. bǫde|tъ bo velei prědъ gm̃ъ.
i vina i sike|ra ne imatъ piti.
ι d̃xa s̃taago isplъ|nitь sn ešte
i-črěva matere svoeę.|

8. Ἐγένετο δὲ ἐν τῷ ἱερατεύειν
αὐτὸν ἐν τῇ τάξει τῆς ἐφημερίας
αὐτοῦ ἔναντι τοῦ θεοῦ,

9. κατὰ τὸ ἔθος τῆς ἱερατείας
ἔλαχεν τοῦ θυμιᾶσαι εἰσελθὼν εἰς
τὸν ναὸν τοῦ κυρίου,

10. καὶ πᾶν τὸ πλῆθος ἦν τοῦ λαοῦ
προσευχόμενον ἔξω τῇ ὥρᾳ τοῦ
θυμιάματος.

11. ὤφθη δὲ αὐτῷ ἄγγελος κυρίου
ἑστὼς ἐκ δεξιῶν τοῦ θυσιαστηρίου
τοῦ θυμιάματος.

12. καὶ ἐταράχθη Ζαχαρίας ἰδὼν καὶ
φόβος ἐπέπεσεν ἐπ' αὐτόν.

13. εἶπεν δὲ πρὸς αὐτὸν ὁ ἄγγελος,
Μὴ φοβοῦ, Ζαχαρία, διότι εἰσηκούσθη
ἡ δέησίς σου, καὶ ἡ γυνή σου
Ἐλισάβετ γεννήσει υἱόν σοι, καὶ
καλέσεις τὸ ὄνομα αὐτοῦ Ἰωάννην.

14. καὶ ἔσται χαρά σοι καὶ
ἀγαλλίασις, καὶ πολλοὶ ἐπὶ τῇ
γενέσει αὐτοῦ χαρήσονται.

15. ἔσται γὰρ μέγας ἐνώπιον [τοῦ]
κυρίου, καὶ οἶνον καὶ σίκερα οὐ μὴ
πίῃ, καὶ πνεύματος ἁγίου
πλησθήσεται ἔτι ἐκ κοιλίας μητρὸς
αὐτοῦ,

Gk. *10* ην του λαου⟧ τ. λ. ην °τη⟧ εν τη   *13* αγγελος⟧ αγγελος κυριου
°Ζαχαρια⟧ Ζαχαριας °αυτου⟧ αυτω   *14* χαρα σοι⟧ σοι χαρα   °επι⟧ εν
15 κυριου⟧ θεου

ASSEMANIANUS

16. ṁnogъi| s͞novъ izlvъ obratıtъ
kъ| g͡u b͡u ixъ ·
17. İ tъ prědъidetъ ·| prědъ nimъ
d͞xmъ i siloǫ i|liinoǫ̈ · Obratıtı
s͞rdca o͡cъ| na čnda · i protıvъnъię
vъ| mǫdrostь pravedъnъiixъ ·|
ugotovatı lüdi sъvrъšenъi ·|

18. İ reče zaxarič kъ anᴋlu · po
česo|mu razumēǫ̈ se · Azь bo
esmъ| starъ · i žena moě
zamatorě|vъšı vъ dьnexъ svoixъ ·

19. ʿİ ωtъ|věɥavъ anᴋlъ reče
emu · ʿAzъ| esmъ gavrıilъ
prěstoęi prě|dъ b͞mъ · İ posъlanъ
esmъ gla|tı kь tebě · i blagověstiti
te|bě sıi ·
20. i se bǫdeši mlъčn i ne| mogъi
progl͞atı · do negože dь|ne bǫdǫtъ
sii · zane ne věrova| slovesemъ
moimъ · eže sъbǫdǫ|tъ sn vъ
vrěmn svoe ·
21. ʿİ běšn lü|dię židǫɥe zaxarię · İ
čüžda|axǫ sn eže muždaaše
vъ| c͞rkvi ·
22. İ išedъ že ne mo|žaaše gl͞atı kъ
nimъ · ʿİ | razumēšn ěko vıděni|e
vıdě vъ c͞rkvi · i tъ| bě pomaę imъ
· i prěbъivaaše| němъ·

ZOGRAPHENSIS

16. i̇ mnogъı s͞novъ | il'evъ ·
ŏbratitъ kъ g͡u b͡u ixъ ·|
17. i̇ tъ prědъidetъ prědь ńi|mь.
d͞xomь i̇ siloǫ̈ i̇liinoǫ̈.| ŏbratiti
s͞rdьca o͡cmъ* na čn|da.
i̇ protivъnъię. vъ mǫ|drostь
pravьdъnъixъ. ugo|tovati g͡vi
l'üdi sъvrъše|nъı.
18. i̇ reče zaxarič kъ aᴋlu.| po
čьsomu razumēǫ̈ se.| Ăzъ bo
esmь starъ. i̇ žena moě|
zamatorěvъši vъ dьnъxъ svo|ixъ.

19. i̇ otъvěštavъ aᴋlъ reče| emu.
ăzъ esmь gavriilъ.| prěstoęı
prědъ* b͞mь. i̇ posъ|lanъ° ěsmь
g͞lati tebě. i̇ bla|gověstitı tebě se.

20. i̇ se bǫ|deši mlъčn.
do ńegože dьne| bǫdetъ se.
za ńe ne věrova.| slovesemъ
moimъ · eže sъ|bǫdǫtъ sn vь
vrěmn svoę.|
21. i̇ běšn l'üdье židǫšte za|xarię. i̇
čüždaăxǫ sn eže| mǫždaăše
vь c͞rkъve.

22. i̇ tъ| bě pomavaę imъ. i̇
prěbъı|vaăše němъ.

Zog. *17* o͡cmъ an o͡cmь dubium. (J) *19* prědъ an prědь dub. (J) °Końcowy jer
w poslanъ budzi wątpliwości. (M = Moszyński)

MARIANUS

16. ι mъnogъı sn̄vъ izdr̄lvъ
obrati|tъ kъ g̅i b̅u ixъ.

17. ι tъ prědьide|tъ prědъ nimь
d̅xomь i siloǫ i|liinoǫ̈. obratiti
srъdьca otьce|mъ na čnda.
ι protivъnъıę vъ| mǫdrostь
pravedъnъıxъ. ugo|tovati g̅vi lüdi
sъvrъšenъı.|

18. ι reče zaxarič kъ ank̄u. po
česomu| razuměǫ̈ se. azъ bo esmъ
starъ i| žena moě zamatorěvъši vъ
dьne|xъ svoixъ.

19. ι otъvěštavъ ank̄lъ.| reče emu.
azъ esmъ gavr̄lъ prě|stoęi prědъ
bm̄ъ. ι posъlanъ| esmъ g̅lti kъ*
tebě. ι blagověsti|ti tebě.

20. ι se bǫdeši mlъčN i ne mogъı
proglagolati. do negože| dьne
bǫdetъ se. zane ne věrova|
slovesemъ moimъ. ěže sъbǫ|dǫtъ
sN vъ vrěmN svoė.

21. ι běšN| lüdьe židǫ̈e zaxarię.
ι čü|ždaaxǫ sN eže kъšněaše tъ vъ
crъ|kъve.

22. ιšedъ že ne možaaše g̅lati| kъ
lüdemъ. ι razuměšN ěko vidě|nie
vidě vъ cr̄kvi. ι tъ bě pomava|lę
imъ. ι prěbъıvaaše němъ.

16. καὶ πολλοὺς τῶν υἱῶν Ἰσραὴλ ἐπι-
στρέψει ἐπὶ κύριον τὸν θεὸν αὐτῶν.

17. καὶ αὐτὸς προελεύσεται ἐνώπιον
αὐτοῦ ἐν πνεύματι καὶ δυνάμει Ἠλί-
ου, ἐπιστρέψαι καρδίας πατέρων ἐπὶ
τέκνα καὶ ἀπειθεῖς ἐν φρονήσει
δικαίων, ἑτοιμάσαι κυρίῳ λαὸν
κατεσκευασμένον.

18. Καὶ εἶπεν Ζαχαρίας πρὸς τὸν
ἄγγελον, Κατὰ τί γνώσομαι τοῦτο;
ἐγὼ γάρ εἰμι πρεσβύτης καὶ ἡ γυνή
μου προβεβηκυῖα ἐν ταῖς ἡμέραις
αὐτῆς.

19. καὶ ἀποκριθεὶς ὁ ἄγγελος εἶπεν
αὐτῷ, Ἐγώ εἰμι Γαβριὴλ ὁ παρεστη-
κὼς ἐνώπιον τοῦ θεοῦ, καὶ ἀπεστάλην
λαλῆσαι πρὸς σὲ καὶ εὐαγγελίσασθαί
σοι ταῦτα·

20. καὶ ἰδοὺ ἔσῃ σιωπῶν καὶ μὴ
δυνάμενος λαλῆσαι ἄχρι ἧς ἡμέρας
γένηται ταῦτα, ἀνθ᾽ ὧν οὐκ
ἐπίστευσας τοῖς λόγοις μου, οἵτινες
πληρωθήσονται εἰς τὸν καιρὸν αὐτῶν.

21. Καὶ ἦν ὁ λαὸς προσδοκῶν τὸν
Ζαχαρίαν καὶ ἐθαύμαζον ἐν τῷ
χρονίζειν ἐν τῷ ναῷ αὐτόν.

22. ἐξελθὼν δὲ οὐκ ἐδύνατο λαλῆσαι
αὐτοῖς, καὶ ἐπέγνωσαν ὅτι ὀπτασίαν
ἑώρακεν ἐν τῷ ναῷ· καὶ αὐτὸς ἦν
διανεύων αὐτοῖς καὶ διέμενεν κωφός.

Mar. *19* kъ прибавл. над строкою. (J) Gk. *16* επι] προς *22* ηδυνατο]
εδυνατο °αυτοις] προς αυτους °διεμενεν] διεμεινεν

38

| ASSEMANIANUS | ZOGRAPHENSIS |

ASSEMANIANUS

23. ʽI bъĩ ěko isplъnišN sN ·|
denie službъi ego · ide vъ| domъ
svoi ·

24. Po sixъ že dьnex| začNtъ
elisaveθь žena e|go · ʼï taěaše sN
mͤcь д̂ · gl̄ꙟı:| Vъⁿo začNtъ
elısaveθ ·| žena zaxariina · i taěše|
sN mͤcь д̂ gl̄ꙟi ·|

25. Ěko tako sъtvori m̀ně gl̄ · vь|
dьnı vъ nNže prızьrě · Ꙏt|ętı
ponošenie moe vъ c̄lc̄ěx ·:·| ěko
tako sъ|tvori mьně gl̄ · vъ dьni
vъ nN|že prizьrě · otъętı
pono|šenie ınoe vь c̄lcěxь ·

26. Vъ še|stъi že mͤcь · posъlanъ
bъistъ| arx̄n̄жlъ gavriilъ oᵗ b̄a · vъ
gra|dъ galileıskъ imN emu
nazareθ ·|

27. kъ děvě obrǫčeně mǫžü ·
emuže| imN iosifъ · Ꙏᵗ domu
d̄dva · i|mN děvě marič ·

28. i vъšedъ kь ne|i anжlъ reč. ·
Radui sN blagodě|tьnač gl̄ sъ
toboǫ̈ · B̄lna tъı| vъ ženaxъ ·

29. ona že viděvъši i sъ|mNte
sN · o slovesi ego · i pomъı|šlěaše·
kako ·· se bǫdetъ cělo|vanie ·

ZOGRAPHENSIS

23. ı bъıstъ| ěko ısplъnišN sN
dьnьe| službьı ego. ıde vъ
do|mъ svoı.

24. po sixъ že dьnьxъ.| začNtъ
elisavьtь žena| ego. ı taěše pNtь
m̄scь* gl̄'ǫ̈|šti.

25. ěko tako sъtvori mně| gl̄ . vъ
dьni vь ńNže prizьrě.| otъęti
ponošenьe moe otъı| c̄kъ.

26. Vъ šestъı že m̄scь.*| posъlanъ
bъĩ ãжlъ gavьriı|lъ. otъ b̄a. vъ
gradъ galile|ıskъ. ěmuže ïmN
nazaretъ.|

27. k̄ъ děvě obrǫ̆čeně mǫževi.|
ěmuže ïmN ïosifъ. ŏtъ| domu
d̄ava. ïmN děvě marič.|

28. ı vъšьdъ kъ ńeı aжlъ reče.|
raduı sN blagodětьnač gl̄| sъ
toboǫ̈. bl̄gs̄vena* tъı| vъ ženaxъ.

29. Ꙏna že slъıša|vъši sъmNte sN
o slovesi| ěgo. ı pomъıšl'ěaše vъ
se|bě. kako se bǫdetъ cělova|nьe.

Zog. **24** W m̄scь... specjalna ligatura ... czytana przez Gr[unskiego] ... jako
mě, a nie nadpisane s .... (M) **26** W m̄scь ligatura j.w. (M) **28** Pкпс.
bl̄gsvena (J). bl̄gsv'ena (M).

MARIANUS

23. ι bы|stъ ěko isplъnišN sN
denьe služь|bы ego ide vъ domъ
svoi.
24. po sixъ| že dьnexъ ·:· z̄c̄ ·:·
začNtъ elisave|tь žena ego. ι taěše
sN d m̄scъ gl̄ǭ|šti.

23. καὶ ἐγένετο ὡς ἐπλήσθησαν αἱ
ἡμέραι τῆς λειτουργίας αὐτοῦ,
ἀπῆλθεν εἰς τὸν οἶκον αὐτοῦ.
24. Μετὰ δὲ ταύτας τὰς ἡμέρας
συνέλαβεν Ἐλισάβετ ἡ γυνὴ αὐτοῦ καὶ
περιέκρυβεν ἑαυτὴν μῆνας πέντε
λέγουσα

25. ěko tako sъtvori mьně ḡъ̄. vь|
dьni vъ nNže prizьrě. otъęti
po|nošenie moe vъ c̄l̄vcěxъ ·:·

25. ὅτι Οὕτως μοι πεποίηκεν κύριος
ἐν ἡμέραις αἷς ἐπεῖδεν ἀφελεῖν
ὄνειδός μου ἐν ἀνθρώποις.

26. Vъ šestы že měsNcъ
posъlanъ bы|stъ an̄ǧ̄lъ gavьrilъ
otъ b̄ā. vъ gra|dъ galileiskъ.
emuže imN naza|retъ.
27. kъ děvě obrǫčeně mǫževi.|
emuže imN iosifъ. otъ domu
da|v̄dva. ι imN děvě mariě.
28. ι vъše|dъ kъ nei an̄ǧ̄lъ reče.
radui sN bla|godatъnaě ḡъ̄ sъ
toboǫ̈. blaḡsna| tы vъ ženaxъ.
29. ona že viděvъši| sъmNte sN o
slovesi ego. ι po|mъišlěaše vъ
sebě kakovo se bǫ|detъ cělovanie.

26. Ἐν δὲ τῷ μηνὶ τῷ ἕκτῳ ἀπεστάλη
ὁ ἄγγελος Γαβριὴλ ἀπὸ τοῦ θεοῦ εἰς
πόλιν τῆς Γαλιλαίας ᾗ ὄνομα
Ναζαρέθ
27. πρὸς παρθένον ἐμνηστευμένην
ἀνδρὶ ᾧ ὄνομα Ἰωσὴφ ἐξ οἴκου Δαυίδ,
καὶ τὸ ὄνομα τῆς παρθένου Μαριάμ.
28. καὶ εἰσελθὼν πρὸς αὐτὴν εἶπεν,
Χαῖρε, κεχαριτωμένη, ὁ κύριος μετὰ
σοῦ.
29. ἡ δὲ ἐπὶ τῷ λόγῳ διεταράχθη καὶ
διελογίζετο ποταπὸς εἴη ὁ ἀσπασμὸς
οὗτος.

Gk. 26 τω μηνι τω εκτω]] τω εκτω μηνι   27 Δαυιδ]] Δαβιδ   28 αυτην]] αυτην
ο αγγελος   °σου]] σου ευλογημενη συ εν γυναιξιν   29 επι τ. λ. δ.]] ιδουσα
(ακουσασα) δ. επι τ. λ. αυτου   °διελ.]] διελ. εν εαυτη

40

ASSEMANIANUS	ZOGRAPHENSIS

ASSEMANIANUS

30. İ reče anᵹlъ kъ nei · Ne boļi
sn marie · obrěte bo blagodětļ otъ
b̄a ·ļ

31. İ se začьneši vъ črěvě ·ļ
i rodiši s̄nъ · i narečeši imN emuļ
ĩsъ ·

32. sь bǫdetъ veliı · i s̄nьļ
vъišьněago narečetъ sn · İ daļstъ
emu ḡb b̄ъ prěstolъ d̄da ōcaļ
ego ·

33. i vъ̄critъ sn vъ domu
iěkoļvlı vъ věkъı · İ c̄rstvu egoļ ne
bǫdetъ konca ·

34. Reče že ıarıěļ kъ anᵹlu ·
Kako se bǫdetъ ideļ mǫža ne
znaǫ·

35. İ ωˡvěᵹavъ anᵹlъ reče ei ·
D̄xъ st̄ьi naidetьļ na tN · i sila
vъišьněago osěniļtъ tN · Těmьže i
eže roditъļ sn · s̄to narečetъ sn
s̄nъ b̄žii ·ļ

36. İ se elısaveθь ǫžika tvoě ·ļ
i tạ začNtъ s̄na vъ starostьļ svoǫ ·
i se m̄cъ šestъi éï estъ ·ļ
narıcaeměi neplodьvı ·

ZOGRAPHENSIS

30. ı reče ěı aᵹlъ. ne boıļ sn
marie. ŏbrěte bo blagoļdětь ŏtъ
b̄a.

31. ı se začьneļšı vь črěvě ·
ı rodiši s̄nъ ·ļ ı narečeši ımN ěmu
ĩs. ļ

32. sь* bǫdetъ veliı. ı s̄nьļ
vъišьńěǎgo narečetь sn.ļ ı dastъ
emu ḡb b̄ъ. prěstoļlъ d̄ada ōca
ego.

33. ı vъ̄critъ snļ vъ domu.
ıěkovl'i. vъ věkъı.ļ ı c̄rstvu ego ne
bǫdetъ koļnьca.

34. Reče že mariě kъ aᵹlu.ļ kako
bǫdetъ se. ıžde mǫļža ne znaǫ.

35. ı otъvěštaļvъ aᵹlъ reče eı.
d̄xъ st̄ьı ļ naidetъ na tN. ı sila
vъıļšьńěǎgo ŏsěnitъ tN. těmьļže
ı eže roditъ sn. s̄to nareļčetъ sn
s̄nъ b̄žii.*ļ

36. ı se ělıļsavьtь. ǫžika tvoě.
ı taļ začьnetъ* vъ starostьļ svoǫ. ı
sь m̄cъ° šestъı ļ estъ eı.
narıcaeměi neploļdъvi.

Zog. *32* Jer miękki w s̲ь̲ na miejscu innej wydrapanej litery. (M) *35* W b̃žii
ligatura ž̲i̲ (M) *36* emend. aliqu. ne erasit, sed vest. app. (J) °Końcowy jer w
za̲č̲ь̲n̲e̲t̲ъ̲ budzi wątpliwości. (M) °Co do ligatury w m̲ᶜ̲ь̲ por. uwagi przy *24*.
(M)

MARIANUS

30. ι reče ei anͷlъ.| ne boi sn
marie. obrěte bo blago|datъ otъ
ба.
31. ι se začьneši vъ črě|vě i rodiši
snъ. ι narečeši imn e|mu
isъ.
32. sь bǫdetъ velii· ι snъ|
vъišьněago narečetъ sn ·:·| ι dastъ
emu gъ bъ prěstolъ davda| otca
ego.
33. ι vъcěsaritъ sn vъ domu
i|ěkovli vъ věkъı· ι csrstviü ego
ne| bǫdetъ konьca ·:·
34. Reče že marič kъ|
anͷlu. kako bǫdetъ se ide
mǫža| ne znaǫ̃
35. ι otъvěštavъ anͷlъ reče| ei.
dxъ stъı naidetъ na tn. ι sila|
vъišьněago osěnitъ tn. těmь že
e|že roditъ sn sto narečetъ sn
snъ bžii.|
36. ι se elisavetь ǫžika tvoě. ι ta
za|čntъ sna vъ starostь svoǫ̃. ι sъ|
měsncъ šestъı estъ ei. naricae|měi
neplodъvi.

30. καὶ εἶπεν ὁ ἄγγελος αὐτῇ, Μὴ
φοβοῦ, Μαριάμ, εὗρες γὰρ χάριν παρὰ
τῷ θεῷ.
31. καὶ ἰδοὺ συλλήμψῃ ἐν γαστρὶ καὶ
τέξῃ υἱόν καὶ καλέσεις τὸ ὄνομα
αὐτοῦ Ἰησοῦν.
32. οὗτος ἔσται μέγας καὶ υἱὸς
ὑψίστου κληθήσεται καὶ δώσει αὐτῷ
κύριος ὁ θεὸς τὸν θρόνον Δαυὶδ τοῦ
πατρὸς αὐτοῦ,
33. καὶ βασιλεύσει ἐπὶ τὸν οἶκον
Ἰακὼβ εἰς τοὺς αἰῶνας καὶ τῆς
βασιλείας αὐτοῦ οὐκ ἔσται τέλος.
34. εἶπεν δὲ Μαριὰμ πρὸς τὸν
ἄγγελον, Πῶς ἔσται τοῦτο, ἐπεὶ
ἄνδρα οὐ γινώσκω;
35. καὶ ἀποκριθεὶς ὁ ἄγγελος εἶπεν
αὐτῇ, Πνεῦμα ἅγιον ἐπελεύσεται ἐπὶ
σέ καὶ δύναμις ὑψίστου ἐπισκιάσει
σοι· διὸ καὶ τὸ γεννώμενον ἅγιον
κληθήσεται υἱὸς θεοῦ.
36. καὶ ἰδοὺ Ἐλισάβετ ἡ συγγενίς
σου καὶ αὐτὴ συνείληφεν υἱὸν ἐν
γήρει αὐτῆς καὶ οὗτος μὴν ἔκτος
ἐστὶν αὐτῇ τῇ καλουμένῃ στεῖρα·

Gk. 30 ο αγγελος αυτη] αυτη ο αγγελος °Μαριαμ] Μαρια °τω θεω] θεου
33 επι] εις 35 σοι] σε °γεννωμενον] γενομενον 36 συνειληφυια] συνειληφεν

ASSEMANIANUS	ZOGRAPHENSIS

ASSEMANIANUS

37. Ěko ne| iznemožetъ отъ б͞а
vsěkь g͞lъ :|
38. Reče že marič · se raba g͞ně ·
bǫ|di мъně po g͞lu tvoému
İ o|tıde отъ neę ànм͠lъ ·:· · –|

39. Vъstavъši marič · i|de vъ
podъgorie sъ tъštanie|mъ · vъ
gradъ iüdovъ ·
40. i vъni|de vъ domъ zaxariinъ ·
ï cělo|va elisaveθь ·
41. İ bъі͠ѕ ěko uslъi|ša elisaveθь ·
cělovanie mari|ino · vъzıgra ѕn
m¹adъncсь rado|ѱamı vь ǫtrobě
eę · i isplъ|nı ѕn d͡xmъ stъimъ
elısaveθь ·|
42. İ vъzъpi ı glasomъ veliemъ| i
reče · B͡lvna tъi vъ ženaxъ ·|
i b͡lvnъ plodъ črěva tvoego ·|
43. İ отъ kǫdu se mně da pridetъ|
m͡tı г͡а moego kь mně ·
44. se bo ěko| bъistъ gla͠ѕ
cělovaně tvo|ego vъ ušiü moeü ·
vъzigra| ѕn m¹adъnecъ radoštamı
vъ| črěvě moemъ ·
45. i blažena ěže vě|rǫ ętъ · ěko
bǫdetъ sъvrъše|nie g͡lanъimъ (ei).
otъ г͡а ·

ZOGRAPHENSIS

37. ěko ne ïznemože|tъ о̌тъ б͞а
vъsěkъ* g͞lъ.*.
38. reče| že marьě. se raba g͞ně.
bǫ|di m'ně po g͞lu tvoemu.|
ï otide о̌тъ ńeę aм͠lъ.|

39. vъstavъši že marič vъ| tъı dni.
ïde vъ gorǫ sъ| tъštanьemь. vъ
gradъ| ïüdovъ.
40. ı vьnide vъ domъ| zaxarıinъ ·
ï cělova eli|savьtь ·
41. ı bъistъ ěko u|slъiša ělisavьtь
· cělo|vanьe marıino · vъzigra| ѕn
mladъnьcь radoštami| vь črěvě eę
· ï isplъni ѕn| d͡xomь stъımь
ělisavь|tь ·
42. ï vъzъpi glasomь ve|lьemь
ï reče · blg͡vna tъı| vъ* ženaxъ ·
ï blg͡svenъ| plodъ črěva tvoego ·
43. ï отъ|kǫdu se · da pridetъ matı|
г͡ı moego kъ mně ·
44. se bo ěko| bъistъ glasъ ·
cělova|nьě tvoego · vъ ušьü
moeü ·| vьzigra ѕn mladěništь |
radoštamı vь črěvě moemь ·|
45. ï blažena ěže věrǫ ętъ ·| ěko
bǫdetъ sъvrъšenьe ·| g͡lanъimъ
о̌тъ г͡ě ·

Zog. *37* form lit. ь et ъ dub. (J) °We vъsěkъ wątpliwy tylko jer pierwszy. (M)
42 Jer w vъ wątpliwy. (M)

MARIANUS

37. ěko ne iznemožetъ| otъ b̄a
vьsěkъ g̅lъ.

38. reče že mariě| se raba g̅ně.
bǫdi mьně po g̅lu tvo|emu. ι otide
otъ neę an̄ẽlъ •:• k̄c •:•

39. Vъstavъši že mariě vъ tъι
dьni.| ιde vъ g̅r̄q sъ tъštaniemь •
vъ gra|dъ iüdovъ.

40. ι vьnide vъ domъ zaxa|riinъ •
ι cělova elisavetь •:•

41. ι bъι|stъ ěko uslъša* elisavetь
• cělovani|e mariino • vъzigra sn
mladьnecъ| vъ črěvě eę • ι isplъni
sn d̄xmь| st̄ъιmъ elisavetь•

42. ι vъzъpi| g̅lasomь veliemь
i reče• b̄lgsna| tъι vъ ženaxъ •
ι blgsl̄vnъ plo|dъ qtrobъι tvoeę •

43. ι otъ kqdq se| mьně • da
pridetъ mati g̅i moego| kъ mьně •

44. se bo ěko bъιstъ glasъ|
cělovaniě tvoego vъ nušiü moeǘ•|
vъzigra sn mladьnecъ radoštami|
vъ qtrobě moeï •

45. ι blažena ěže vě|rq ętъ • ěko
bǫdetъ sъvrъšenie g̅la|nъιmъ otъ
g̅i•

37. ὅτι ᵒοὐκ ἀδυνατήσει παρὰ τοῦ
θεοῦ πᾶν ῥῆμα.‟ (Gen. 18.16)

38. εἶπεν δὲ Μαριάμ, Ἰδοὺ ἡ δούλη
κυρίου· γένοιτό μοι κατὰ τὸ ῥῆμά
σου. καὶ ἀπῆλθεν ἀπ' αὐτῆς ὁ
ἄγγελος. 39. Ἀναστᾶσα δὲ Μαριὰμ
ἐν ταῖς ἡμέραις ταύταις ἐπορεύθη
εἰς τὴν ὀρεινὴν μετὰ σπουδῆς εἰς
πόλιν Ἰούδα, 40. καὶ εἰσῆλθεν εἰς τὸν
οἶκον Ζαχαρίου καὶ ἠσπάσατο τὴν
Ἐλισάβετ. 41. καὶ ἐγένετο ὡς
ἤκουσεν τὸν ἀσπασμὸν τῆς Μαρίας ἡ
Ἐλισάβετ, ἐσκίρτησεν τὸ βρέφος ἐν
τῇ κοιλίᾳ αὐτῆς, καὶ ἐπλήσθη
πνεύματος ἁγίου ἡ Ἐλισάβετ,

42. καὶ ἀνεφώνησεν κραυγῇ μεγάλῃ
καὶ εἶπεν, Εὐλογημένη σὺ ἐν γυναιξίν
καὶ εὐλογημένος ὁ καρπὸς τῆς
κοιλίας σου.

43. καὶ πόθεν μοι τοῦτο ἵνα ελθη ἡ
μήτηρ τοῦ κυρίου μου πρὸς ἐμέ;

44. ἰδοὺ γὰρ ὡς ἐγένετο ἡ φωνὴ τοῦ
ἀσπασμοῦ σου εἰς τὰ ὦτά μου,
ἐσκίρτησεν ἐν ἀγαλλιάσει τὸ βρέφος
ἐν τῇ κοιλίᾳ μου.

45. καὶ μακαρία ἡ πιστεύσασα ὅτι
ἔσται τελείωσις τοῖς λελαλημένοις
αὐτῇ παρὰ κυρίου.

Mar. *41* tak w podl. (J) *41* τον α. τ. Μ. η Ε.⟧ η Ε. τον α. τ. Μ. ᵒτο
βρεφος⟧ το βρεφος εν αγαλλιασει, cf. v. 44. *44* εν α. το β.⟧ το β. εν α.

44

46. İ re|če marıě · Velıčıtъ d̄ša
mo|ě ḡa ·

47. i vъzdradova sɴ d̄xъ moi| o
b̄ӡě s̄p̄sě moemъ ·

48. ěko prizbrě| na sъměrenıe
rabъı svoeę · se| bo otъ selě
blažɴtъ mɴ vъ|si rodı ·

49. Ěko sъtvori mně veli|čıe
sılъnъı i s̄t̄o imɴ ego ·

46. ı rečе| marıě · veličitъ d̄ša
moě| ḡě ·

47. ı vьzdradova* sɴ d̄xъ| moı · o
b̄ӡě s̄pě moemь ·|

48. ěko pri|zьrě na sъměrenье
rabъı svo|eę · se bo őtъ selě
blažɴtъ*| mɴ vьsi rodi ·

49. ěko sъtvori| mьně veličie
silьnъı ·| ı s̄t̄o ımɴ ěgo ·

50. ı milostь | ěgo vъ rodъı ı rodъ
boęštiı|mъ sɴ ego* ·

51. sъtvori drъza|vǫ mъıšьсeǫ̈
svoeǫ̈ · ra|stoči grъdъię mъıslьǫ̈|
srъdьca ıxъ* ·

52. nizъloži si|lьnъię sъ prěstolъ·
ı vь|znese sъměrenъię ·

53. lačǫ|štɴę* ısplьni blagъ · ı
bo|gatɴštɴę sɴ otъpusti tъ|štɴ ·

54. priętъ ıl͡ě őtroka| svoego ·
pomęnǫti milo|stь ·

55. ěkože ḡla kъ o͡cemъ na|šimъ ·
ǎvramu ι sěmene| ěgo do věka ·

56. Prě|bъı͡s že marıě sъ neǫ̈ ěko
tri m͡ĕcę ·| i vъzvrati sɴ vъ domъ
svoi ·:· –|

56. prěbъıstъ že| marıě sъ ńeǫ̈ ·
ěko tri m͡scɴ*| ı vъzvrati sɴ vъ
domъ| svoı ·

Zog. *47* vъzdr. an vъzdr. dub. (J) *48* Jer w blažɴtъ wątpliwy. (M) *50* Nad e w
ego łuczek lub plamka. (M) *51* Jer w ıxъ wątpliwy. (M) *53* Głag. lačǫštɴę
poprawiacz cyrylski Nr 6 przerobił na alъčǫštɴę w ten sposób, że przed wyra-
zem dopisał głag. a, które oczywiście jest czarne jak cała cyrylica Nr 6, a głag.

MARIANUS

46. ι reče mariě · veliči|tъ d̄ša
moě ḡa ·

47. ι vъzdradova sn d̄xъ| moi o
b̄z̄ě s̄p̄s̄ě moemь ·

48. ěko prizъrě na| sъměrenie
rabъı svoeę̨ · se bo otъ| selě
blažntъ mn vьsi rodi ·

49. ěko sъ|tvori mьně veličьě
silъnъı · ι svn|to imn ego ·

50. ι milostь ego vъ rodъ i ro|dъ
boęštiimъ sn ego ·

51. sъtvori drъ|žavǫ mъıšъceǫ̈ ·
svoeǫ̈ rastači| grъdъıę̨ mъısliǫ̈
s̄rdca ixъ.

52. nizъ|loži silъnъıę̨ sъ prěstolъ·
ι vъzne|se sъměrenъıę̨ ·

53. alčǫštnę̨ isplъ|ni blagъ ·
ι bogatnštnę̨ sn otъpu|sti tъštn·

54. prię̨tъ il̄ě otroka svo|ego ·
poměnǫti milostь ·

55. ěkože ḡla| kъ o̅t̅cmъ našimъ ·
avramu i sě|meni ego do věka ·:·

56. Prěbъıstъ že| mariě sъ neǫ̈
ěko i tri m̄s̄cn · ι vъ|zvrati sn vъ
domъ svoi ·:· ·:· ko̅c̅ ·:·

46. Καὶ εἶπεν Μαριάμ, Μεγαλύνει ἡ
ψυχή μου τὸν κύριον,

47. καὶ ἠγαλλίασεν τὸ πνεῦμά μου
ἐπὶ τῷ θεῷ τῷ σωτῆρί μου,

48. ὅτι ἐπέβλεψεν ἐπὶ τὴν
ταπείνωσιν τῆς δούλης αὐτοῦ. ἰδοὺ
γὰρ ἀπὸ τοῦ νῦν μακαριοῦσίν με
πᾶσαι αἱ γενεαί,

49. ὅτι ἐποίησέν μοι μεγάλα ὁ
δυνατός. καὶ ἅγιον τὸ ὄνομα αὐτοῦ,

50. καὶ τὸ ἔλεος αὐτοῦ εἰς γενεὰς
καὶ γενεὰς τοῖς φοβουμένοις αὐτόν.

51. Ἐποίησεν κράτος ἐν βραχίονι
αὐτοῦ, διεσκόρπισεν ὑπερηφάνους
διανοίᾳ καρδίας αὐτῶν·

52. καθεῖλεν δυνάστας ἀπὸ θρόνων
καὶ ὕψωσεν ταπεινούς,

53. πεινῶντας ἐνέπλησεν ἀγαθῶν καὶ
πλουτοῦντας ἐξαπέστειλεν κενούς.

54. ἀντελάβετο Ἰσραὴλ παιδὸς αὐτοῦ,
μνησθῆναι ἐλέους,

55. καθὼς ἐλάλησεν πρὸς τοὺς
πατέρας ἡμῶν, τῷ Ἀβραὰμ καὶ τῷ
σπέρματι αὐτοῦ εἰς τὸν αἰῶνα.

56. Ἔμεινεν δὲ Μαριὰμ σὺν αὐτῇ ὡς
μῆνας τρεῖς, καὶ ὑπέστρεψεν εἰς τὸν
οἶκον αὐτῆς.

---

a po l przerobił na cyrylski ъ, wpisując go na nie naruszone głag. a. (M) 56 W
m̄s̄cn specjalna ligatura .... (M) °Wyraz ko̅c̅ z nadpisanym c jest wprowadzony
z marginesu kreską za wyraz svoi. (M) Gk. 50 γεν. και γεν.] γενεαν και
γενεαν] γενεας και γενεων

ASSEMANIANUS	ZOGRAPHENSIS

57. Elisaveti že isplъnišn sn|
denie rodıti ei · i rodı s͠nъ ·

57. ělisaveti že i̇|splъnišn sn
dъnьe roditi| eı · ι rodi s͠nъ ·

58. Ι̇ slъišašn ok͞rstъ živǫ|ѱii
roždenie éę · Ěko vъzve|lιčilъ
estъ g͞b m͞lstъ svo|ǫ sъ neǫ̈ ·
Ι̇ radovaaxǫ sn| sъ neǫ̈ ·

58. ι̇ slъiša|šn ŏkrъstъ živǫšteı · ι̇
ro|žденьe eę · ěko vъzveli|čilъ
estъ g͞b · milostь svo|ǫ sъ ńeǫ̈ ·

59. Ι̇ bъi͡s vъ ósmъı d͡ne ·| pridǫ
obrězatъ otročnte ·| Ι̇ naricaaxǫ e
imenemъ o͞ca svo|ěgo zaxarič ·

59. ι̇ bъıstъ vъ osmъı| dъnь ·
pridǫ ŏbrězatъ ŏtro|čnte · ι̇
naricaăxǫ e · ι̇me|nemь · o͞ca
svoego zaxarię ·|

60. i ótъvěѱavъ|ši m͞tι ego re ni ·
nъ da nare|četъ sn imn emu
iоanъ ·

60. ι̇ otъvěštavъši m͞tι ego| reče ·
ni · nъ da narečetъ sn| ι̇mn ěmu
ι̇oanъ ·

61. Ι̇ rěšn kъ nei · ěko niktože
estъ| otъ roždenič tvoego · ιže
na|rιcaetъ sn imenemъ těmь ·

61. ι̇ rěšn ei ·| ěko* nikъtože ěstъ
otъ rožde|nьě tvoego · iže
naricaetъ| sn ι̇menemь těmь ·

62. pomavaaxǫ že o͞cü ego · kako|
bı xotělъ nareѱı e ·

62. poma|vaăše že o͞cь ego · kako
bi xo|tělъ narešti e ·

63. Ι̇ isprošъ| dъѱicǫ · Napısa g͞īn:
ioanъ| estъ imn emu · i čüždaaxǫ|
sn vъsı ·

63. ι̇ isprošъ| dъšticǫ napsa · g͞īn ·
ι̇oanъ| estъ ι̇mn ěmu · ι̇ čüdišn| sn
emu v'si ·

64. ʿOtvrěsn že sn usta| ego abie ·
i ęz͞kъ ego · Ι̇ g͞laaše| B͞ıvǫ b͞a ·

64. otvrъzošn| že sn usta ego
ăbьe · ι̇ ęzъı|kъ ěgo · ι̇ g͞laăše ·
bgs͞vstn b͞a ·|

65. Ι̇ bъi͡s na vъsěx| straxъ ·
živǫѱiixъ ok͞rstъ · i| vъ vsei
gornιι iüdeistěi ·| povědaemi
běaxǫ vъsi g͞li| sı ·

65. ι̇ bъi͡s na vsěxъ straxъ ·|
živǫštiıxъ ŏkrъstъ ι̇xъ ·| ι̇ vъseı
strěně ι̇üděιscěi ·| povědaemi
běăxǫ vsi g͞li| sıi ·

---

61 Nad ě w ěko raczej plamka niż łuczek. (M)

MARIANUS

57. Eli|saveti že isplьni sn vrěmn
rodi|ti ei · ι rodi sn̄ъ ·

58. ι slъišašN okrъ|stь živǫštei
ι roždenie eǫ· ěko| vьzveličilъ
estь g̃ъ milostь| svoǫ sъ neǫ·
ι radovaxǫ sn sъ neǫ·|

59. ι bъistь vъ osmъι denь pridǫ
o|brězatъ otročNte· ι naricaxǫ e|
imenemь oͭca svoego zaxarič·

60. ι o|tъvěštavъši mati ego reče ·
ni nъ| da narečetъ sn ioanъ ·

61. ι rěšN ei·| ěko niktože estь otъ
roždeně tvoego ·| ιže naricaatъ sn
imenemь těmь ·|

62. Pomavaaxǫ že otьcü ego ·
kako bi xo|tělъ narešti e ·

63. ι isprošь dъšticǫ| napisa g̃N ·
ιoanъ estь imN emu·| ι čüdišN
(sn)* vьsi

64. ótvrěsN že sn u|sta ego abie i
ęz̃kъ ego · ι gͫaše bla|goslovN b̃a ·

65. ι bъistь na vьsěxъ| straxъ
živǫštiixъ okrъstь ixъ ·| ι vъ
vьsei straně iüdeistčěi| povědaemi
běaxǫ vьsi gͫi sii ·

57. Τῇ δὲ Ἐλισάβετ ἐπλήσθη ὁ
χρόνος τοῦ τεκεῖν αὐτήν, καὶ
ἐγέννησεν υἱόν.

58. καὶ ἤκουσαν οἱ περίοικοι καὶ οἱ
συγγενεῖς αὐτῆς ὅτι ἐμεγάλυνεν
κύριος τὸ ἔλεος αὐτοῦ μετ᾽ αὐτῆς καὶ
συνέχαιρον αὐτῇ.

59. Καὶ ἐγένετο ἐν τῇ ἡμέρᾳ τῇ
ὀγδόῃ ἦλθον περιτεμεῖν τὸ παιδίον
καὶ ἐκάλουν αὐτὸ ἐπὶ τῷ ὀνόματι τοῦ
πατρὸς αὐτοῦ Ζαχαρίαν.

60. καὶ ἀποκριθεῖσα ἡ μήτηρ αὐτοῦ
εἶπεν, Οὐχί, ἀλλὰ κληθήσεται
Ἰωάννης.

61. καὶ εἶπαν πρὸς αὐτὴν ὅτι Οὐδείς
ἐστιν ἐκ τῆς συγγενείας σου ὃς
καλεῖται τῷ ὀνόματι τούτῳ.

62. ἐνένευον δὲ τῷ πατρὶ αὐτοῦ τὸ
τί ἂν θέλοι καλεῖσθαι αὐτό.

63. καὶ αἰτήσας πινακίδιον ἔγραψεν
λέγων, Ἰωάννης ἐστὶν ὄνομα αὐτοῦ.
καὶ ἐθαύμασαν πάντες.

64. ἀνεῴχθη δὲ τὸ στόμα αὐτοῦ
παραχρῆμα καὶ ἡ γλῶσσα αὐτοῦ, καὶ
ἐλάλει εὐλογῶν τὸν θεόν.

65. καὶ ἐγένετο ἐπὶ πάντας φόβος
τοὺς περιοικοῦντας αὐτούς, καὶ ἐν
ὅλῃ τῇ ὀρεινῇ τῆς Ἰουδαίας
διελαλεῖτο πάντα τὰ ῥήματα ταῦτα,

Mar. *63* sn после čüdišN прип. над стр. (J) Gk. *56* ωϛ〛 ωσει *59* τη ημερα
τη ογδοη〛 τη ογδοη ημερα °Ζαχαριαν〛 Ζαχαρια *60* Ιωαννηϛ〛 το ονομα αυτου
Ιωαννηϛ *63* αυτου〛 αυτω

48

66. i položišN vsi slъišN|štii na
sr̄dciixъ svoixъ · čь|to ubo otročN
se bǫdetъ · i rǫka ḡně bě sъ
nimъ ·

67. i zaxa|riě o͞cь ego · isplъni sN
d͞xmъ| st͞biimъ · i pr͞rčъstvova
g͞iN ·

68. B̄lnъ g͞b b͞ъ iz̄lvъ · Ěko
posě|tı i sъtvorı izbavleni|e
lüdemъ svoimъ ·

ZOGRAPHENSIS

66. i položišN vsi slъı|šavъšeı na
sr'dьcixъ svo|ixъ · ḡl'öšte · čьto
ubo| ötročN se bǫdetъ · i rǫka| ḡně
bě sъ ńimъ ·

67. i zaxariě| o͞cь ego · isplъni sN
d͞xomь| st͞bımь · i proročьstvo|va
g͞iN

68. Blḡsnъ g͞b b͞ъ| il'evъ · ěko
posěti i sъtvo|ri izbavl'enьe
l'üdьmъ| svoimъ · *°

69. i vъzdviže ro|gъ sp͞enьě
našego · vъ domu| dāvě · ötroka
svoego ·

70. Ěkože| ḡla ustъı st͞bıxъ ·
sǫ|štiıxъ otъ věka · prorokъ| ěgo ·

71. sp͞enьe ötъ vragъ na|šixъ ·
izdrǫkъı vъsěxъ ·| nenavidNštixъ
nasъ ·|

72. Sъtvoriti milostь| sъ o͞ci
našimi · i pomě|nǫti zavětъ st͞oı
svoı ·|

73. KlNtvǫ eǜže klNtъ sN| kъ
ăvramu o͞cü našemu ·| dati namъ

74. bestraxa · izdrǫ|kъı vragъ
našixъ izba|vl'ьšemъ sN · Služiti|
ěmu

75. prěpodobьemь · i pra*|vъdoǫ
prědь ńimь vsN| dьni života
našego ·

Zog. *68* Za svoımъ · po kropce jest jeszcze krzyżyk. (M)   *75* Litera r w
pravъdoǫ nadpisana nad wierszem. (M)

MARIANUS

66. ι| položišn vьsi slъišavъšei na
srъ|dьcixъ svoixъ glǭšte · čto ubo
o|tročn se bǫdetъ · ι rǫka gn̄ě bě
sъ| nimь ·

67. ι zaxarič o͡tcъ e · ιsplъni| sn
d͡xmь stͧыmъ · ι proročьstvo|va
gl̄n ·:·

68. Blgͫn̄ъ g͡ъ b͡ъ iͧzlvъ · ěko|
posěti i sъtvori izbavlenie
lü|demъ svoimъ·

69. ι vъzdviže rogъ| sp͡snič našego
· vъ domu dav͡da o|troka
svoego ·

70. ěkože gl͡a ustъι| stͧыxъ
sǫštiixъ otъ věka pr̄kъ ·|

71. sp͡snie otъ vragъ našixъ ·
ι izdǫ|kъ vъsěxъ nenavidnštiixъ
na|sъ ·

72. sъtvoriti milostь sъ o͡ci|
našimi · ι pomnnqti zavětъ| st͡oi
svoi ·

73. klntvoǫ eǫ̈že klntъ| sn · kъ
avraamu o͡tcü našemu| dati namъ

74. bestraxa · izdrǫ|kъı vragъ
našixъ izbavlьšemь| sn · sluužiti
emu

75. prěpodobiemь ·| ι pravъdoǫ
prědъ nimь vьsn dьni ži|vota
našego ·

66. καὶ ἔθεντο πάντες οἱ ἀκούσαντες
ἐν τῇ καρδίᾳ αὐτῶν, λέγοντες, Τί
ἄρα τὸ παιδίον τοῦτο ἔσται; καὶ γὰρ
χεὶρ κυρίου ἦν μετ' αὐτοῦ.

67. Καὶ Ζαχαρίας ὁ πατὴρ αὐτοῦ
ἐπλήσθη πνεύματος ἁγίου καὶ
ἐπροφήτευσεν λέγων,

68. Εὐλογητὸς κύριος ὁ θεὸς τοῦ
Ἰσραήλ, ὅτι ἐπεσκέψατο καὶ ἐποίησεν
λύτρωσιν τῷ λαῷ αὐτοῦ,

69. καὶ ἤγειρεν κέρας σωτηρίας ἡμῖν
ἐν οἴκῳ Δαυὶδ παιδὸς αὐτοῦ,

70. καθὼς ἐλάλησεν διὰ στόματος
τῶν ἁγίων ἀπ' αἰῶνος προφητῶν
αὐτοῦ, 71. σωτηρίαν ἐξ ἐχθρῶν ἡμῶν
καὶ ἐκ χειρὸς πάντων τῶν μισούντων
ἡμᾶς,

72. ποιῆσαι ἔλεος μετὰ τῶν πατέρων
ἡμῶν καὶ μνησθῆναι διαθήκης ἁγίας
αὐτοῦ,

73. ὅρκον ὃν ὤμοσεν πρὸς Ἀβραὰμ
τὸν πατέρα ἡμῶν, τοῦ δοῦναι ἡμῖν

74. ἀφόβως ἐκ χειρὸς ἐχθρῶν
ῥυσθέντας λατρεύειν αὐτῷ

75. ἐν ὁσιότητι καὶ δικαιοσύνῃ
ἐνώπιον αὐτοῦ πάσαις ταῖς ἡμέραις
ἡμῶν.

Gk. 66 τε καρδια] ταις καρδιαις °και γαρ χειρ] και χειρ 71 ημων και εκ]
ημων εκ 75 ημων] της ζωης ημων [cf. Josh. 1.5, 1 Kings 7.14.]

50

ASSEMANIANUS

76. İ tъı o|tročn · prrk̄ъ vъišněago
nare|češi sn · prědъideši bo prědъ|
lıcemъ g̃nemъ · ugotovati pǫti
ego ·

80. Otročn že rastča|še ·
i krěplěaše sn d̄xmъ · i bě| vъ
pustъiněxъ · do dьne ěvle|niě
svoego · kъ iz̄lü ·:· –

ZOGRAPHENSIS

76. ı̇ tъı*| ŏtročn prorokъ
vъıšьńĕgo| narečeši sn ·
prědъıdeši| bo prědъ licemь
g̃nemь ·| ŭgotovati pǫtь ego ·|
77. dati razumъ sp̃enьě| l'üdemъ
ego vъ ŏstavl'e|nьe vъ
ŏtъpuštenьe grě|xъ našixъ ·
78. milosrъdъı| radi milosti b̃a
našego ·| vь ńixьže* posěti nasъ ·|
vъstokъ sъ vъıše
79. prosvě|titi šĕdnštnę vъ tъmě|
ı̇ v' sěni sъmrъtьněı ·| napraviti
nogъı našn na| pǫtь mirenъ ·
80. ŏtročn že ra|stěăše ·
ı̇ krěpl'ěăše sn| d̄xomь · ı̇ bě vъ
pustъıńexъ ·| do dьne ăvl'enьě
svoego| kъ ı̃l'ü · kō^c* ·

Zog. *76* tъi an tъi dub. (J) *78* Jer w ńixьže wątpliwy. (M) *80* c w kō^c nadpisane. (M)

MARIANUS

76. ι тъι otročN prorkъ
vъıšь|něago narečeši sN ·
prědъideši bo prě|dъ licemъ
ḡnemь ugotovati pǫti| ego ·
77. dati razumъ sp̄sniě lüdemъ|
ego vъ otъpuštenie grěxovъ ixъ ·

78. mi|losřdei radi ба našego · vь
nixъže po|sětilъ estъ nasъ
vъstokъ sъ vъı|še ·
79. prosvětiti sědnštnę vь tьmě :|
ι sěni sъmrьtьně · napraviti
nogъı| našN na pǫtь mirenъ ·
80. otročN že ra|stěaše i krěplěaše
sN d̄xmь · ι bě vъ| pustъıněxъ do
dьne avleniě svoe|go kъ izdrailü ·
·:· k̄͞c ·:·

76. Καὶ σὺ δέ, παιδίον, προφήτης
ὑψίστου κληθήσῃ· προπορεύσῃ γὰρ
ἐνώπιον κυρίου ἑτοιμάσαι ὁδοὺς
αὐτοῦς,
77. τοῦ δοῦναι γνῶσιν σωτηρίας τῷ
λαῷ αὐτοῦ ἐν ἀφέσει ἁμαρτιῶν
αὐτῶν,
78. διὰ σπλάγχνα ἐλέους θεοῦ ἡμῶν,
ἐν οἷς ἐπισκέψεται ἡμας ἀνατολὴ ἐξ
ὕψους,
79. ἐπιφᾶναι τοῖς ἐν σκότει καὶ σκιᾷ
θανάτου καθημένοις, τοῦ κατευθῦναι
τοὺς πόδας ἡμῶν εἰς ὁδὸν εἰρήνης.
80. Τὸ δὲ παιδίον ηὔξανεν καὶ
ἐκραταιοῦτο πνεύματι, καὶ ἦν ἐν ταῖς
ἐρήμοις ἕως ἡμέρας ἀναδείξεως
αὐτοῦ πρὸς τὸν Ἰσραήλ.

Gk. 77 αυτων] ημων [cf. Gal. 1.4, 1 John 2.2, Rev. 1.5].

Zographensis 242v.6–243v.1: John 6.35–45

35. reče že ї|mъ їs. Azъ esmь xlěbъ| životъnъi. grNdӂi po mь|ně. ne їmatъ vъzlakati sN.| ї věruęı vъ mN. ne їma|tъ vъždNdati sN ni|kogdaže.

36. nъ rěxъ va|mъ. ěko ι viděste mN ї ne| věruete mi.

37. Vьse eže| dastъ mьně ōcь. kъ mьně| pridetъ. ї grNdǫšta|go kъ mьně. ne їždenǫ vъ|nъ.

38. ěko sъnidъ sъ n̄se.| da ne tvořǫ volˊN moeę.| nъ volˊǫ posьlavъšaego| mN

39. Se estъ volˊě posъ|lavъšaego mN ōca. da vъ|sěko eže dastъ mi. ne po|[243r]gublˊǫ otъ ńego. nъ vъskrě|šǫ ę vъ poslědьńi dьnь.|

40. Se bo estъ volˊě ōca moego.| da vьsěkъ vidNι s̄na. ї vě|ruęı vь ńego. ї vъskrěšǫ| ї ǎzъ vъ poslědьni dьnь.|

41. Rъpъtaxǫ že ïüdei o ńemь.| ěko reče ǎzъ esmь xlěbъ| sъšьdъι sъ n̄se.

42. ї glāxǫ.| ne sь li estъ s̄nъ ïosifovъ.| emuže mъι znaemь ōca| ї materь. kako ubo sь gle|tъ. ěko sъ n̄se sъnidъ.|

43. Ѡtъvěšta že ïs. ї reče| ιmъ. ne rъpъštite me|ždü soboǫ.

44. nikъtože ne| možetъ priti kъ mьně.| ǎšte ne ōcь posьlavъι mN| privlěčetъ ego. ї azъ| vъskrěšǫ ego vъ poslě|dьńi dьnь.

45. estъ p'sano| vъ prorocěxъ. ї bǫdǫtъ| vьsi učeni(ci) b̄mь| [243v] Vьsěkъ slъιšavъι otъ| ōca. ї navъιkъ pridetъ| kъ mьně.

46. ne ěko ōca vidě|lъ estъ kъto. tъkъmo sӂi| otъ b̄a tъ vidě ōca.

47. ǎmin, ǎmin, glǭ vamъ. věru|ęı vь mN їmatъ život̃a| věčьnaego.

48. Azъ esmь xlěbъ životъnъι.

49. Ѡ̄ci| (n)aši ěšN mannǫ vъ pu|stъιńi ї umrěšN.

50. Sь e|stъ xlěbъ sъxodNι sъ nb̄se.| da ǎšte kъto ōtъ ńego ě|stъ ne umьretъ.

51. Ǎzъ e|smь xlěbъ živъι. sъšь|dъι sъ nb̄se. ǎšte kъto| sъněstъ otъ xlěba sego| živъ bǫdetъ vъ věkъ.| xlěbъ bo ïže ǎzъ damь.| plъtь moě estъ. ǫže ǎzъ| damь za životъ vьsego mira.

52. pьѓѣӑхǫ že sɴ ʼüǀdei. meždü soboǫ̈

g҃ʼǫ̈ǀ[244r]šte. kako možetъ sь datiǀ plъtь svoǫ̈ namъ ѣsti.ǀ

53. reče že ʼimъ ī҃s. ӑminǀ ӑmin, g҃lǫ̈ vamъ. ӑšteǀ ne sъnѣste plъti s҃na

čs̅kaǀgo. ʼi pieti krъvi ego.ǀ života ne ʼimate vъ sebѣ.ǀ

54. ѣdѫ́i moǫ̈ plъtь. ʼi pięǀi moǫ̈ krъvь. ʼimatъ žiǀvota vѣčьnaego.

ʼi azʼъǀ vъskrѣšǫ ɪ vъ poslѣdьǀɴ́i dьnь.

55. Plъtь bo moѣ ʼiǀstinъnoe estъ brašьno.ǀ ʼi krъvь moѣ ʼistinъno estъǀ

pivo.

56. Ědъi moǫ̈ plъǀtь. ʼi pięɪ moǫ̈ krъvь.ǀ vъ mьnѣ prѣbъi ʼi azъ vъǀ

ɴ́emь.

57. ѣkože posъla mɴǀ živѫ́i ō҃сь. ʼi azъ živǫǀ ō҃ca radi. ʼi ѣdъi mɴ tъǀ živъ

bǫdetъ mene radi.ǀ

58. sь estъ xlѣbъ sъšьdъiǀ sъ n҃se. ne ѣkože ѣšɴ ō҃ciǀ[244v] vaši man'nǫ

ʼi umrѣšɴ.ǀ ѣdѫ́i xlѣbъ sь živъ bǫǀdetъ vъ vѣkъ.ǀ

59. si reče na sъǀnъmišti. učɴ vъ kaperъǀnaumѣ.

60. mnoʒi že slъišaǀvъšei. otъ učenikъ ego rѣǀšɴ. žestoko estъ slovo se.ǀ

kъto možetъ ego slušati.ǀ

61. Vѣdъi že ī҃s vъ sebѣ. ѣkoǀ гъръштǫtъ o semь učeniǀci ego. reče ʼimъ

se li vъiǀ blaznitъ.

62. Ašte ubo uǀzьrite s҃na čskago. vъxoǀdɴšta ʼideže bѣ prѣ́ždeǀ

63. D҃xъ estъ ʼiže živ(e)tъ. otъǀ plъti nѣstъ polьzɴ nikaǀ koęže. g҃lъi ęže

ӑzъ g҃laǀxъ vamъ d҃xъ sǫtъ. ʼi živoǀtъ sǫtъ.

64. nъ sǫtъ otъ vaǀsъ eteri. ʼiže ne vѣruǫtъ.ǀ Vѣdѣӑše bo ʼiskoni ī҃s. kъtoǀ

sǫtъ ne vѣruǫšteɪ. ʼi kъǀto estъ xotɴi prѣdati ɪ.ǀ[245r]

65. ʼi g҃laaše sego radi rѣхъǀ vamъ. ѣko nikъtože neǀ možetъ priti kъ

mьnѣ.ǀ ӑšte ne bǫdetъ dano emuǀ otъ ō҃ca moego.

66. otъ sego mnoǀʒi otъ učenikъ ego ʼidǫǀ vъspɴtь. ʼi kъ tomu ne

xoǀždaxǫ sъ ɴ́imь.

67. Reče žeǀ ī҃s. obѣma na desɴte. edaǀ ɪ vъi xoštete ʼiti.

68. otъǀvѣšta emu simonъ petrъ.ǀ g҃i kъ komu ʼidemъ. g҃lъiǀ života

vѣčьnaego ʼimaši.ǀ

69. ʼi mъi vѣrovaxomъ. ʼi poǀznaxomъ. ѣko tъi esi x҃ъ s҃nъ б҃a živago.

70. otъvěšta| ı͡mъ i͡s. ne azъ li vasъ.| dъva na desɴte izbъraxъ.| i otъ
vasъ edinъ diěvo|lъ estъ.

71. G͡laše iüdq| simonova. iskariota.| sь bo xotěaše prědati ı.| edinъ sъı
otъ oboü na desɴte.

Marianus 71v.29–72r.26: Mark 14.41–52

41. ı pride tretiici. i g͡la i|mъ. sъpite pročeė i počivaite.| prispě konьčina
pride časъ. se|| prědaatъ sɴ s͡nъ člv͡čskъı| vъ rq|cě grěšъnikomъ.

42. vъstaněte idě|mъ. se prědaęi mɴ približi sɴ|

43. ı abie ešte emu g͡lǫⱷü. pride iüda| edinъ otъ obоǫ na desɴte. i sъ
ni|mь narodъ mъnogъ. sъ orǫžii i drъ|kolьmi. otъ arxierei i
kънižъni|kъ i starecъ ·:·

44. Dastъ že prědaęi e|go znamenie imъ g͡lɴ. egоže ašte| lobъžǫ iměte
i tъ estъ. i veděte| sъxranьno.

45. ı prišedъ abie pristǫpь| kъ nemu g͡la. ravvi ravvi. i oblo|bъiza i.

46. oni že vъzложišɴ rǫcě na| nь i ęsɴ i.

47. edinъ že otъ stoęšti|xъ. izvlькъ nožъ udari raba arxi|ereova. i urěza
emu uxo.

48. i otъvě|štavъ i͡sъ reče imъ. ěko na razboi|nika li izidete sъ
orǫžьemь i drъ|kolьmi ęti mɴ.

49. po vьsɴ dьni bě|xъ vъ vasъ učɴ vъ crkve| i ne ęste| mene. nъ da
sъbǫdǫtъ sɴ kъni|gъı.

50. ı ostavьše i vьsi běžašɴ.|

51. ı edinъ ünoša eterъ po nemь ide. o|děnъ vъ plaštanicǫ nagъ. ı ę|sɴ
i ünošɴ.

52. onъ že ostavь plašta|nicǫ. nagъ běža otъ nixъ.

Clozianus. Excerpt 1: On the treason of Judas

(II, 111) ... čъto xoštete mi

4r.35 dati i azъ vamъ prědamь ı· ω nevěždъstvьe
ω nečüvьstvьe mnogoe· ı azъ vamъ sNtъ
prědamь ı· česo radı rьcı mi· koǫ vı

(115) nъ imъ · li malǫ· lı velıkǫ prědaše
učıtelě · ımьže li ti oblastь dalъ e

40 стъ· na nečıstъıхъ běsěхъ. ı tolıkǫ

4v sılǫ dastъ tı da nedǫžъпъıę ubalu
ešı · ı prokaženъıę očıštaešı · ı slě

(120) ръıę tvorıšı prozьrětı· ı ina mnoga čü
desa takova tvorıti· za tъı lı dobrъıę

5 dětělı sьę mъzdъı vъzdaeši emu·
čъto xoštete mı dati sNtъ ı azъ vamъ prě
damь ı · ω neıstovъstvo velikoe pače že

(125) ω sъrebrolübьbьstvьe vьse se zъloe to sъ
tvorılo estъ· to vъzlübь sь učıtelě·

Τί θέλετέ μοι δοῦναι, κἀγὼ ὑμῖν παραδώσω αὐτόν; ὦ τῆς ἀπονοίας. Τίνος ἕνεκεν, εἰπέ μοι, (115) παραδίδως τὸν διδάσκαλον; ὅτι τὴν κατὰ τῶν δαιμόνων ἐξουσίαν σοι παρέδωκεν, ὡς καὶ νοσήματα θεραπεύειν, καὶ λεπροὺς καθαίρειν, (120) καὶ ἕτερα πολλὰ θαύματα ἐπιδείκνυσθαι; ἀντὶ οὖν τῶν εὐεργεσίων τούτων αὐτὰς ἀποδίδως τὰς ἀμοιβάς; τί θέλετέ μοι δοῦναι, κἀγὼ ὑμῖν παραδώσω αὐτὸν; ὦ τῆς ἀπονοίας, μᾶλλον δέ, (125) ὦ τῆς φιλαργυρίας. πάντα γὰρ ἐκείνη ἔτεκε τὰ κακά. Ἐκείνης αὐτὸς ἐπιθυμήσας, παρέδωκε

Quid vultis mihi dare, et ego vobis tradam eum (Matt. 26.15)? O stultitiam! Cur, quaeso, magistrum (115) prodis? an quia potestatem tibi dedit adversus daemoniam, ita ut morbos curares, lamprosos mundares, (120) et alia miracula perpetrares? pro hisne beneficiis haec illi praemia retribuis? Quid vultis mihi dare, et ego vobis eum tradam? O stultitiam! imo potius, (125) o avaritiam! nam haec tot

56

svoego prědastъ· takъ bo estъ zъlы tъ

korenь · běsa gorы d̃šǫ našǫ buǫ̈ tvoritъ·

tvoritъ vьsɴ· ne vědětɪ i sebe ɪskrъnixъ

(130)   ɪ tělesъnago obъɪčaě· ɪ otъ samogo sъ

mъɪsla ɪzgъna nы· ɪ ne pomnɪtъ nɪ

15   družьbы· nɪ obъɪčaě· nɪ roda nɪ ino

go nɪkogože· nъ oslěpɪ očɪ uma našego.

ěkože vъ tъmě tako tvorɪtъ nы xodɪ(tɪ)

(135)   ɪ vъ brěgы metaetъ· ɪ da uvěsɪ se vъ ɪ

stɪnǫ · ɪ vɪždъ ɪ togda to vъšedъ

20   kolɪko vъɪnese· otъ d̃šɴ ɪüdov. ɪ

besědǫ obъɪčaɪ· obьštenьe eže na

ɪrapězaxъ · ɪ dɪv ьпoc učenьe ɪ · naka

τὸν διδάσκαλον. Τοιοῦτον γὰρ ἐστὶν ἡ πονηρὰ ῥίζα ἐκείνη, δαίμονος
χαλεπώτερον· τὰς ἁλούσας ἐκβακχεύει ψυχάς, καὶ ποιεῖ πάντας ἀγνοεῖν, καὶ
ἑαυτὸν καὶ ὑπὸ πλησίον, (130) καὶ ὑπὸ τῆς φύσεως νόμους, καὶ αὐτῶν
ἐκβάλλει τῶν φρενῶν, καὶ παράπληγας ἐργάζειν, καὶ οὐκ ἀφίησιν οὔτε
φιλίας οὔτε συγγενείας οὔτε ἄλλου τινὸς μεμνῆσθαι· ἀλλὰ καθάπαξ
πηρώσασα ἡμῶν τὰ ὄμματα τῆς διανοίας, οὕτως ἐν σκότει ποιεῖ βαδίζειν.
(135) Καὶ ἵνα μάθῃς τοῦτο σαφῶς, ὅρα τότε πόσα ἐξέβαλεν ἐκ τῆς τοῦ
Ἰούδα ψυχῆς, τὴν ὁμιλίαν, τὴν συνήθειαν, τὴν κοινωνίαν τὴν ἐν τραπέζῃ, τὰ
θαύματα, τὴν διδασκαλίαν,

mala peperit: hujus ille concupiscentia magistrum prodidit, Talis
quippe est illa mala radix; quas invahit animas plus quam daemon in
furorem vertit, omnium ignorantiam parit, et sui et proximi (130) et
naturalium legum, ab ipsa mente excedere facit, et furiosos efficit.
neque permittit ut vel amicitiae, vel cogitationis, vel alterius
cujuspiam recordemur: sed semel excaecans oculos mentis nostrae,
nos in tenebris incedere facit. (135) Et ut hoc clare discas, vide quanta
tunc ejecerit ex anima Judae conversationem, consuetudinem, mensae
societatem, miracula, doctrinam,

(140)   zanьe· vьse to sъrebrolübьstvьe sъ

          tvorιlo estь zabъiti · pravъι·

4v.25   blaženъι pavelъ g͞laše ěko

          korenь vьsěmъ zьlomъ (e)

          stь sъrebrolüblenьe

(145)   čъto xoštete mι sɴtь

          datι ι azь vamъ prěda

30   mь ι· velьě drъzostь

          velьe bestudьe· rьcι

          mi togo li prědaešι iže vъ

(150)   sěčъskaa odrъžιtъ. vladǫštago bě

          sъι · povelěvaǫštago mιru · vladъι

35   kǫ vьsěkoι tvarι · tvorɴšta slovo

          mь · ι povelěnьmь vьse· nъ xotɴ u

          čιtι · ι bezumьe go utolιtι· vo

(155)   leǫ prědanъ bъι͞· ι poslu

τὴν παραίνεσιν, τὴν νουθεσίαν· (140) πάντα ταῦτα εἰς λήθην ἐνέβαλεν ἡ φιλαργυρία. Καλῶς ἔλεγε Παῦλος, ὅτι ῥίζα πάντων τῶν κακῶν ἐστιν ἡ φιλαργυρία. (145) Τί θέλετέ μοι δοῦναι. κἀγὼ ὑμῖν παραδώσω αὐτόν; Πολλὴ ἡ ἀπόνοια τοῦ ῥήματος. Παραδίδως, εἰπέ μοι, (150) τὸν πάντα κρατοῦντα, τῶν δαιμόνων ἐξουσιάζοντα, τῇ θαλάττῃ ἐπιτάττοντα, τὸν τῆς φύσεως ἁπάντων δεσπότην; τὸν λόγῳ καὶ νεύματι τα πάντα συστησάμενον; ἵνα οὖν αὐτοῦ καταστείλῃ τὴν ἀπόνοιαν, καὶ (155) δείξῃ, ὅτι εἰ μὴ ἐβούλετο, οὐκ ἄν παρεδόθη.

---

cohortationem, admonitionem, (140) omnia, inquam, illa in oblivionem adducit. Pulchre dicebat Paulus, Radix omnium malorum est avaritia. (1 Tim. 6.10) (145) Quid vultis mihi dare, et ego vobis tradam eum. Magna dicti stultitia. Tradisne, quaeso, eum qui (150) omnia continet, daemonibus imperat, mari praecipit, universae naturae Dominum? qui verbo et nutu omnia constituit? Ut igitur ejus arrogantiam comprimeret, et (155) ostenderet se, si noluisset, numquam traditum iri,

58

šaı čьto stvorı · vъ to vrĕmn prĕda
40   nьü· egda prıdǫ na nь· sъ orǫžı i drъ
5r (161) kolьmı· svĕštn ı svĕtilьnıkъı i
        mǫšte· gl̄a kogo ıštete· ı ne znaxǫ e
        gože xotĕaxǫ ętı· tolьmı· ʽüda ne mo
        žaše ego prĕdatı· ašte ne bı samъ xotĕlъ.
5 (165) ı togo ne možaaše zьrĕtı· egože xotĕaše prĕ
        datı· ıbo svĕtilьnıkomь sǫštemъ
        ı svĕštamъ tolikamъ· se bo sьkazaę
        evanǥlıstъ reče· ĕko svĕtılьnıkъı
        svĕštn nošaxǫ· ı tako ego ne obrĕtaaxǫ
10 (170) sntъ· ı üda stoĕše sъ nımı· tъ rekъı·
        čьıо xoštete mı datı ı azъ vaıııь prĕda
        mı i·

ἄκουσον τί ποιεῖ. Κατ᾽ αὐτὸν τὸν καιρὸν τῆς προδοσίας, ὅτε ἐπῆλθον αὐτῷ μετὰ μαχαιρῶν καὶ (160) ξύλων λαμπάδας καὶ φανοὺς ἔχοντες, λέγει αὐτοῖς, Τινα ζητεῖτε; καὶ ἠγνόουν ὃν ἤμεινον συλλαμβάνειν. Τοσοῦτον ἀπεῖχε τοῦ δυνηθῆναι παραδοῦναι αὐτὸν ὁ Ἰούδας, (165) ὅτι οὐδὲ ἑώρα παρόντα ὃν ἤμεινε παρα δώσειν, καὶ ταῦτα λαμπάδων οὐσῶν καὶ φωτὸς τοσούτου. Ὅτι γὰρ τοῦτο ἠνίξατο ὁ εὐαγγελιστής φησι· ὅτι λαμπάδας καὶ φανοὺς εἶχον, καὶ οὐδὲ οὕτως αὐτὸν ηὕρισκὸν, (170) φησι, (γὰρ) καὶ Ἰούδας εἰστήκει μετ᾽ αὐτῶν· ἐκεῖνος εἰπών, ἐγὼ ὑμῖν παραδώσω αὐτόν.

audi quid faciat. Ipso proditoris tempore, quando invaserunt cum gladiis et (160) lignis lampadibus et laternis instructi, dicit eis: Quem quaeritis (John 18.4)? Et ignorabant eum, quem capturi erant. Tantum aberat, ut eum Judas tradere posset, (165) ut neque praesentem cerneret eum, quem traditurus erat, licet cum lampadibus et lumine tanto: hoc subindicans evangelista dicit. eos et lampades et laternas habuisse, neque sic eum invenisse, (170) id innuit cum ait, Et Judas stabat cum illis, is qui dixerat, Ergo vobis tradam eum.

Clozianus. Excerpt 2: Epiphanius on the Entombment

12r (I, 752) S̄TAAGO EPİFANIĒ · ARXİEPISKUPA KYPRЬSKA

AGO · O POGREBENI TĒLA ḠNĒ· 1 B̄A NAŠEGO ĪY X̄A · I O I

OSIFĒ · IŽE OTЪ ARIMATĒĘ · ı NİKODIMĒ ı O SЬ

35 · NIİ ḠI NAŠEGO GROBЬNĒMЬ· PO SЪPASNĒI MYCĒ DIVЪ

NO BЬIVЪŠÜ · -+-+

12v.1 Čъto se dьnesь bezm¹ьvьe mnogo

na zemı· čъto se bezmlъvь

e mnogo· ı m¹ъčanьe m'nogo· be

(760) zmlьvьe mnogo· ěko cěsarь sъpıtъ·

5 zemlě uboě sn i umlъča· eko b̄ъ plъ

tьǫ u.sъpe· b̄ъ plъtьǫ· umrětъ· ı a

dъ vъstrepeta· b̄ъ vъ malě usъpe·

i sъpnštnę otъ věka· otъ adama vъ

(765) skrěsı · kъde nъıně sǫtъ· vъčerašъ

Τοῦ ἐν ἁγίοις πατρὸς ἡμῶν Ἐπιφανίου ἀρχιεπισκόπου Κύπρου λόγος εἰς τὴν
θεόσωμον ταφὴν τοῦ Κυρίου ἡμῶν Ἰησοῦ Χριστοῦ, και εἰς τὸν Ἰωσὴφ τὸν ἀπὸ
Ἀριμαθαίας, τῷ ἁγίῳ καὶ μεγάλῳ σαββάτῳ. Κύριε εὐ. (757) Τί τοῦτο; σήμερον
σιγὴ πολλὴ ἐν τῇ γῇ· τί τοῦτο; σιγὴ πολλὴ καὶ ἠρεμία πολλή· σιγὴ (760)
πολλή, ὅτι ὁ βασιλεὺς ὑπνοῖ· γῆ ἐφοβήθη καὶ ἡσυχάσεν, ὅτι ὁ θεὸς ἐν σαρκὶ
τέθνηκεν· καὶ ὁ ἅδης ἐτρόμαξεν· ὁ θεὸς πρὸς βραχὺ ὕπνωσεν καὶ τοὺς ἀπ'
αἰῶνος ὑπνοῦντας ἐκ τοῦ θανάτου (765) ἀνέστησεν· ποῦ ποτὲ νῦν εἰσὶν αἱ

Sancti Patris nostri Epiphanii episcopi Cypri oratio in divini corporis
sepultrum Domini et Servatoris nostri Jesu Christi, et in Josephum qui
fuit ab Arimataea, et in Domini in infernum descensum, post salutarem
passionem admirabiliter factum. Sancto et magno Sabbato. (757) Quid
istud rei est? hodie silentium magnum in terra, silentium magnum, et
solitudo deinceps; (760) silentium magnum, quoniam Rex dormit; terra
timuit et quievit, quoniam Deus in carne obdormivit, et a saeculo
dormientes excitavit. Deus in carne mortuus est, et infernus contremuit.
Deus paululum obdormivit, et eos qui in inferno sunt,
(765) suscitavit. Nunc tandem ubi sunt

60

10   пṉę mlъvъɪ i glasɪ· ɪ govorɪ· bъɪ
            vaǫ̈šteɪ na x̃a· otъ zakonoprě̃stǫ
            pьnɪkъ· kъde narodi· ɪ kovi· ɪ čɪnɪ·
            ɪ orǫžbě ɪ drъkoli· kъde cě̃sare· ɪ i
     (770) erěi ɪ sǫdbę osǫ̌ždenъɪę· kъ
15   de svě̃štɴ ɪ mečɪ· ɪ govorɪ bešti
            slъnɪ· kъde lüdьe i šɴtanbě· ɪ
            trǫtъ nepravedьnъii· vъ ɪstinǫ
            ubo zělo vъ ɪstɪnǫ lüdьe po
     (775) učɪšɴ sɴ tъštetъnъɪmъ· ɪ sue
20   tъnъɪmъ· potъkǫ sɴ vъ akrogonie·
            ɪ kamenь x̃ъ· ɪ sami sъkrušɪšɴ sɴ·
            prɪvrъgǫ sɴ vъ tvrъdъɪ kamenь·
            пь vь pě̃пьɪ vlьпьɪ ixь ɪɑzidǫˢᴺ· pо

πρὸ βραχέως ταραχαὶ καὶ φωναὶ καὶ θόρυβοι κατὰ Χριστοῦ ὦ παράνομοι; ποῦ
οἱ δῆμοι καὶ αἱ στάσεις καὶ ἐνστάσεις καὶ τὰ ὅπλα καὶ δόρατα; ποῦ οἱ
βασιλεῖς καὶ (770) ἱερεῖς καὶ κριταὶ οἱ κατάκριτοι; ποῦ αἱ λαμπάδες καὶ αἱ
μάχαιραι καὶ οἱ θρύλλοι οἱ ἄτακτοι; ποῦ οἱ λαοὶ καὶ τὸ φρύαγμα καὶ ἡ
κουστωδία ἡ ἄσεμνος; ἀληθῶς ὄντως, ἐπεὶ καὶ ὄντως ἀληθῶς λαοὶ
μεμελέτηκαν (775) κενὰ· κενὰ. Προσέκοψαν τῷ ἀκρογωνιαίῳ λίθῳ Χριστῷ, ἀλλ'
αὐτοὶ συνετρίβησαν προσέρρηξαν τῇ πέτρᾳ τῇ στερεᾷ, ἀλλ' εἰς ἀφρὸν τὰ
κύματα διελύθησαν.

nuperae illae turbae, et vociferationes, et tumultus adversus Christum,
o impii? ubi populi, et insultus, et ordines, et arma, et lanceae? ubi
reges et (770) sacerdotes, et judices condemnati? ubi lampades, et
enses, et clamores inconditi? ubi vulgus, et fremitus, et custodia
inhonesta? vere reipsa, quando reipsa vere populi (775) meditati sunt
inania et facta. Impegerunt in angularem lapidem Christum, sed ipsi
contriti sunt; alliserunt petrae solidae, verum ipsi contriti sunt, et in
spumam fluctus eorum dissoluti;

(780) tьkǫ sn o nakovalě nepobědıměemъ·

25   nъ sami sъtь(re)ni bъišN· vъzněsN

na drěvo kamenь· ı sъšedъ umrьtvi

ę· sъvNzašN velikaago s(m)pssa· slъ

nьca x̅a̅· nъ razdrěšъ věčьnъıę ǫ

(785) zъı· ınoplemen'nikъı· ı zakonoprě

30   stǫpьnıkъı· pogubı· zaıde b̅ъ̅

slъnъce podъ zemlǫ· ı tьmǫ prě

mračьnǫǫ̈ ıüdeomъ sъtvorı· dь

nesь sp̅snbe· sǫšti(m)ъ na zemı· ı

(790) otъ věka podъ zemleǫ̈ sъpNšti

35   mъ· dьnesь sp̅senbe vьsemu miru·

eliko vidimъ· ı eliko nevidimъ·

(780) Προσέκρουσαν τῷ ἀηττήτῳ ἄκμονι, ἀλλ' αὐτοὶ κατεκλάσθησαν. "Υψωσαν ἐπὶ ξύλου τὴν πέτραν καὶ κατελθοῦσα αὐτοὺς ἐθανάτωσεν. Ἐδέσμησαν τὸν μέγαν Σαμψὼν ἥλιον θεὸν, ἀλλὰ λύσας τὰ ἀπ' αἰῶνος δεσμὰ, (785) τοὺς ἀλλοφύλους καὶ παρανόμους ἀπώλεσεν. "Εδυ θεὸς ἥλιος Χριστὸς ὑπὸ γῆν καὶ σκότος πανέσπερον τοῖς Ἰουδαίοις πεποίηκεν. Σήμερον σωτηρία τοῖς ἐπὶ γῆς καὶ τοῖς ἀπ' αἰῶνος ὑποκάτω τῆς γῆς. Σήμερον σωτηρία τῷ κόσμῳ, ὅσος ὁρατὸς καὶ ὅσος ἀόρατος.

(780) offenderunt ad indomitam incudem, et ipsi confracti sunt; sustulerunt in ligno petram vitae, quae descendens ipsos occidit; colligarunt magnum Sampsonem solem Deum, sed solutis a saeculo vinculis, (785) alienigenas et impios perditit. Occidit Deus sol Christus sub terram, et tenebras perpetuas Judaeis fecit. Hodie salus his qui sunt supra terram, et his qui sunt (790) a saeculo subtus terram. Hodie salus universo mundo, quantuscunque visibilis, et quantus invisibilis.

Clozianus. Excerpt 3: On adultery

2r   ... vъ sto̅e ı spsaǫ̈

        štee krъštenьe dlъženъ estъ· vьsěkъ krъ

30 (I, 110) štenъ sъ straxomъ· ı trepetomь xranıtı·

        to že stu̅mu ı blaženumu pavъlu ap̅s̅lu

        glǫ̅štü kъ věrъnъmъ· lüboděanьe že

        ı vьsěka nečıstota vъ vasъ da ne ımenu

        etъ sn· ěkože podobaetъ stu̅ımъ· ı nıkъ

35 (115) tože vasъ da ne slъišıtъ tъštımı slo

        vesъı· ne lübodě́ı bo nı klevetьnıcı·

        nı obıdьlıvi csr̅stvıe bž̅ıe naslědъstvu

        ǫ̈tъ· sıxъ bo radı grndetъ gněvъ bž̅ı· na

        sn̅ъı protıvъnъıę· dlъženъ estъ vьsě

40 (120) kъ krъštenъı· samъ sebe čısta xranıtı·

2v   ěko crk̅ve bu̅ stǫ̈· ı o svoeı ženě dovъlě

        ti sn· nıčъže ıno dalьnee sъmъišlětı·

        nı vъ skota město vъ slědъ nesъmъıslъ

        nъ poxoti ımъ xodıtı· ıže ubo otъ selě

5 (125) krъštenъ sъı· tvorn obrětaetъ sn po bž̅ıü

Tout homme baptisé dans le saint baptême de salut doit le (110) garder
avec crainte et tremblement, alors que le saint et bienheureux apôtre
Paul dit aux fidèles: "Que l'impudicité et toute impureté ne soient pas
nommées parmi vous, ainsi qu'il convient aux saints; et que (115)
personne ne vous séduise par de vaines paroles; car ni les impudiques,
ni les calomniateurs, ni les injustes n'hériteront le royaume de Dieu;
car c'est à cause de ces choses que la colère de Dieu vient sur les fils
de la rébellion". Tout (120) baptisé doit se garder lui-même pur
comme (étant) le saint "temple de Dieu", et se contenter de sa propre
femme, ne porter sa pensée au loin sur rien d'autre, et ne pas suivre des
désirs insensés, tel un animal. Celui donc, qui, désormais (125)
baptisé, est trouvé agissant ainsi,

zakonu· da osǫdıtъ sn to že b̅u̅ ı sp̅s̅u
našemu ı̅s̅x̅u̅ vъprošenu бъıvъšü· ašte
e lьzě puštati ženǫ svoǫ̈· na vьsěko vrě
mn· ı otъrekъšü· vьsěkъ puštaǫı ženǫ
10 (I,130) svoǫ razvě slovese lüboděanьnago· tvori
tъ ǫ̈ prělübъı tvorıtı· ı vьsěkъ prılě
plěeı sn potьpězě prělübъı děetъ· ěže
bo b̅ъ̅ sъvelъ estъ c̅k̅a̅· da ne razlüčaete sn·
fropıtu že malaxeu sъızvěstuǫ̈štü
15 (135) b̅v̅ı· ı gl̅ǫ̅štü· ı ženǫ ünostı tvoeę·
da ne ostavıšı· nъ ašte· [v]ъznenaviděvь
otъpustıšı· ı pokrıetъ nečъstьe na tn·
gl̅etъ g̅ъ̅· takožde s̅t̅ı apᵒlı· ı blaženı o̅c̅i
sъ st̅ъ̅ımь zakonomь otъnǫdь · velьe ı
20 (140) ӡěluto· takovoe posǫždenьe rekъše velьü
ıspъıtanьü· ı poštenьü se sъpodobıšn·

qu'il soit condamné selon la loi de Dieu, dès lors que notre Dieu et Sauveur Jésus-Christ, à qui on demandait s'il est permis de répudier sa femme en toute circonstance, l'a dénié (en disant): "Quiconque répudie (130) sa femme, en dehors du cas d'impudicité, lui fait commettre un adultère, et quiconque s'unit à une répudiée commet un adultère; car ceux que Dieu a joints, que l'homme ne les sépare pas"; et que le prophète Malachie ajoute son témoinage (135) à celui de Dieu et dit: "Et n'abandonne pas la femme de ta jeunesse; mais si, par haine, tu la renvoies, l'impiété te recouvrira, dit le Seigneur". De même les saints apôtres et les bienheureux Pères, prononçant avec la loi sainte qu'une telle autorisation est tout à fait grave et (140) très cruelle, ont jugé qu'elle appelait une grande enquête et des jeûnes ....

64

Psalterium sinaiticum: Psalm 3

2b 14	(III*, 1)	PSALMъ
		DAD̄OVЪ EGDA BĒGAŠE OT LIC-A-
		VESELUMA S̄ÑA SVOEGO
	(2)	Ḡı čto sę umьnožišę sъtǫ
		žaǫ̈ψe mı: Mnoӡıı vъsta
		šę na mę: Mnoӡıı vьsta
20		šę na mę:
[20, cont]	(3)	Mnoӡi glǫ̈tъ
		d̄šı moeı nēstъ sp̄ньĕ
3a 1		o b̄ӡĕ ego: di͡ep̄s͡la:
	(4)	Tъı že ḡı zastǫpьnıkъ moı esı:
		slava moĕ vьznese glavǫ moǫ̈:
	(5)	Glasьmъ moımъ kъ ḡvı vozь
5		vaxъ: I usl̕ъıša mę otъ gorъ
		ı st̄ъıę .... svoeę:[1]
	(6)	Azъ že usъnǫxъ ı sъraxъ: vъ
		staxъ ĕko ḡъ zastǫpitъ mę:
	(7)	Ne uboǫ̈ sę otъ tьmъı lü
10		deı: Napadaǫ̈ψıxъ na mę

[1] Ψαλμὸς τῷ Δαυιδ, ὁπότε ἀπεδίδρασκεν ἀπὸ προσώπον Ἀβεσσαλώμ τοῦ υἱοῦ αὐτοῦ. 2 Κύριε, τί ἐπληθύνθησαν οἱ θλίβοντές με; πολλοὶ ἐπανίστανται[2] ἐπ᾽ ἐμέ· 3 πολλοὶ λέγουσιν τῇ ψυχῇ μου. Οὐκ ἔστιν σωτηρία αὐτῷ[3] ἐν τῷ θεῷ αὐτοῦ. Διάψαλμα. 4 σὺ δέ, κύριε, ἀντιλήμπτωρ μου εἶ, δόξα μου καὶ ὑψῶν τὴν κεφαλὴν μου. 5 φωνῇ μου πρὸς κύριον ἐκέκραξα, καὶ ἐπήκουσέν μου ἐξ ὄρους ἁγίου αὐτοῦ. Διάψαλμα. 6 ἐγὼ[4] ἐκοιμήθην καὶ ὕπνωσα· ἐξηγέρθην, ὅτι κύριος ἀντιλήμψεται μου. 7 οὐ φοβηθήσομαι ἀπὸ μυριάδων λαοῦ τῶν κύκλω συνεπιτεθεμένων[5] μοι.

*Numbering is according to the Septuagint; beyond Psalm 9, numbers in the Western Bible typically are higher by one. [1]Точки означают вытертое место приблизительно 4-х знаков (2-я буква была g, а на 4-м месте двоеточие. (S = Sever'janov) [2]επανεστησαν. [3]om. [4]add. δε. [5]om. συν.

okrъstъ:

(8) Vъskrъsnı g̃ı s̃pı mę bže moi:
     ěko tъı porazı vьsę vražь
     dυǫ̈ψę̈ mně vъsue:
15   zǫbъı grěšьnъıxъ sъkru
     šılъ esı:
(9) G̃ne estъ s̃pnьe: i na lüdexъ
     tvoıxъ bl̃goslovewvenьe
     tvoe: slava:

Psalm 25

30 a 13 (XXV, 1)   DAVъ PъSALOMъ
                 Sǫdı mı g̃ı ěko azъ nezъ
15   loboǫ̈ moǫ̈ xodıxъ:• i na
                 G̃ě upъvaę ne iznemogǫ
        (2)   İskusı mę g̃ı ı tъı tęžı¹ mę:•
                 raždъzı ǫtrobǫ moǫ̈ i srъdь
                 ce moe:
20   (3)   Ěko mılostь tvoě prědъ oči
                 ma moıma estъ:• İ ugodı
30b 1   xъ vъı-istıně tvoeı:

8 ἀνάστα, κύριε, σῶσόν με, ὁ θεός μου, ὅτι σὺ ἐπάταξας πάντας τοὺς
ἐχθραίνοντάς μοι ματαίως, ὀδόντας ἁμαρτωλῶν συνέτριψας. 9 τοῦ κυρίου ἡ
σωτηρία, καὶ ἐπὶ τὸν λαόν σου ἡ εὐλογία σου.

Τοῦ Δαυίδ. 1 Κρίνον με, κύριε, ὅτι ἐγὼ ἐν ἀκακίᾳ μου ἐπορεύθην καὶ ἐπὶ τῷ
κυρίῳ ἐλπίζων οὐ μὴ ἀσθενήσω. 2 δοκίμασόν με, κύριε, καὶ πείρασόν με,
πύρωσον τοὺς νεφρούς μου καὶ τὴν καρδίαν μου. 3 ὅτι τὸ ἔλεός σου
κατέναντι τῶν ὀφθαλμῶν μού ἐστιν, καὶ εὐηρέστησα ἐν τῇ ἀληθείᾳ σου.

---

¹ı tъı tęžı писца изменено в ı sъtęžı переделкою и разурою tъı в
sъ. (S)

66

(4) Ne sědъ sъ sonъtomъ suetъno[1]

mъ:· İ sъ zakonoprěstǫpъ

nъi[i]mi[2] ne vъnidǫ:

5 (5) Vъznenaviděxъ cr̄kovъ lǫka

vъnъixъ:· İ sъ nečъstivъi

imi ne sędǫ:

(6) Umъiǫ̈ vъ nepovinъixъ rǫ

cě moi: İ obidǫ olъtarъ

10 tvoi g̃i:

(7) Da uslъišǫ glasъ xvalъi tvoe

ę:· İspověmъ vъsě čüdesa tvoě:·

(8) G̃i vъzlübixъ krasotǫ domu

tvoego:· İ město vъselenъě

15 slavъi tvoeę:·

(9) Ne pogubi sъ nečъstivъii

mi d̃šę moeę:· i sъ mǫži

krъvъi života moego:

(10) Vъ nixъže rǫku bezakonenъě

sǫtъ:· Desnica ixъ isplъ

31a 1 ni sę mъita[3]

4 οὐκ ἐκάθισα μετὰ συνεδρίου ματαιότητος καὶ μετὰ παρανομούντων οὐ μὴ εἰσέλθω. 5 ἐμίσησα ἐκκλησίαν πονηρευομένων καὶ μετὰ ἀσεβῶν οὐ μὴ καθίσω. 6 νίψομαι ἐν ἀθῴοις τὰς χεῖράς μου καὶ κυκλώσω τὸ θυσιαστήριόν σου, κύριε, 7 τοῦ ἀκοῦσαι φωνὴν αἰνέσεως καὶ διηγήσασθαι πάντα τὰ θαυμάσιά σου. 8 κύριε, ἠγάπησα εὐπρέπειαν οἴκου σου καὶ τόπον σκηνώματος δόξης σου. 9 μὴ συναπολέσῃς μετὰ ἀσεβων τὴν ψυχήν μου καὶ μετὰ ἀνδρῶν αἱμάτων τὴν ζωήν μου, 10 ὧν ἐν χερσὶν ἀνομίαι, ἡ δεξιὰ αυτῶν ἐπλήσθη δώρων.

1-по- писца переделано справщиком в –пъı припиской ı и допол-нением к глаголич. знаку для о специфич. части знака для глухого, качество которого не ясно. (S) ²i над строкой писцом. (S) 3-ъita справщиком по стертому месту 4-х букв писца (δώρων мъzdъı Бол., мъitomъ Пог.). (S)

(11)   Azъ že nezloboǫ̈ moe⁴ xodı
         xъ izbavı mę g̃ı ı pomılu
         ı mę:•
(12)   Noga moě sta na pravъdě:•
         vъ⁵ cr̃kъvaxъ blagoslove
         sъstuǫ̈ tę:

11 ἐγὼ δὲ ἐν ἀκακίᾳ μου ἐπορεύθην· λύτρωσαί με⁶ καὶ ἐλέησόν με. 12 ὁ γὰρ
πούς μου ἔστη ἐν εὐθύτητι· ἐν ἐκκλησίαις εὐλογήσω σε, κύριε.

⁴moe(ǫ̈). (S) ⁵vъ ili vь? (S) ⁶add. κύριε.

Psalm 129

172a 13   (CXXIX, 1)   SLAVA PĚSNь STEPENŃA:¹
                        ız glǫbinъı vozъvaxъ
15   kъ tebě g̃ı: G̃ı uslъıši
                        glasъ moı:
         (2)   Bǫděte uši tvoı vъnem¹ǫ̈²
                        šte glasъ molitvъı moeę:
**   (3)   Ašte bezakonenič nazъriši
20   g̃ı: G̃ı kъto postoıtъ ěko
                        otъ tebe ocěštenie estъ:
         (4)   ımeni tvoego radi potrъpě
                        xъ tę g̃ı: Potrъpě d̃ša mo

1 Canticum graduum. De profundis clamavi ad te, Domine; Domine,
exaudi vocem meam. 2 Fiant aures tuae intendentes in vocem
deprecationis meae. 3 Si iniquitates observaveris, Domine, Domine,
quis sustinebit? Quia apud te propitiatio est; 4 et propter legem tuam
sustinui te. Domine. Sustinuit anima mea

---

¹-nńa (sic) со знак. паерка (вм. –ńna). (S) ²mᴸ лигатура. (S)

ě vъ slovo tvoe: Upьva d̃ša

25 moě na g̃ě:

172b 1 (5) Otъ stražę utrьnę do no

štı: Otъ stražę utrьnę

da upьva³ iĩlь na g̃ě:

(6) Ěko otъ g̃ı milost-ı mьno

5 go otъ nego ızbavlenie:

ı tь ızbavitъ iĩlě oto

vьsěxъ bezakonъnъıxъ ego:

in verbo ejus; speravit anima mea in Domino. 5 A custodia matutina usque ad noctem, speret Israel in Domino; 6 quia apud Dominum misericordia, et copiosa apud eum redemptio. Et ipse redimet Israel ex omnibus iniquitatibus ejus.

---

³-va(etъ) (S)

Psalm 30

35a 18 (XXX, 1) SLAVA: Vъ KONECъ PSLMь

DAṼъ Vь UŽASĚ

20 (2) Na tę g̃ı upьvaxъ da ne

postьıždǫ sę ᵛь věkъ:

Pravьdoǫ̈ tvoeǫ̈ izba

vı mę ızъmı mę:

(3) Prıklonı ko mьně uxo

tvoe uędrı izętı mę:·

Bǫdı mı vъ b̃a zaštıtı

telъ:· Ì vъ domъ prıběžı

ψü sъpastı mę:

(4) Ěko drьžava ı prıběžıšte

moe esı tъı: Ìmenı tvoe

go radı nastavıšı mę i prěpı

těešı mę:

(5) İ ızvedešı mę otъ sětı esę

q̈že sъkгъıšę mně:• Ěko tъı

esı zaštıtıtelъ moı g̃ı:•

(6) Vъ rǫcě tvoı prědamъ d̃хъ:

İzbavılъ mę esı g̃ı b̃že rě

snotъı:

(7) Vьznenavıdě xranęštę su

etьna za tъštee:

(8) Azъ že na g̃ě upъvaxъ: İ vъzradu

q̈ sę i vьzveselǫ sę o mı

lostı tvoeı:

Ěko prızьrě na sъměrenьe mo

e:• S̃plъ esı otъ bědъ d̃šǫ

(9) moq̈:• İ něsı mene zatvo

rılъ vъ rǫkaxъ vгažьěxъ:

Postavılъ esı na prostra

(10) ně noзě moı:• Pomıluı

mę g̃ı ěko skrъblǫ:

Sъmętе sę otъ ěrostı o

ko moe: D̃ša moě i qtrǫ

ba moě:

(11) Ěko oskodě bolěznъq̈ žıvo

tъ moı:• İ lěta moě vъzdъı

xanьıi: ıznemože nı

štetoq̈ krěpostь moě:•

İ kostı moę sъmęšę sę:

(12) Pače vъsěxъ vгagъ moı

бъıxъ ponošenьü:•

i sǫsědomъ moımъ зě

lo:• İ straxъ znaemъıımъ

moımъ:

Vıdęšteı mę vonъ běža

(13) šę otъ mne:· Zabъvenъ

bъıxъ ěko mrъtvъ otъ srь

dьca:· Vъıxъ ěko sъsǫdъ

pogublenъ:

(14) Ěko slъıšaxъ rǫženье mno

go žıvǫštııxъ okrьstь

ego ᵈᵃ sъbıraaxǫ sę kupь

no na mę:· Prıętı d͞šǫ mo

ǫ̈ sъvěštašę:·

(15) Azъ že na tę g͞ı upъvaxъ rě

(16) xъ tъı esı b͞ъ moı:· Vъ rǫ

ku tvoeü žıěbъı moı:

ızbavı mę izdrǫkъı

vragъ moıxъ otъ gonęštı

(17) ıxъ mę:· · Prosvьtı lıce

tvoe na raba tvoego:· S͞pı

mę mılostьǫ̈ tvoǫ̈:

(18) G͞ı da ne postъždǫ sę ěko prı

zъvaxъ tę:· Da postъıdę

tъ sę nečьstıvı-i sъnı

dǫtъ vъ adъ:·

(19) Němъı da bǫdǫtъ ustъnъı

lьstıvъıę: gl͞ǫštę na pra

vedьnago bezakonenье:· Grъdъ

ıneǫ̈ ı unıčьženьетъ:·

(20) Kolъ mъnogo množьstvo bla

gostı tvoeę g͞ı:· Ǫ̈že sъkъ

ı boęštıımъ sę tebe:· Sъ

vrьšılъ esı upъvaǫ̈štę

ę na tę: prědъ s͞nъı čl͞včskъı:·

(21) Sъkrъıešı ę vъ taıně lıca
tvoego:· Ѡtъ męteža čĪvča:
Pokrъıešı ę vъ krově otъ prě
rěkanъě ęzъıkъ:

(22) Blagoslovestvenъ g͠ı ěko u
dıvılъ estъ mılostь svo
ǫ̈ vъ gradě ostoěnъě:·

(23) Azъ že rěxъ vъ užěsě moemъ

37b 1 otьvrъženъ esmъ < · otъ lı
ca očьü tvoeü:
Sego radı slъıša glasъ mo
lıtvъı moeę:· Egda vozъ

5 vaxъ kъ tebě:

(24) Vъzlübıte g͠ě vъsı prěpodo
bınıı ego:· Ěko rěsnotъı vь
zıskaetъ g͠ъ :· I vъzda
etъ tvoręštıımъ izlı

10 xa grъdъınǫ:

(25) Mǫžaıte sę ı da krěpıtъ
sę srъdьce vaše:· Vъsı
upъvaǫ̈šteı na g͠a:

Psalm 22

27a 16	(XXII, 1)	G͞ь pasetъ mę ı nıčesože
	(2)	mene lıšıtъ:· Na městě
		pastvınъně tu mę vъselı
		Na vodě pokoıně vъspıtě mę:·
	(3)	D͞šǫ moǫ obratı:· Nastavı
27b 1		lъ mę esı na stьзǫ pravъıę:
	(4)	İmenı ego radı ěšte bo ı
		poıdǫ posrědě sěnı sъmrъ
		tъnъıę:
5		Ne ubоǫ sę zъla ěko tъı ˢo mno
		ǫ esı: Žezlъ tvo-ı palıca
		tvоě ta mę utěšıste
	(5)	Ugotovalъ esı prědo mnоǫ
		trapezǫ:· Prědъ sъtǫžаǫ
10		štıimi mně:
		Umastılъ esı оlěemъ gla
		vǫ моǫ: İ čěša tvоě upa
		ěǫštı mę kolь drъžavъ
		na estъ:
15	(6)	İ mılostъ tvоě poženetь mę
		vьsę dъnı žıvota moego:·
		İ da vъselǫ sę vъ domъ
		g͞нъ vъ dlъgotǫ dьnъı:

The Kiev Missal

1v		vъ ĪV DN KLIMENTA
	(1)	Bъ̋ ïže nъi · lěta ȯgrędǫčě
		blaženago klímenta mǫ
		čenıka tvoego ï papeža
5		čьstьǫ̋ veselïšı: podá
		zь mılostıvъî · dȁ ȇgože
		čьstь čьstımъ. silȯǫ̋
		ȗbo mǫčenïě ȇgo naslědue
		mъ : · : gm̄ь : · :
		NADь OPLATMь
10	(2)	Rovanïę̋ ḡı prınesenъïę
		svętí · ï xodataěcü
		blaženumu klimentu
		mǫčeniku tvoemu · sïmь
		nъ̀î ȯtъ grěx̄ъ skvrьnostiɩ
15		našıxъ ȯčıstı : gm̄ь :
		PRĔFACIĔ: DO věčnъî bže.
	(3)	(Č)ьstьnǎgo klimenta zako
		nьnïka ï mǫčenïka čьs̄ʰı
		čьstęce · ïže ȗtěže bъi
20		ti blaženûmu ápȯsto
		lu tvoemu pétru · vъ ï

Cod. Pad. D47 VIIII. Kal. Dec.
Sancti Clementis Papae.
(1) Deus qui nos annua beati Clementis martyris tui atque pontificis
solemnitate laetificas, concede propitius, ut cuius natalitia colimus
uirtutem quoque passionis imitemur, per dominum. Super oblatum. (2)
Munera domine oblata sanctifica, et intercedente beato Clemente
martyre tuo per haec nos a peccatorum nostrorum maculis emunda, per
dominum. U[ere] D[ignum] aeterne Deus. (3)Veneranda Clementis
sacerdotis et martyris solemnia recurrentes, qui fieri meruit beati Petri

nokostı podrugъ · vъ ı̇spo
2r   vědı ůčenıkъ · vъ čьstı na
městьnĭkъ : vъ mǫčenii na
slědьnĭkъ : xm̄ь gm̄ь našmь:
PO VъSQDĚ : · :
5   (4)   Télese svętago ı̇ prědra
gъı̇ę̇ krъve naplьnenı̇ vъ
litĭě prosĭmъ g̃ı b̃že našь :
da eže milostıvač óběcě
nı̇é̇ nosĭmь · rěsnotívьnač
10   ı̇zdŕěšenı̇é̇ óbьmemь : gm̄ь .·.
Vъ TъZE DьNь ΘELICTЬI:
(5)   Podázь námь prosımь tę
vь́semogъı̇ı b̃že · blaženъi
ę̇ radı̇ mǫčenıcę̇ tvoeę̇
15   θelıcıtъı̇ vьkupьnǫ̈
molitvǫ: ı̇ toęze radı̇
zaščı̇tı nъı̇: gm̄ь: NDъ OPL
(6)   Na služьbъı lüdiı tvoıxь
milostiǫ̈ prızьrı́ · ı̇ (...)
20   se nъı̇ čьstьǫ̈ svętъixъ čь
stĭmъ: sъtvorı nъı̇ rado
stьnъi · vъ věčьně̇mь život(ě)

in peregrinatione comes, in confessione discipulus, in honore successor, in passione secutor, per Christum. (4) Ad complendum. Corporis sacri et pretiosi sanguinis repleti libamine quaesumus domine Deus noster, ut quod pia deuotione gerimus, certa redemptione capiamus, per. EODEM DIE NATL. SANCTAE FELICITATIS VIA SALARIA. (5) Praesta quaesumus omnipotens Deus, ut beatae Felicitatis martyris tuae solemnia recensentes, meritis ipsius protegamur et precibus, per. Super oblatam. (6) Uota populi tui propitiatus intende, et quorum nos tribuis solemnia celebrare, fac gaudere suffragiis, per.

2v

PO VЪSQDĚ :•

(7) Sъmĕrъno tę molĭmъ vĕse
mogъî bže· molitvami svę
tъixъ tvoıxъ· ı tъi samъ
bǫdı· ı darъ tvoı vъselı
vъ nъî· ı vrĕmę naše vъ
pravьdǫ postávı :• gm̃ь :•
MьŠĚ NA VĔSĘ DьNь Vь
SEGO LĚTA ȮBIDǪCĚ :•

(8) Bъ ıže tvarь svóǫ ve
lьmı pomílova· ı po gnĕ
vĕ svoemь · ızvolı vъ
plъtitı sę sъpásenĭĕ ra
dı človĕcьska· ı vъsxo
tĕvъ námъ ûtvrьdı srь
dьcĕ nášĕ· ı milostıǫ
tvoéǫ prosvĕtı nъî: gm̃ь:
NADь ȮPLATъMь:

(9) Blızъ násъ bǫdı g̃ı prósı
mъ tę· ı molítvǫ našǫ
uslъ́išı· dà ûpъvaníe
(vъ)nьmémъ dĕlĔ svoıxъ·
ı vъ lübъvь darъ sь té
bĕ prınosımъ: gm̃ь:•

(7) Supplices te rogamus omnipotens Deus, ut interuenientibus sanctis tuis, et tua in nobis dona multiplices et tempora nostra disponas, per. INCIPIUNT ORATIONES COTTIDIANAE GREGORII PAPAE. (8) Deus qui creaturae tuae misereri potius eligis quam irasci, cordis nostri infirma considera, et tuae nos gratia pietatis inlustra, per. Super oblatam. (9) Adesto nobis quaesumus domine, et preces nostras benignus exaudi, ut quod fiducia non habet meritorum, placationis obtineat hostiarum, per.

3r   PRĒΘACIĒ: VĒCЬNЪÎ B͠ZE:

(10)   Nebesьskъȉę tvóę sılъȋ

prosȉmъ ȉ mólımъ· dà sъ

vъȉšьnȉmı tvoımı· do

5   stoȉnъi sъtvorȉšı nъȋ: ȉ

věčьnáě tvóě ȉxъže žęda

emъ podăsь námъ mılostı

vьno: x͞mь g͞mь nášımь · ȉmь

PO VъSQDĒ :·

10 (11)   Prósımъ tę g͞ı dazь námъ·

dà svętб̌ı tvoı vъsqdъ

prıemlǫ̈ce dóstoını bǫ̂

demъ očȉščenȉě tvoego·

ȉ věra tvoě vь násъ da vъ

15   zdrăstetъ: g͞mь našımь ȋsm·

*   MьŠĒ · B͞ · O TOMьZE :·

(12)   Prosımъ tę vьsemogб̌ı vě

čьnб̌ı b͠že· prızьrı na mo

lıtvǫ našǫ· ȉ vъnǫ

20   trьněě našě očıstı· ěže

nъȉ sušętъ grěxб̌ı našı

mı: dà mılostıǫ̈ tvoe

ǫ̈ ȉzbavı nъi: g͞mь našı

NADъ ÓPLATъMь:

UD aeterne Deus (10) Maiestatem tuam suppliciter deprecantes, ut opem tuam petentibus dignanter impendas, et desiderantibus benignus tribuas profutura, per Christum. Ad complendum. (11) Praesta quaesumus domine, ut sancta tua nos expient dignosque semper sui perceptione perficiant, per. ITEM ALIA MISSA. (12) Quaesumus omnipotens Deus, preces nostras respice, et tuae super nos uiscera pietatis impende, ut qui ex nostra culpa affligimur, ex tua pietate misericorditer liberemur, per. Super oblatam.

3v (13) Sы prınosъ prınesenŏı tébĕ
ḡı prosımъ tę prıımî: ı
že ésı blagoslovestılъ
na sъpasenıe naše: gm̃ь našı:·

5 PREΘACiÈ: DO vĕčьn b̃že:

(14) Da sę tébe drьžımъ ı mılo
stı tvoeę prosımъ: prı
zъvalъ nъı ésı ḡı · da ıspra
vı nъı ı̓ ôčıstı: ne náśı

10 хъ dĕlŏ radı· nъ ôbĕta tvo
ego radı ıže ésı obĕcĕlъ
námъ: da vъzmožemъ du
šĕmı ı tĕlesъî ı mъıslь
mı našımı · prıęti zapo

15 vĕdı tvoę: ę̓že ésı posъ
lalъ kъ namъ: xm̃ь gm̃ь na
šımь · ı̓mъže velıčь :·
PO VъSQDÈ :·

(15) Svętŏı tvoı vъsqdъ

20 ḡı ıže ésmъ vъzęlı mo
lımъ tę̓· da ôčıstitъ
nъı ôtъ grĕxъ našıхъ: ı
kъ nebesьscĕ̓ı lübъvı
privedetъ nъ́ı: gm̃ь naš:

(13) Hostias domine quaesumus suscipe placatus oblatas, quae te
sanctificando nobis perficiantur salutares, per dominum. UD aeterne
Deus. (14) Ut qui te auctore subsistimus, et dispensante dirigamur, non
nostris sensibus relinquamur, sed ad tua reducti semper tramitem
ueritatis haec studeamus exercere quae praecipis, ut possimus dona
percipere quae promittis, per Christum. Ad complendum. (15) Sancta
tua nos domine quaesumus et a peccatis exuant, et caelestis uitae uigore
confirment, per.

4r   MьŠË̃ · ṽ · O TOMьZE :·

(16) Prosı̇mъ tę vsemogѣ̃ı
b̃že da ěkože ésmъ skrъbьnı
grěxѣ̃ı našımı : mılostь
5   ö tvoeö̈ ȯtъ vьsěxъ zъ
lıı našıxъ ȯčıstı nъ̀ı:
g̃mь:· NADъ OPLATъMъ :

(17) Prıımı g̃ı prosımъ tę pri
nosъ sь̀ · prınesenѣ̃ı tébě·
10   i̇zbavleni̇ě radı člově
čьska· ı̇ sъdravı́e námъ
dázь · ı̇ dušę našę ı̇ tě
lesa ȯčıstı· á molıtvǫ
našǫ prıımı:· g̃mь : PREθ
15   DO věčьnѣ̃ı b̃že :·

(18) Tъı ésı životъ nášь g̃ı o
tъ nebъıtı̇ě bo vъ bъit(ıe)
sъtvorı̇lъ nъı esı· ı̇ otъ
pádъšę vъskrěsı pakъı·
20   dà namъ ne dostoıtъ tebě
sъgrěšatı: tvoě že sǫ
tъ vьsě̊· nebesьskaě ı ze
mlьskaě g̃ı· da tъı samъ
ȯtъ grěxѣ́ našıxъ i̇zbavi
25   nъı: x̃mь g̃mь :·

ITEM ALIA. (16) Praesta quaesumus omnipotens Deus, ut qui pro nostris excessibus incessanter affligimur, tuae pietatis in omnibus protectione consolemur, per. Super oblatam. (17) Suscipe quaesumus domine hostiam redemptiones humanae et salutem nobis mentis et corporis operare placatus, per. UD aeterne Deus. (18) Tuum est enim omne quo uiuimus quia licet peccati uulnere natura nostra uitiata sit, tui tamen est operis, ut a terrena generati ad caelestia renascamur, per Christum.

4v   PO VЬSQDĚ

(19) Dázь námъ vьsemogȗı b̃že·
da ěkože nȗi ési nebesьskȇı̨ę
pıcę̨ nasьıtılъ : takozé

5   že ı̇ životъ náśь sılo
ǫ̈ tvoeǫ̈ ûtvrьdı: g̃mь :·

MьŠĔ : G̃ : O TOMьZE :·

(20) (C)ěsarьstvě našemь g̃ı mı
lostьǫ̈ tvoeǫ̈ prızьrî :

10   ı̇ ne ótьdázь našego tu
zı̆mъ· ı̇ ne óbratı násъ
vъ plĕnъ narodomъ poga
nьskȇımъ: x̃a radı g̃ı na
šego· ı̇že cĕsarıtъ sъ ótь

15   cemь ı̇ sъ svę̇tьımь :·

NADъ ÓPLATЬMь :

(21) Tvoě cirkьnaě tvrьdь za
šč̆ıtı nȗi g̃ı· ǫ̈že ési
óbrazъmь svoımь ûpo

20   dobılъ· ǫ̈že nȗı̂ čьstı
mъ ná balьstvo náše· to
(go) radı ési námъ věčь
noe óbĕcěnie prineslъ :·
g̃mь našımь :·

Ad complendum. (19) Da, quaesumus onmipotens Deus, ut mysteriorum uirtute satiati uita nostra firmetur, per. ITEM ALIA MISSA. (20) Rege nostras domine propitius uoluntates, ut nec propriis iniquitatibus implicentur, nec subdantur alienis, per dominum. Super oblatam. (21) Tua sacramenta nos Deus circumtegant et reforment, simulque nobis temporale remedium conferant et aeternum, per dominum.

5r PREθ(ACIĚ)

(22) Da ěkъiže sǫtъ tvoę si
slǔžьbъi vъžlüblenъi
ę · tăkъiže mъislьmi svo
5 imi nъi tvorimъ· a tъi
samъ g̃i prisno nъi priemli:
da vъzmožemъ pravьdь
naě tvoe naslědovati·
i otъ neprněznině dělě
10 očistiti sę: xm̃ь gm̃ь náš
mь: imьže veličьstvo :·
PO VъSQDĚ:

(23) Tvoě svętaě vьsemogěi
bže· eže se nъi priemlemъ:
15 na razdrěšenie · i na očišče
nie námъ bǫdǫ: a tъi sa
mъ pomocьǫ tvoeǫ vě
čьnoǫ zaščiti nъi: gm̃ь
* MьŠĚ · D · O TOMьZE :·
20 (24) Prosimъ tę g̃i vъzdvi
gni srьdьca náš kъ tebě o
tъ zemlьskъixъ poxot(ii)
da vъzmožemъ xotěti (ne)
besьskъimъ tvoimъ ·:·

UD aeterne Deus. (22) Ut quia tui est operis, si quod tibi placitum est aut cogitemus aut agamus, tu nobis semper et intelligendi quę recta sunt et exsequendi tribuas facultatem. Per Christum. (Cod. S. Gall. 348, n. 1536.) Ad complendum. (23) Tua sancta nobis omnipotens Deus quae sumpsimus: et indulgentiam praebeant, et auxilium perpetuae defensionis impendant, per. ALIA MISSA. (24) Erige quaesumus domine ad te corda nostra, ut a terrenis cupiditatibus in caelestia desideria transeamus, per.

5v   (NADъ OPLAT)ъMь.

(25) Ėkъiže darьi imamъ· prědъ

toboǫ sǫtъ· i prosimъ

tę priimi ę · da i nъi vъzmo

5   žemъ vъ vъžlüblenii tvo

emь: g̃mь našimь: PRĖΘA

CIĖ · DO věčьnѣi b̃že :·

(26) Zъloba našě ne vъrěsni sę vъ

násъ · nѣ izdrěšenie věčь

10   noe prisno námъ bǫdi · g̃i

našego radi: tъ bo nъi sǎ

mъ otъ tьmьnъixъ ötьve

de: i öčisti· i zaklepe·

i dostoino izbavi: x̃mь

15   g̃mь našimь : PO VъSQDĖ:

(27) Vъsǫdьnaě molitva našě

ùtvrьdi nѣi g̃i věčьnъimi

tvoimi: i podázь námъ sъ

pasenie tvoe: g̃mь našimь:·

20   MьŠĖ · Ẽ : O TOMьZE :·

(T)ъi g̃i otьmi nъi ötъ lǫkavь

stva našego : i tvoeǫ milo

stiǫ öbrati nъi na pravьdǫ

tvoǫ : g̃mь našimь :

Super oblatam. (25) In tuo conspectu domine quaesumus talia nostra sint munera: quae et placare te ualeant, et nos tibi placere perficiant, per. UD aeterne Deus. (26) Ut non in nobis nostra malitia, sed indulgentiae tuae praeueniat semper affectus, qui nos a noxiis uoluptatibus indesinenter expediat, et a mundanis cladibus dignanter eripiat, per Christum dominum nostrum. Ad complendum. (27) Cotidianis domine quaesumus munera sacramenti: perpetuae nobis tribuas salutis augmentum, per. ITEM ALIA. (28) Tu domine semper a nobis omnem remoue prauitatem, et ad tuam nos propitius conuerte

6r   NADъ OPLATъMь ː.

(29)   Prinesenѣı tébě g̃ı sьı darъ

ıže tьi ésı dalъ i sъtvo

rılъ· cırъkъve raďi tvoe

5   ę̂ · i žıvota i prěstavle

niě našego radı ː i sъvěstu

emъ nъı̀ · ěko balьstvo é

stъ tò žıvota věčьnago:

g̃mь: PRЕѲACIÉ · DO

10   věčьnѣı b̃že:·

(30)   Molımъ sę ı̃su x̃u sъinu

tvoemu g̃ı našemu· da

mılostьǫ svoeǫ zaščı

tıtъ nъi i sъpasetъ: be

15   ž negože bo mılostı ne vъ

zmožemъ nıčьsože sъtvo

rıtı: těmьže samogo

égo radı darьi i mılostь

prıemlemъ i vъ lübъvı

20   živemъ: x̃mь g̃mь našımь

PO VъSQDÉ ·.

(31)   Vъsǫda tvoego g̃ı nasьi

cenı prosımъ tę: ótъ vь

6v   sěxъ protıvęcĭxъ sę ná

iustitiam, per. Super oblatam. (29) Offerimus tibi domine munera quae dedisti, ut creationis tuae circa mortalitatem nostram testificentur auxilium et remedium nobis immortalitatis operentur, per dominum. UD aeterne Deus. (30) Precantes ut Iesus Christus filius tuus dominus noster sua nos gratia protegat et conseruet, et quia sine ipso nihil recte ualemus efficere ipsius semper munere capiamus, ut tibi placere possimus, per quem maiestatem. Ad complendum. (31) Quos caelesti domine alimento satiasti, praesta quaesumus ab omni aduersitate

mъ sъpası nъı : g̃mь našı :•

MьŠĔ O MǪČENICĔXъ :

(32) Mǫčenıkĕ tvoıxъ g̃ı čь

5   stı čьstęcè molımъ tę

prosęce : da ĕkože ę ĕsı

slavoǫ tvoeǫ nebesьsku[1]

ǫ utvrьdılъ : takoze že

i̇ nъi̇ mılostıǫ tvoeǫ

10   prĭmi̇ g̃mь :• NADъ OPLATMь:

(33) Prınosъ g̃ı prınesenĕı tébĕ

mǫčenıkъ svętъıxъ ra

dı primi̇ : i̇ molıtvamı

i̇xъ ı zapovĕdьmı tvoı

15   mı prıspĕı namъ pomocь

tvoĕ • g̃mь : PO VъSQDĔ :•

(34) Ȯčístı nъı g̃ı prosımъ tę

nebesьskĕıxъ tvoıxъ ra

dı̇ zapovĕdъı̇: i̇ utvrь

20   dı̇ nъi̇ da slavımъ tę prĕ

dъ svętĕımı tvoımı

molıtvamı našımı :

g̃mь našımь :•

custodias, per. IN UIGILIA PLURIMORUM SANCTORUM. (32) Martyrum tuorum domine ill. natalitia praeeuntes supplices te rogamus, ut quos caelesti gloria sublimasti, tuis concede adesse fidelibus, per. Super oblata. (33) Sacrificium domine quod pro sanctis martyribus ill. praeuenit nostra deuotio eorum meritis nobis augeat te donante suffragium, per. Ad communionem. (34) Purificet nos domine quaesumus et diuini perceptio sacramenti et gloriosa sanctorum tuorum oratio, per. Sacram. Fuld.

---

[1] nebesьkoo (Kul'bakin, *Le vieux slave*, 43)

7r   *   MьŠÊ O VьSÉXъ NEBESьSKъI

Xъ SιLAXъ : Pomlιmъ sę :·

(35) B̄ъ ïže nъ̀i molιtvъi radî

blaženъiȩ̂ b̄cȩ̂ ι prιsno

5   děvêi marιȩ̂ : ι blaženêi

xъ radî ánκelê tvoíxъ· ι

vьsěxъ nebesьskъixъ sιla

xъ : ι apostolê · ι mǫče

nιkê · ι prěpodobьnêixъ·

10   ι čιstêixъ děvê· ι vьsěxъ

svętêixъ tvoιxъ molι

tvamι · prιsno nъ̀i vъzve

selιlъ ésι : prosιmъ tę

ḡι · da ěkože nъ̀i čьstïmъ

15   čьstι sïïxъ na vьsę dьnι

milostьǫ̈ tvoéǫ̈ dázь

námъ prïsno naslědovátι·

nebesьskêię̈ tvóę̈ sílьi :·

ḡm̄ь našmь : NAD ÓPLATMь :

20   (36) Darъ sь prinesenêi tebě ḡι

vьsěxъ svętêixъ nebesь

skêixъ sιlê radî : ι vьsě

xъ svętêixъ · tvoιxъ radι

7v   ι pravьdьnêixъ radî : bǫ

MISSA COTIDIANA DE SANCTIS. (35) Deus qui nos beatae Mariae semper uirginis et beatorum caelestium uirtutum et sanctorum patriarcharum, prophetarum, apostolorum, martyrum, confessorum et uirginum atque omnium simul sanctorum continua laetificas commemoratione, praesta quaesumus, ut quos cotidiano ueneramur officio etiam piae conuersationis sequamur exemplo, per. (36) Munera tibi domine nostrę deuotionis offerimus, quę et pro omnium sanctorum tuorum tibi sint

di tebĕ vъ xvălǫ : á namъ

molitvami ixъ dostoi

noe ótъplati : g̃mь našimь

5   PO VъSQDĔ :•

(37)   Prosimъ tę g̃i • dazь namъ

molitvami vъsĕxъ nebe

sьskĕixъ silaxъ • i vьsĕxъ

svętĕixъ tvoixъ • i dĕlĕ

10   ixъ radî pravьdьnъixъ : vъ

sǫdъmь sïmь vъzętĕi

mь • óčisti srьdьcĕ našĕ

ótъ grĕxĕ našixъ : g̃mь na :•

MOLITVA • B̄ :

15 (38) Sьtvorí nъì g̃i b̄že pričę

stьnĕi svętĕi b̄ci i pri

snodĕvĕ marîi : i dostoi

nъi svętĕixъ anѫelĕ • i

blaženъixъ ápostolĕ • mǫ

20   čenikĕ • i prĕpodobьnъixъ

(i) čistъixъ dĕvĕ • i vьsĕ

(xъ) svętъixъ tvoíxъ : mo

litvami ixъ zaščití

nъì

grata honore et nobis salutaria te miserante reddantur, per. (37) Praesta
nobis quaesumus domine intercedentibus omnium sanctorum tuorum
meritis, ut quę ore contingimus, puro corde capiamus, per. ALIA. (38)
Fac nos domine Deus sanctae Mariae semper uirginis subsidiis attolli et
gloriosa beatarum omnium caelestium uirtutum et sanctorum
patriarcharum, prophetarum, apostolorum, martyrum, confessorum,
uirginum et omnium simul protectione defendi, ut dum eorum pariter
cotidie commemorationem agimus, eorum pariter cotidie ab omnibus
aduersis protegamur officio, per.

Euchologium Sinaiticum. *Excerpt 1: Against fever*

45a   16   •:• MO͞L NA͞D VS E͠M TRNSOMO͠M TRNSAVICE͡Q •/•

Zaprěψaetъ ti ιmenemь g͞ne

mь • trɴsavice poslědьněě

ęze• ukorena sǫψi• slaběi

20 šič v͠sěxъ ęzь • Ne tъι li sa

ma i v͠sɴ tvoę • boite sɴ v͠sě

xъ mǫdrostei zemъпъιxъ.

mǫdrъιxъ• ι krěpostei krě

рькъιxъ• mǫžьstva mǫžьska•

45b   ι ženьstva ženьska• Posьla

nič poslušьlivъιxъ• poslě

dь že vъ buesti buiixъ• Em͡le

tъ žɛ ɴɛposlušьlivъιę • Xu

5 dɵumъιę• ι xudosilьпъι

ę• těmъ pakosti tvorite• na

vrěmena měsɴčьnaa• Xodite

skozě nɴ• ěko skozě čьto• Drugoe

mɴkъko• ι skozě tvorɴψɴę vo

10 lɴ vašɴ• ne tъι li sama • ι v͠sɴ

tvoę• boite sɴ prětъιkanei•

French translation (Frček 1933). Prière sur toute personne agitée par la fièvre. ‹Je› te conjure par le nom du Seigneur, fièvre, la dernière des maladies, qui es méprisée, la plus faible (20) de toutes les maladies: toi-même et toutes tes fièvres, ne craignez-vous pas toutes les sagesses des sages de la terre et les vigueurs des vigoureux, la virilité des virils (45b) et la féminité des femmes, la ‹docilité› des dociles, enfin la folie des fous? Vous saisissez les indociles, les faibles (5) d'esprit et de corps, c'est à eux que vous faites du mal selon les phases de la lune, vous cheminez à travers eux comme à travers toute autre chose molle et (comme) à travers ceux qui font (10) votre volonté. Toi-même et toutes tes fièvres, ne craignez-vous pas les obstacles

prětъikaemъixъ vamъ· ι vsĕ

xъ postrašenei č͡lskъ· strašN

ψiixъ vъι· KričNψe izbĕgaite·

15 ι otъxodite· Nъinĕ že samoi

tebĕ zaprĕψaǫ trNsavice· u

boi sN imeni g͡nĕ· ι vĕrъi vĕru

ǫψiixъ vь nь· egože trepeψǫ

tъ. Vidimaa i nevidimaa.

20 A͡ѫli ι arx͡ѫli· Prĕstoli ι g͡de

stviĕ· Vlasteli ι drъžavъι·

ι silъι· mnogorazličьnii

xerovimi· Egože trep(ǫ)eψǫtъ

n͡bsa· zem^lĕ i more· ι v͡sĕ ĕže sǫ

25 tъ vъ nixъ· tъi pače v͡sĕxъ

46a trepeψǫψi· ιzbĕgni ιsego

raba g͡nĕ· Vĕruǫψaago vъ imN

g͡ne· otъbĕgni otъ nego· ι ne i

mĕi pamNti na nemъ· ne vъspo

5 mNni ego· ne bǫdi po semь ime

ni tvoego vъ nemь· ni tebĕ sa

moę vъ nemь· ni tvoixъ· Vъ

qui vous sont opposées et toutes les menaces des hommes qui vous menacent? Fuyez en criant (15) et retirez-vous. Maintenant c'est toi-même, fièvre, que je conjure: crains le nom du Seigneur et la foi de ceux qui croient en lui, devant qui tremblent le visible et l'invisible, (20) les anges et les archanges, les Trônes et les Dominations, les Principautés, les Puissances et les Vertus, les Chérubins ‹aux yeux› multiples; devant qui tremblent les Cieux, la terre et la mer et tout ce qui s'y trouve. Toi qui trembles plus que tous, (46a) enfuis-toi de ce serviteur du Seigneur qui a foi dans le nom du Seigneur, sauve-toi de lui et ne garde pas souvenance de lui, ne (5) fais pas mention de lui, qu'il n'y ait pas dorénavant en lui ton nom, ni toi-même, ni tes fièvres.

zbranĕetъ bo ti g̃ъ· V̄sĕxъ ča

sъ· ι v̄sĕxъ godinъ· ι v̄sĕxъ

10 že vrĕmenъ· Vъ godinǫ em|ǫ̈

ψiixъ· Vъzbranĕetъ ti v̄sĕ

xъ pǫtei· ι vsĕxъ stezъ vъ

xodъnъixъ· ι zatvarĕǫ̈tъ

ti sn v̄sn dvьri vъxodъnъię·

15 V̄sĕlĕetъ že vo nь sьdravie·

Daetъ že slavǫ imeni tvoe

mu· v̄s̄ Ĕko proslavlĕetъ sn

imn tvoe· ōca i s̄na ι s̄taago ·/·

Car le Seigneur t'interdit tous les instants et toutes les heures, et toutes les (10) époques (des fièvres) intermittentes, il t'interdit tous les chemins et tous les sentiers d'accès, et toute porte d'accès t'est fermée; il (15) établit la santé dans le malade, et il donne la gloire à ‹son› nom. A haute voix: Car ton nom est glorifié, Père, Fils et Saint ‹Esprit›.

Euchologium Sinaiticum. Excerpt 2: Against pests

59a 5 MO̅L STAA̅G̅ T̅ROFONA̅ · ω VSE̅M̅ GA

dĕ zъlĕ· GubNψiimъ · Vina i

nivъi· ι vrьtъi ·/·

Vъ imn ōca i s̄na· ι s̄taago d̄xa·

PomolNψü mi sn· g̃vi ι b̄u· sъ

10 lĕzъ otъ n̄bse am̄lъ sedmъ· Da

Greek text (Frček 1933). Προσευχὴ τοῦ ἁγίου Τρύφωνος. Ἐν ὀνόματι τοῦ Πατρὸς καὶ τοῦ Υἱοῦ καὶ τοῦ ἁγίου Πνεύματος. Προσευξαμένου μου τῷ θεῷ

PRIERE DE SAINT TRYPHON contre toute vermine mauvaise qui détruit les vignes, les champs et les jardins. Au nom du Père et du Fils et du Saint-Esprit. Pendant que je priais le Seigneur Dieu, (10) sept anges ‹sont› descendus du ciel pour

otъženqtъ v̄se zъlo· ι v̄sǫ̈ zъ
lobǫ· ι g̃a gadovъ· ι v̄se eže obi
ditъ vina· ι nivъı· ι vrъtogra
dъı· Začъnǫ nъıně g̃lati· i
15 mena gadomъ· prǫgъ· slanǫ·
črъvenъı prǫgъ· kataarosъ·
filosъ· ιlosъ· Vilitisъ· Karъ
kinos· Vrъxosъ· Ѡtъxodn otъ
xodn· otъ sěmeni grozdovъ· ι o
20 suša eǫ̈ · ι velikъı vrъxъ · V̄sě
kъı gadъı· Ѡtiděte otъ lo
ziě· Ѡtъ nivъ· Ѡtъ vrъtogra
dъ· Ti otidi vъ gorъı pustъıę·
59b Vъ drěvo eže ne tvoritъ sěme
ni· tamo vъı estъ dalъ g̃ъ· Denъ
nǫ̈ǫ̈ piψǫ̈· Pakъı zaklinaǫ̈ va

.... (10) κατῆλθον ἐκ τοῦ οὐρανοῦ ἑπτὰ ἄγγελοι τοῦ διῶξαι πᾶν φαῦλον καὶ πάντα τὰ κακοῦργα καὶ τὰ δεκατέσσαρα [?] θηρία καὶ πάντα τὰ ἀδικοῦντα τὰς ἀμπέλους καὶ τὰς χώρας καὶ τοὺς κήπους. Ἄρξομαι δὲ λέγειν τῶν θηρίων τὰ (15) ὀνόματα· ... (20) [Ἐξορκίζω ὑμᾶς] πάντα τὰ θηρία, ἐξέλθετε ἀπὸ τῆς ἀμπέλου ταύτης καὶ τῆς χώρας καὶ τοῦ κήπου, καὶ ἀπέλθετε εἰς τὰ ἄγρια ὄρη, (59b) εἰς τὰ ἄκαρπα ξύλα, ἐκεῖ γὰρ ὑμῖν ἔδωκεν ὁ Κύριος τὴν καθημέρινὴν τρόφην.

chasser tout mal et toute malignité, ›les quatorze‹ vermines et tout ce qui nuit aux vignes, aux champs et aux jardins. Je commencerai maintenant à dire les noms des vermines: la sauterelle, la gelée blanche, (15) la sauterelle rouge, le scarabée, le puceron, l'ichneumon (?), le scolopendre (?), le karkinos, le bruche. Qu'ils s'en aillent, qu'ils s'en aillent du germe des raisins; toute vermine (qui desseche les rameaux (?) (20) et la cime, allez-vous-en des vignes, des champs, des jardins. Puis: Va-t'en dans les montagnes désertes, (59b) dans l'arbre qui ne porte pas de fruit, c'est là que le Seigneur vous a ménagé la nourriture quotidienne. Ensuite: Je vous conjure

sъ· Vъ imN g̅a̅ našego is̅x̅a· ěko a̅m̅li

5 g̅d̅ьscii· mixailъ gavъrilъ· u

rilъ· Rafailъ· Pakъı zaklina

Q̧ vъı v̅sěkъ gadъ· ωtiděte otъ

lozič· ωtъ nivъı· ωtъ vrъtogra

dъ. Aψe ne poslušaete m̅n̅e bědъ

10 naago· čľskъıę pьticN izědN

tъ vasъ· ωtiděte vъ pustъıę

gorъı· Vь drěva neplodьnaa· Į

dadite slavQ̧ b̅u̅· sъ o̅cemъ i s̅t̅

mъ d̅xomъ· nъıně i prisno i vъ vě ·/·

Εἰ δὲ παρακούσητε ἐμοὶ τῷ ταπεινῷ καὶ (10) ἐλαχίστῳ δούλῳ τοῦ θεοῦ Τρύφωνι, οὐκ ἔχϲτϲ μϝτἐμοὐ ἀλλ ἔχετε μετὰ τοῦ μεγάλου ὀνόματος τοῦ θεοῦ καὶ Πατρὸς καὶ τοῦ Σωτῆρος Χριστοῦ καὶ τοῦ ἁγίου Πνεύματος, ὅς καὶ ἀποστελεῖ στρουθία μικρὰ καὶ καταναλώσουσιν ὑμᾶς. Ἐξέλθετε οὖν τάχιον, ὅπως δότε δόξαν τῷ Πατρὶ καὶ τῷ Υἱῷ καὶ τῷ ἁγίῳ Πνεύματι, νῦν καὶ ἀεὶ καὶ εἰς τοὺς αἰῶνας τῶν αἰώνων. Ἀμήν.

au nom de notre Seigneur Jésus-Christ, (moi) de même que les anges du Seigneur: Michel, Gabriel, Uriel, Raphaël. Ensuite: Je vous conjure, toute vermine: allez-vous-en des vignes, (des) champ(s), des jardins. Si vous ne m'écoutez pas, moi misérable, (10) les oiseaux (du ciel) vous dévoreront. Allez-vous-en dans les montagnes désertes, dans les arbres qui ne portent pas de fruits, et rendez gloire à Dieu, avec le Père et le Saint-Esprit, maintenant et toujours et dans les (siècles des siècles). Amen).

Euchologium Sinaiticum. Excerpt 3: Confessional prayer

72a ·:· I PO TO͞M VьLĔZÉTE Vь CR͞K͞Vь·
·:· ι padeᵗ nicь na zemi. XotNι ιspo
·:· vĕdati sN. ι gleᵗ ierĕi nadъ nimь
·:· MOL͞IT͞VQ SIᵠ ·/·
5 G͞ı b͞že v͞semogъı· tebĕ bQdQ azъ i
spovĕdenъ· V͞sĕxъ moixъ grĕxъ· ι
moego lixa sъtvorenič sego· eže ko
ližьdo izḡlaxъ· İ lixo sъtvori
xъ· ι lixo mъıslixъ· G͞lomь li
10 dĕlomь· Li pomъıšleniemь·
V͞sego eže azъ pomьnQ· Lübo
ne pomьnQ· Éže azъ sъvĕdъı
sъgrĕšixъ· lübo ne sъvĕdъı· nQ
ždeQ lübo ne nQždeQ· sъpN li
15 bьdN· lixoklNtvъı· ι lьžN· ι vъ
pomъıšlenьı nepravedьnĕ· pu

Old High German parallel text (Repp 1954). (5) Trohtîn, dir uuirdu ih
pigihtîg allero mînero suntôno enti mînero missatâteô, alles des ih eo
missasprâhhi oda missatâti oda missadâhti, uuortô enti (10) uuerchô
enti gadanchŏ, des ih kihugku oda nigihugku, des ih uuizzanto geteta
oda unuuizzanto, nôtag oda unnôtag, slâffanto oda (15) uuahhento:
meinsuertô enti lugîno, kiridôno enti unrehterô

(72a) Et ensuite qu'ils entrent dans l'église. Et celui qui veut se
confesser se prosterne face contre terre, et le prêtre dit sur lui la prière
suivante: (5) Seigneur Dieu tout-puissant, je me confesserai à toi de
tous mes péchés et de mes mauvaises actions, de ‹tout› ce que j'ai dit
‹de mauvais›, fait de mauvais et pensé de mauvais, en parole ou (10) en
action ou en pensée, de tout ce don't il me souvient ou dont il ne me
souvient pas, en quoi j'ai péché consciemment ou inconsciemment, par
contrainte ou sans contrainte, dormant ou éveillé: (15) faux serments,
mensonges, vanités et sottises malintentionnées, de quelque manière

stoši ι blɴdi· ěkože azъ koližъ
do sъtvorixъ· ι v̄sě iz lixa· Vь ě
denьι · ι vь pitьι · ι vъ neprave
20 dьněmь sъpanьι · Molǫ tɴ g̃i
b̃že moi · Da tьi mi račilъ · ži
votъ i milostъ podati · Da i a
zъ neposram¹eṇ prědъ očima
tvoima bǫdǫ · ι da i azъ eψe na
72b semь světě · moixъ grěxъ poka
ǫ sɴ · ι dostoino pokaanie imě
ti mogǫ · Ěkože tvoę ψedrotьι
sǫtъ · V̄sevĩko g̃ι · troice b̃že
5 v̄semogъι · bǫdi mi pomoψьni
kь · ι bǫdi mi podavъì silǫ ·
ι mǫdrostь · ι pravьdenъ za
mъιslъ · ι dobrǫ volǫ · sъ pra

vizusheitô, hûrôno sô uuê sô ih siô giteta, enti unrehterô firinluslo in
mûsa enti in trancha enti in unrehtemo (20) slâffa; ... daz dû mir,
trohtîn, kenist enti ginâda farkip [B¹: kauuerdos fargepan], daz ih fora
dînên ougen unscamanti môzzi uuesan [AB¹ : unscamanti sî] enti daz ih
in (72b) desaro uueraltî mînerô missatâtô [A: suntono] riuûn enti
harmscara hapan môzzi, sôlîho sô dîno miltadâ sîn, alles uualtanto
trohtîn, got (5) almahtîgo, kauuerdô mir helfan enti gauuerdô mir
fargeban keuuizzida enti furistententida, [A add.: ia] cûtan uuillun mit

que j'en aie commis, et tous les excès dans le manger et le boire et dans
le sommeil (20) déréglé. Je te prie, Seigneur mon Dieu, de daigner
m'accorder la vie et la grâce, pour que moi aussi je ne sois pas en
confusion devant tes yeux, et pour que, dès (72b) ce monde-ci, je me
repente de mes péchés et que je puisse avoir un repentir convenable,
conformément à tes miséricordes, Seigneur Maître de tout. Trinité,
Dieu (5) tout-puissant, prête-moi assistance et sois celui qui m'accorde
la force, la sagesse, l'intention juste et la bonne volonté avec une foi

vedъnoǫ věroǫ · Na tvoǫ slu
10 žъbq g̃ı · Tъı edinъ na sъ svě
tъ pride grěšъnikъ ızbavitъ ·
Bǫdi mN sp̃sъı · ızbavi mN
g̃ı b̃že s̃ne g̃ı · Ěkože tъı xoꟅeši
ěkože ti lübo · Sъtvori sъ mno
15 ǫ rabomь tvoimь · milosti
vъı̇ · Ei b̃že · Rači mi pomoꟅi
tvoemu rabu · tъı edinъ věsi
g̃ı · Kakъı moę sǫtъ bědъı ·
Vь tvoǫ mil̄stь prědaǫ azъ
20 moe s̃rce · ı moǫ mъıslь · ı
moǫ lübovь · ı moi životъ ·
ı moę grěxъı · otъloži · moě
slovesa · ı moe dělo okonьča
i g̃ı · ı tvoǫ mil̄stь · Vь m̃ně

rehtan galaupon za dînemo deonosta. (10) Trohtîn, du in desa uuerolt quâmi suntîga za generienna, kauuerdô miń gahaltan enti ganerien. Christ, cotas sun, trohtîn, sôso dû uuellês enti sôso dir gezeh sî, tua pî mih (15) scalh dînan. Trohtîn, ganâdîgo kot, keuuerdô mir helfan dînemo scalhe. Dû eino uuêst, trohtîn, uuemo [A: uueo mino] durftî sint. In dîno genâdâ, trohtîn, pifilhu (20) mîn herza, [A add.: ia] mîna gadanchâ, [A add.: ia] mînan uillun, [A add.: ia], mînan môt, [A add.: ia] mînan lîp, [A add.: ia] mîniu uuort, [A add.: ia] mîniu uuerh. Leisti, trohtîn, dîno ganâdâ uper mih

juste pour ton service. (10) Seigneur, tu es seul venu en ce monde pour délivrer les pécheurs: sois mon sauveur ‹et› délivre-moi. Seigneur, fils ‹de› Dieu, Seigneur, fais de moi, ton serviteur, (15) ce que tu veux ‹et› ce qu'il te plaît. Dieu, ‹Seigneur› miséricordieux daigne me secourir, moi ton serviteur. Tu es le seul qui saches, Seigneur, quelles sont mes misères: je confie à ta miséricorde (20) mon coeur, ma pensée, mon désir, ma vie, [remets mes péchés,] mes paroles, mon action. Parachève, Seigneur, ta miséricorde en moi,

25 grěšъně rabě tvoimъ avi • ι i

zbavi mN g̅ı̅ otъ v̅sego zъla

73a nъıně i prisno i • vь věkъı věko m̅ •/•

(25) suntîgan dînan scalh. Kaneri mih, trohtîn, fonna allemo upila.

(25) pécheur, ton serviteur, [manifeste-la] et délivre-moi, Seigneur, de tout mal, maintenant et toujours et dans les siècles des siècles.

Euchologium Sinaiticum. Excerpt 4: Penitence

102a 5   ZAPOVĚDI STЪIXЪ w̅Cь • O •

•:• pokaanъı razboě • ι o v̅semь grěsě •/•

Aѱe k̅to razboi sъtvori͡ꞇ • ı̂li otъ ro

ždeniě svoego ubietъ •ı͡ꞇ lě͡ꞇ da po

•:• kaeꞇ͡sN • Vъ inoi oblasti • Toli po

10 •:• tomь da prię͡ꞇ bǫde͡ꞇ vъ svoe ote

•:• c̃stvo • Aѱe bǫde͡ꞇ prave dno pokaa

•:• lъ͡s • o xlěbě o vodě • ι da poslušъ

•:• stvuetъ emu epi͡spъ • i p͡ꝓove • Vь ni

•:• xъže sN estъ pokaalъ •/• Къ roždenьü

15 •:• ubienaago •/• Aѱe li͡s bǫde͡ꞇ nedobrě

•:• pokaalъ͡s • To da ne priętъ bǫde͡ꞇ vъ

•:• svoe otc̃stvo •/• Aѱe k̅to razboi   Ƃ

•:• sъtvori͡ꞇ ne xotN • d̅ lě͡ꞇ da pokae

COMMANDEMENTS DES SAINTS PÈRES relatifs à la pénitence pour l'homicide et à tout péché. ‹I› Si quelqu'un commet un homicide ou s'il tue (quelqu'un) de sa race, qu'il se repente pendant 10 années dans un autre pays. Après (10) cela qu'il soit admis dans sa patrie, à condition qu'il se soit bien repenti au pain (et) à l'eau; que l'évêque et les prêtres auprès de qui il s'est repenti en témoignent à la famille (15) de la victime. S'il s'est mal repenti, qu'il ne soit pas admis dans sa patrie. II. Si quelqu'un commet un homicide involontaire, qu'il se repente

•:• ῑ sn • v̄ oͭ niˣ o xlěᵇ • o vodě •/•

20 v̄ Aψe kotorы pričetьniᵏ • sodomъ

skы blǫdъ sъtvoriͭ •῍ι lěͭ da

•:• pokaetъˢ • v̄ oͭ niˣ o xlěᵇ o vod̄ •/•

g̃ Aψe kotorы pričetьnikъ blǫd̄

102b sъtvori • z̄ lěͭ da pokaetъ sn •/•

d̄ Aψe k̄to proklinaetъˢ • z̄ lěͭ da pok̄eῑ sn •/•

Aψe k̄to nǫdьmi klьnetъˢ • v̄ lěͭ da

ẽ •:• pokaetъˢ •/• Aψe k̄to ukradeͭ • glavъ

5 •:• no č̃to • ili skotъ • ιli domъ podьko

•:• paeͭ • ιli č̃to dobro • zělo drago u

•:• kradetъ • d̄ lěͭ daᵖ̄ kaetъˢ • A li ma

•:• lo č̃to ukradeͭ • v̄ lěͭ da pokaeῑ sn •/•

z̄ Aψe kotorьì pričetьniᵏ blǫd̄ sъtvo

10 riͭ • sъ tuždeǫ̈ ženoǫ̈ • li sъ děvi

•:• ceǫ̈ • v̄ lͭě da pokaetъˢ • o xlěᵇ o vod̄ •/•

z̄ Aψe li estъ diěkъ • li črьnecь • g̃ lěͭ

da pokaetъˢ • v̄ oͭ niˣ o xlěᵇ o vod̄ •/•

z̄ Aψe li estъ epsp̄ъ • to da izvrьže

15 tъˢ sana • iῑ lěͭ daᵖ̄ kaetъˢ •/•

pendant 5 années, dont 3 au pain (et) à l'eau. (20) III. Si un ecclésiastique commet le péché de sodomie, qu'il se repente pendant 10 années, dont 3 au pain (et) à l'eau. IV. Si un ecclésiastique fornique, (102b) qu'il se r. pendant 7 années. V. Si quelqu'un commet un parjure, qu'il se r. pendant 7 années. VI. Si quelqu'un commet un parjure par nécessité, qu'il se r. pendant 3 années. ‹VII.› Si quelqu'un commet un vol capital (5) ou (qu'il vole) du bétail, ou s'il mine une maison, ou s'il vole quelque bien très précieux, qu'il se r. pendant 5 années. ‹VIII.› S'il commet un vol peu important, qu'il se r. pendant 3 années. IX. Si quelque ecclésiastique fornique (10) avec la femme d'autrui ou avec une jeune fille, qu'il se r. pendant 3 années au pain (et) à l'eau. S'il est diacre ou moine, qu'il se r. pendant 4 années dont 3 au pain (et) à l'eau. S'il est évêque, qu'il soit déposé (15) et qu'il se r. pendant 10 années.

Codex Suprasliensis

75   29   ПРѢБЫШѦ ЖЕ ВЪ ТѪ НОШТЬ ВЕСЕ-

          ЛАШТЕ СѦ· О НАКАЗАНИИ ГОСПОДЬНИ·

76   ОУТРОУ ЖЕ БЫВЪШОУ· ВЪ ТЪ ДЬНЬ ПОВЕЛѢ

          ИЗВЕСТИ Ѧ ИС ТЕМНИЦѦ· И ПРИВЕСТИ· И

          СТАВ'ЪШЕ ПРѢДЪ ПАКОСТЬНИКЫ РѢШѦ·

          ЄЖЕ ХОШТЕТЕ ТВОРИТЕ· ІАВИ ЖЕ СѦ ДИІА-

      5   ВОЛЪ О ДЕСНѪІѪ ДРЪЖѦ МЕУЬ· О ЛѢВѪІѪ

          ЖЕ ЗМИИ· ГЛАГОЛААШЕ ЖЕ КЪ ОУХОУ АГРИ-

          КОЛАУ· МОИ ЄСИ ПОДВИЗАИ СѦ· ПОВЕЛѢ ЖЕ

          ВОЄВОДА· СЪВѦЗАВЪШЕ ЗА ВЫІѪ ВЕСТИ

          ВЬСѦ ВЬКОУПѢ КЪ ЄЗЕРОУ· ЄСТЪ БО ВЬ СЕ-

     10   ВАСТИИ ЄЗЕРО ИМЫ ВОДѪ МНОГѪ· ВЪ ТО

          ЖЕ ВРѢМѦ ЄГ'ДА СТЫІА МѪУДААХѪ· БѢАШЕ

          СТОУДЕНЬ ВЕЛИКА· ВЪВЕДЪШЕ ЖЕ Ѧ НАГЫ

          ПОСТАВИША ПОСРѢДѢ ЄЗЕРА· БѢАШЕ ЖЕ

          И ВЪЗДОУХЪ СТОУДЕНЪ· И УАСЪ БРИДЪКЪ·

     15   КЪ ВЕУЕРОУ БО БѢАШЕ ДЬНИ· ПРИСТАВИ-

          ША ЖЕ ИМЪ СТРАЖА ВОИНЫ· И КАПИКЛА-

          РИІА· ВЪСКРАИ ЖЕ БѢАШЕ ЄЗЕРА БАНѢ· РА-

Διῆγον δὲ καὶ τὴν νύκτα ἐκείνην ἀγαλλιώμενοι ἐπὶ τῇ προτροπῇ τοῦ Χριστοῦ.
(76.1) Πρωΐας δὲ γενομένης ἐκέλευσεν αὐτοὺς ἐκβληθῆναι ἐκ τῆς φυλακῆς· καὶ
σταθέντες ἔμπροσθεν τῶν τυράννων εἶπον· ὃ ἐὰν θέλετε ποιεῖν, ποιεῖτε·
Ἐφάνη δὲ καὶ ὁ διάβολος (5) τῇ δεξιᾷ χειρὶ κατέχων μάχαιρα[ν] καὶ τῇ
ἀριστερᾷ δράκοντα· ἔλεγεν δὲ πρὸς τὸ οὖς τοῦ Ἀγρικολάου· ἐμὸς εἶ,
ἀγωνίζου. Ἐκέλευσεν δὲ αὐτοὺς δε θέντας καὶ σχοινισθέντας εἰς τοὺς
τραχήλους ἄγεσθαι πάντας ὁμοῦ ἐπὶ τὴν λίμνην· ἔστιν δὲ ἐ[ν] τῇ Σεβαστείᾳ
(10) λίμν[η] ἔχουσα ὕδωρ πολ[ύ]· κατὰ δὲ τὸν καιρὸν ἐ[κεῖ]νον, ὅτε οἱ ἅγιοι
ἐμα[ρ]τύρησαν, εἶχεν κρ[ύ]ος μέγα· ἀγαγόντ[ες] δὲ αὐτοὺς ἔστησα[ν] ἐν μέσῳ
τῆς λίμν[ης] γυμνούς· ἦν γὰρ ἀὴρ χειμέριος καὶ ὥρα δριμυτάτη (15) [πρὸς]
ἑσπέραν γὰρ ἦν· [πα]ρεκατέστησαν δὲ αὐ[τοῖς] στρατιώτας φύλα[κας] καὶ τὸν
καπικλά[ριον]· ἐγγὺς δὲ τῆς λίμνη[ς] ἦν βαλανεῖον

ЖДЕЖЕНА· ДА АШТЕ К’ТО ХОШТЕТЪ ПРНЕТѪ-
ПНТН Н ЇꙀБѢГНѪТН· ПРНБѢЖНТЪ КЪ БА-
20 НН· БЪ ЧАСЪ ЖЕ ПРЬБꙀꙊН НОШТН· СЪКЛѢ-
ШТААХѪ СА ОТЪ СТОУДЕНН СТꙊН· Н ТѢ-
ЛО НМЪ РАСПАДААШЕ СА· НѤДННЪ ЖЕ ОТЪ
ЧНСЛА М҃ ОТЪПАДЪ ПРНБѢЖЕ КЪ БАНН·
Н ПРНКОСНѪВЪ СА КЪ ТОПЛОТѢ· АБНѤ РА-
25 СТАА СА· Н ТАКО ОТЪДАСТЪ Д҃ШѪ СВОІѪ·
СТꙊН ЖЕ ОТЪПАДЪШЕ РѢША· ІАКО НꙀЪ НѤДН-
НѢХЪ ОУСТЪ ГЛАСОМЪ ВЕЛНѤМЪ· НѤДА БꙊ
РѢКАХЪ ПРОГНѢВАНѤШН СА Г҃Н· ЛН БꙊ РѢ-
КАХЪ ІАРОСТЬ ТВОІА· НЛН ВЪ МОРН ОУСТРꙊ-
30 МЬНѤННѤ ТВОНѤ· НЖЕ БО ОТЪЛѪЧНВЪ СА
77 ОТЪ НАСЪ АКꙊ ВОДА РАꙀЛНІА СА· Н РАꙀНДО-
ША СА ВЬСА КОСТН НѤГО· МꙊ ЖЕ НЕ ОТЪСТѪ-
ПНМЪ ОТЪ ТЕБЕ ДОНЬѪДЕЖЕ ОЖНВНШН
НАСЪ· Н НМА ТВОНѤ ПРНꙀОВЕМЪ· НѤГОЖЕ
5 ХВАЛНТЪ ВЬСА ТВАРЬ· ꙀМНѤВЕ Н ВЬСА БЕ-
ꙀДЕННІА· ОГНЬ ГРАДЪ СНѢГЪ ЛЕДЪ· ДОУ-
ХЪ БОУРЕНЪ ТВОРАШТНН СЛОВО НѤГО· ХО-

ὃ κ[ατ]εξεπύρωσαν, ὅπ[ως], ἐάν τις θέλει ἐξ αὐ[τῶν] παραβῆναι, πρ[οσ]φύγῃ τῷ βαλανείῳ· (20) [Ὥ]ρᾳ δὲ πρώτῃ τῆς [νυ]κτὸς ἐσφίγγοντ[ο ὑπὸ] τοῦ κρύους οἱ ἅγι[οι καὶ] περιταθέντα τὰ [σώ]ματα αὐτῶν διερρήγνυντο· Εἷς δέ τις ἐκ τοῦ ἀριθμοῦ τῶν τεσσαράκοντα λιποτακτήσας προσέφυγε τῷ βαλανείῳ καὶ ἁψάμενος τῆς θέρμης εὐθέως διελύθη (25) καί οὕτως ἀπέδωκε τὴν ψυχήν. [Ο]ἱ δὲ ἅγιοι ἰδόντες ἐκεῖνον λιποτακτήσαντα καὶ οὕτως ἀποπνεύσαντα ὡς ἐξ ἑνὸς στόματος εἶπον· [Μ]ὴ ἐν ποταμοῖς ὠργίσθης κύριε· ἤ ἐν ποτα[μ]οῖς ὁ θυμός σου· ἤ ἐν [θ]αλάσσῃ τὸ ὅρμημά [σ]ου· ὁ γὰρ ἀποχω[ρ]ισθεὶς (77.1) ἀφ᾽ ἡμῶν, ὡς [ὕ]δωρ ἐξεχύθη πάν[τ]α τὰ ὀστᾶ αὐτοῦ [ἡ]μεῖς δὲ οὐ μὴ ἀπο[στ]ῶμεν ἀπό σου, ἕ[ω]ς οὗ ζωώσεις ἡμᾶς, [κ]αὶ τὸ ὄνομά σου ἐπικαλεσόμεθα· ὃν (5) ὑμνεῖ πᾶσα κτίσις, δράκοντες καὶ πᾶσαι ἄβυσσοι, πῦρ, χάλαζα, χιών, κρύσταλλος, πνεῦμα καταιγίδος τά ποιοῦντα τὸν λόγον αὐτοῦ· ὁ περιπατῶν

ДАЙ ПО МОРОУ АКЪІ ПО СОУХОУ· Й СВЕРѢ-
ПЪІЙМЪ ВЛЪНАМЪ ПОМАІАННЙЙМЪ РѪКЪ

10 ТВОЄІѬ КРОТАЙ· Й НЪІНІА ТЪІ ЄСЙ ГЙ ЙЖЕ
ОУСЛЪІШАВЪ МѠУСЙѬ Й ДАІѬШТА ЗНА-
МЕНЙІА Й ЧОУДЕСА ВЪ ЄГУПТѢ· ВЪ ФАРАѠ-
НѢ Й ВЪ ЛЮДЕХЪ ЄГО· РАЗДѢЛѢА МОРЕ Й
ВЪ ПОУСТЪІНЙ НАСТАВ[НВЪІН] ЛЮДЙ

15 СВОА· ЙЖЕ ОУСЛЪІШАВЪ ЙІАКѠВА МОЛА-
ШТА СА· БѢЖАШТА ВЪСПРѢШТЕННІА Й-
САЛВОВА· ЙЖЕ СЪ ЇѠСНФОМЪ ПРОДАВЪ СА
Й СЪПАСЪ ЄГО· ЙЖЕ ОУСЛЪІША СТЪІА АПО-
СТОЛЪІ· Й НАСЪ ОУСЛЪІШН ГЙ· Й ДА НЕ ПОТО-

20 ПНТЪ НАСЪ БОУРА ВОДЬНАА· НН ПОЖЬРЕТ
НАСЪ ГЛѪБННА· ІАКО ОБННШТАХОМЪ ЗѢ-
ЛО ПОМОЗН НАМЪ БЕ С'ПАСЕ НАШЬ· ІАКО СТА-
ХОМЪ ВЪ ГЛѪБННѢ МОРУ· Й МОКРЪІ БЪІ-
ША НОГЪІ НАША· КРЪВЬІѪ НАШЕІѪ· ОБЛЕГЪ-

25 УН ТАГОСТН НАША· Й ЛЮТОСТН ВЪЗДОУ-
ХА ГЙ БЕ НАШЪ· Й ДА ОУВѢДАТЪ ВЬСН ІАКО
К' ТЕБѢ ВЪЗВАХОМЪ Й СЪПАСЕНН БЪІХОМЪ·
К' ТЕБѢ ОУПВАХОМЪ Й НЕ ПОСТЪІДѢХОМЪ

ἐπὶ θαλάσσης ὡς ἐπὶ ἐδάφους καὶ ἀγριαινομένην αὐτὴν τῷ νεύματι τῆς
χειρός (10) σου καταπραΰνων· καὶ νῦν οὖν αὐτὸς εἶ κύριε ὁ ἐπακούσας Ἰακὼβ
φεύγοντος τὴν ἀπειλὴν Ἡσαῦ· ὁ τῷ Ἰωσὴφ συμπραθεὶς καὶ σώσας αὐτόν· ὁ
ἐπακούσας Μωυσῆν διδόντος σημεῖα καὶ τέρατα ἐν Αἰγύπτῳ, ἐν Φαραὼ καὶ
ἐν τῷ λαῷ αὐτοῦ, ῥηγνύντος τὴν θάλασσαν καὶ ἐν ἐρήμῳ ὁδηγοῦντος τὸν λαὸν
[15] αὐτοῦ· ... ὁ ἐπακούσας τῶν ἁγίων σου ἀποστόλων καὶ ἡμῶν ἐπάκουσον
κύριε καὶ μὴ καταποντισάτω (20) ἡμᾶς βυθός, ὅτι ἐπτωχεύσαμεν σφόδρα·
βοήθησον ἡμῖν ὁ θεός, ὁ σωτὴρ ἡμῶν, ὅτι ἔστημεν ἐν βυθῷ θαλάσσης καὶ
ἐβάφησαν οἱ πόδες ἡμῶν ἐν τῷ αἵματι ἡμῶν· ἐλάφρυνον (25) τὸ βάρος καὶ τὴν
πικρότητα τοῦ ἀέρος κύριε ὁ θεὸς ἡμῶν καὶ γνώτωσαν πάντες, ὅτι πρὸς σὲ
ἐκεκράξαμεν καὶ ἐσώθημεν.

ГД҃· И СЖШТОУ ЧАСОУ ТРЕТИꙊꙐМОУ НОШТИ·

30 СЛЪНЬЦЕ Ѡ НИХЪ ВЪСИꙗ ТОПЛО ꙗКО ВЪ ЖАТВЖ·

И РАСТААВЪ СѦ ЛЕДЪ БꙐСТЪ ВОДА ТОПЛА· ВЬ-

СИ ЖЕ СТРѢГЖШТИИ СЬНОМЬ СЪДРЪЖИМИ

БѢАХЖ· ИEДИНЪ ЖЕ КАПИКЛАРИИ БѢАШЕ

БЬДА· И ПОСЛОУШАꙗ МОЛАШТЬ СѦ ИХЪ· И ПО-

5 МꙐШЛѢꙗ· КАКО ИЖЕ ПРИБѢГЪ КЪ БАНИ·

НЕ ВЬЧЬТЕ СѦ СЪ ЧЕТꙐРЬМИ ДЕСѦТꙐ· НЪ АБЬ-

ИE ѠТЪ ТОПЛОТꙐ РАСТАА СѦ· А СИИ ВЪ КОЛИЦѢ

МРАЗѢ СЖШТЕ ДОСЕЛѢ ЖИВИ СЖТЪ· И ЗЬРА

СВѢТА ИЖЕ Ѡ НИХЪ· И ВЪЗЬРѢВЪ НА НЕБО·

10 ХОТА ВИДѢТИ ѠТЪКЖДОУ ИEСТЪ СВѢТЪ·

ВИДѢ ВѢНЬЦА СЪХОДАШТА НА ГЛАВꙐ СТꙐ-

ХЪ· ЧИСЛОМЪ Л҃Ѳ· И ПОМꙐШЛꙗАШЕ ВЬ СЕБѢ

ГЛАГОЛꙗ· ЧЕТꙐРЕ ДЕСѦТЕ ИХЪ ИEСТЪ· ТО КА-

КО ИEД'НОМꙊ НѢСТЪ ВѢНЬЦА· И РАЗОУМѢВꙐ

15 ꙗКО ПРИБѢГꙐИ ВЪ БАНЖ· НЕ ПРИЧ'ТЕНЪ БꙐ-

СТЪ К НИМЪ И ВЪЗБОУЖДЬ ВЬСА СТРѢГЖ-

ШТАꙗ· И СЪВРЪГЪ РИЗꙐ СЬ СЕБЕ НА ЛИЦА И-

ХЪ· ВЪСКОЧИ ВЬ ИEЗЕРО ВЬПИꙗ И ГЛАГОЛꙗ·

И АЗЪ КРЬСТИꙗНЪ ИEСМЪ· И ВЬШЕДЪ ПОСРѢ-

Καὶ ὡς περὶ τρίτην ὥραν τῆς νυκτὸς ἥλιος ἔλαμψε περὶ αὐτοὺς θερμὸς ὡς ἐν θέρει (78.1) καὶ ἐλύθη τὸ κρύος καὶ ἐγένετο τὸ ὕδωρ θερμόν. Πάντες δὲ οἱ φυλάσσοντες αὐτοὺς ὕπνῳ βαθεῖ κατείχοντο, μό[νος] δὲ ὁ καπικλάριο[ς] ἦν γρηγορῶν καὶ ἀ[κ]ουλόμενος προσευχομένων αὐτῶν καὶ ἐννοῶν, (5) πῶς ὁ προσφυγὼν τὸ βαλανεῖον εὐθέως ἀπὸ τῆς θέρμης ἐτελεύτησεν κα[ὶ] οὗτοι μέχρι τοῦ νῦν ζῶσι, καὶ ἦν ὁρῶν φῶς μέγα περὶ αὐτούς· ἀτενίσας δὲ εἰς τὸν οὐρανὸν (10) ἰδεῖν, πόθεν τὸ φῶς, καὶ εἶδεν στεφάνους κατερχομένους ἐπὶ τοὺς ἁγίους τὸν ἀριθμὸν τριάκοντα ἐννέα. Καὶ διελογίζετο λέγων· τεσσαράκοντά εἰσιν καὶ πῶς ὁ εἷς στέφανος λείπει; καὶ ἔγνω, (15) ὅτι ὁ προσφυγὼν τῷ βαλανείῳ οὐ συγκατεριθμήθη μετὰ τῶν τεσσαράκοντα. Καὶ ἐξυπνίσας τοὺς σὺν αὐτῷ καὶ ῥίψας τὰ ἱμάτια αὐτοῦ εἰς τὰς ὄψεις αὐτῶν εἰσεπήδησεν εἰς τὴν λίμνην κράζων καὶ λέγων· κἀγὼ χριστιανός εἰμι· καὶ

20 ДѢ ЙХЪ РЕУЕ҃• Г҃И Б҃Е ВѢРОГⰶ ВЬ ТА҃• ВЬ НЬ-
ЖЕ Й СИ ВѢРОВАША҃• Й ВЪYЬТИ МА ВЬ Н҃А• Й
СЪПОДОБИ МА ЙСКОУШЕННЙЕ МⰶКЪ ПРИѦ-
ТИ• ӤКО ДА Й АZЪ ЙСКОУШЕНЪ БⰶДⰶ• ПО-
БѢЖДЕНЪ ЖЕ БЪIВЪ ДНЙⰶВОЛЪ ПРѢМѢНИ

25 СА ВЪ МⰶЖЕСКЪ ОБРАZЪ• СЪВАZАВЪ Рⰶ-
ЦѢ СВОЙ Й КОЛѢНѢ СВОЙ ДРⰶЖА ГЛАГОЛАА-
ШЕ• ОҮВЪI МЬНѢ ОҮВЪI МЬНѢ • ПОБѢЖДЕ-
НЪ БЪIХЪ МⰶЖИ СИМИ СВАТЪIЙМИ • Й БЪI-
ХЪ ВЬСѢМЪ ВЪ РⰶГЪ• НЕ ЙМЪI ЙЕДНОДОУ-

30 ШЕНЪ СЛОУГЪ• АШТЕ БО БЪIХЪ ЙМѢЛЪ• ТО
79 НЕ БЪIХЪ ПОБѢЖДЕНЪ БЪIЛЪ• Й НЪIНѢ ҮТⷪ
СЪТВОРⰶ• РАZБРАШТⰶ СРѢДЬЦИ КНАZЕ-
МА МОЙМА• Й СЪЖЕГⰶТЪ ТѢЛЕСА СТ҃ЪIЙХ'•
Й ВЬ РѢКⰶ ВЪВРЬГⰶТЪ• Й СЕ СЪТВОРⰶ ДА

5 Й ОСТАТЪКА ЙХЪ НЕ БⰶДЕТЪ• СТ҃Й ЖЕ КУ-
РИѠНЪ РЕУЕ• К'ТО БОГЪ ВЕЛИКЪ ӤКО БОГЪ
НАШЪ• ТЪI ЙЕСИ БОГЪ ТВОРАЙ УОУДЕСА•
СⰶШТⰶА БО НА НЪI ПО НАСЪ СЬТВОРИ• Й ЛИ-
ШЕННЙЕ УЕТЪIРЬ ДЕСАТЪ НАПЛЬНИЛⰶ ЙЕСИ•

10 Й НАУАША ПѢТИ• СЪПАСИ НЬН Г҃И ӤКО ОСКⰶ-

(20) εἶπεν· κύριε ὁ θεὸς πιστεύω εἰς σέ, εἰς ὃν καὶ οὗτοι ἐπίστευσαν, κἀμὲ
μετ' αὐτῶν καταρίθμησον καὶ ἀξίωσόν με βασάνων καὶ πειρατηρίων, ἵνα κἀγὼ
δόκιμος εὑρεθῶ. Ὁ δὲ σατανᾶς ἡττηθεὶς καὶ μεταβαλὼν (25) ἑαυτὸν εἰς ἄνδρα,
δήσας αὐτοῦ τὰ γόνατα ταῖς χερσὶν ἔλεγεν ἔμπροσθεν πάντων· οὐαί μοι,
νενίκημαι ὑπὸ ἁγίων ἀνδρῶν καὶ γέγονα πᾶσι κατάγελως οὐκ εἶχον ὁμοψύχους
ὑπουργούς, (79.1) ἐπεὶ οὐκ ἂν ἐνικήθην· καὶ νῦν διαστρέψω τὰς καρδίας τῶν
ἀρχόντων καὶ καύσωσι τὰ σώματα τῶν ἁγίων καὶ εἰς τὸν ποταμὸν ρίψωσι·
καὶ οὕτως ποιήσω, ἵνα (5) μηδὲ λείψανον αὐτῶν εὑρεθῇ. Ὁ ἅγιος Κυρίων λέγει
τίς θεὸς μέγας, ὡς ὁ θεὸς ἡμῶν; σὺ εἶ ὁ θεὸς ὁ ποιῶν θαυμάσια· τοὺς γὰρ
καθ' ἡμῶν ὑπὲρ ἡμῶν ἐποίησας καὶ τὸν χωρισμὸν τῆς τετάρτης δεκάδος
ἀνεπλήρωσας καὶ τὸν σατανᾶν κατῄσχυνας· (10) καὶ ἤρξατο ψάλλειν σῶσόν με
κύριε, ὅτι ἐκλέλοιπεν ὅσιος.

дѣ пр︢ѣпод︢обьнъїй· ѹ︢тро́ѹ же бъївъшѹ̈
прид︢оста неѹ̈ьстивам мꙋꙗнтелꙗ· и̇ о-
брѣтоста капиклариꙗ съ нн︢ꙇмн сѣд︢а-
штл· и̇ въпросиста воин︢ъꙇ· у̇то видѣвъ
15 съ︢творн се· рекоша же вонни мъꙇ ꙗ̈ко-
же и̇ꙁмръ︢ли бѣхомъ сьномъ· о̇нъ же бь-
дѣ въ вьсꙗ ношть· и̇ вьнеꙁаапꙗ въꙁбоу-
ди нъꙇ· и̇ видѣхомъ свѣтъ велнкъ на нн︢-
хъ· о̇нъ же а̇бнꙗ съвръꙁгъ рнꙁъꙇ своꙗ· въ-
20 скоун вь ны вьпнꙗ и̇ глаголꙗ· и̇ а̇ꙁъ кр︢ь-
стнꙗнъ ꙗ̈смъ· и̇ раꙁгнѣвавъша сꙗ мꙋ-
 унтелꙗ· повелѣста и̇ꙁвлѣштн-ꙗ· и̇ и̇-
ꙁваꙁавъше ꙗ вестн на брѣгъ морѣ· и̇ др-
колмн ногъꙇ и̇хъ прѣбнватн· ꙗд︢'ного
25 же матн прнлежаꙗше и̇хъ· бѣ бо съꙁнъ
ꙗ︠ю︠ꙇꙗⷪ вьсѣхъ· и̇ боꙗ̈ше сꙗ ꙗ̈да как︦о
о̇тъврь︢жетъ сꙗ· и̇ на н︠ь︡ прнсно въꙁнра-
ше· въꙁлагаꙗ︠ штн на н︠ь︡ рꙋцѣ и̇ глаг︦о-
лꙗ︠ штн· уꙗдо мо︠ꙗ̈ слад︦окоꙗ̈· ꙗ̈ште ма-
30 ло пр︢ѣтрꙋпн да съвръ︢шенъ бꙋдешн·

Πρωίας δὲ γενομένης ἦλθον οἱ ἀσεβέστατοι τύραννοι καὶ εἶδον τὸν
καπικλάριον σὺν αὐτοῖς ὄντα καὶ ἐμάνθανον παρὰ τῶν στρατιωτῶν, τί ἰδὼν
(15) πεποίηκε τοῦτο. Λέγουσιν αὐτοῖς οἱ στρατιῶται· ἡμεῖς ἀπὸ τοῦ ὕπνου
ἀπενεκρώθημεν, ἐκεῖνος δέ δι᾽ ὅλης τῆς νυκτὸς ἦν γρηγορῶν καὶ ἄφνω
ἐξύπνησεν ἡμᾶς· καὶ εἴδομεν φῶς μέγα περὶ αὐτούς· ἐκεῖνος δὲ ῥίψας τὰ
ἱμάτια αὐτοῦ εἰς τὰς ὄψεις ἡμῶν εἰσεπήδησεν (20) εἰς αὐτοὺς κράζων καὶ
λέγων· καγὼ χριστιανός εἰμι. Πληθέντες δὲ θυμοῦ οἱ τύραννοι ἐκέλευσαν
συρέντας ἀχθῆναι αὐτοὺς ἐπὶ τὸν αἰγιαλὸν καὶ βάκλοις τὰ σκέλη αὐτῶν
κατεαγῆναι. Ἑνὸς (20) δὲ μήτηρ ἦν προσκαρτεροῦσα αὐτοῖς – ἦν γὰρ ὁ υἱὸς
αὐτῆς ὑπὲρ πάντας νεώτερος καὶ ἐφοβεῖτο μή ποτε δειλανδρίσῃ – καὶ εἰς
αὐτὸν πάντοτε ἠτένιζεν· ἐκτείνουσα δὲ εἰς αὐτὸν τὰς χεῖρας ἔλεγεν· τέκν[ον]
γλυκύτατον ἔτι μικρὸν ὑπόμεινον, ἵνα τέλειος γένῃ

80 НЕ БОН СА ѴАДО• СЕ БО ХС ПРѢДЪСТОИТЪ ПО-
МАГАѦ ТЕБѢ• ІЕ҃ГДА ЖЕ ИМЪ ПРѢБИВАА́ХѪ
ГОЛѢНИ• ПРѢДААХѪ ДШ҃А СВОѦ ГЛАГОЛѪ-
ШТЕ• ДШ҃А НАША ІА́КО П'ТИЦА И́ЗБАВИ СА О́-
5   ТЪ СѢТИ ЛОВѦШТИИХЪ• СѢТЬ СЪКРОУШИ
СА И́ МЪІ И́ЗБАВЬІЕ́НИ БЪІХОМЪ• ПОМОШТЬ
НАША ВЪ И́МѦ ГОСПОДЬ̃НІЕ• СЪТВОРЬШААГО
НЕБО И́ ЗЕМЬІѪ̃• И́ ВЬСИ ВЬКОУПѢ РЕК'ШЕ А́-
МИНЪ• ПРѢДАША ДШ҃А СВОѦ• СЪІНЪ ЖЕ
10 О҃ѴѴНМЪІЙ МАТЕРИІѪ̃• И́МЕНЕМЬ МЕЛИТЪ•
ІЕ́ШТЕ ДЪІХААШЕ• ПОВЕЛѢСТА ЖЕ МѪѴ҃НТЕ-
ЛѢ ПРИВЕСТИ ВОЗЪІ• И́ ВЪСКЛАДЪШЕ ТѢЛЕ-
СА СВѦТЪІИ́ХЪ ПРѢВЕЗОША Ѧ НА БРѢГЪ РѢ-
КЪІ• О́СТАВЬШЕ Ю̃НОШѪ ҮАІѪШТЕ ІЕ́МОУ• ЖИ-
15 ВОУ БЪІТИ• ВИДѢВЪШИ ЖЕ МАТИ ІЕ́ГО ТЪ
ІЕ́ДИНЪ О́СТАВЬІЕ́НЪ• О́ТЪВРЪГЪШИ ЖЕНЬ-
СКѪІѪ̃ НЕМОШТЬ• ВЬЗЕМЪШИ ЖЕ МѪЖЬСКѪ-
ІѪ̃ КРѢПОСТЬ И́ МѪДРОСТЬ• И́ ВЬЗЕМЪШИ
СН҃А СВОІЕГО НА РАМОУ КРѢПЪКО• ВѢСЛѢДЪ
20 КОЛЪ И́ДѢАШЕ• НОСИМЪ ЖЕ СН҃Ъ МАТЕРЬІѪ̃

(80.1) μὴ φοβοῦ, ὁ Χριστὸς παρέστηκε βοηθῶν σοι. Κατακλανόμενοι δὲ καὶ ἀποδιδόντε[ς] τὰς ψυχὰς ἔλεγον. ἡ ψυχὴ ἡμῶν ὡς στρουθίον ἐρρύσθη (5) ἐκ τῆς παγίδος τῶν θηρευόντων· ἡ παγὶς συνετρίβη καί ἡμεῖς ἐρρύσθημεν· ἡ βοήθεια ἡμῶν ἐν ὀνόματι κυρίου τοῦ ποιήσαντος τὸν οὐρανὸν καὶ τὴν γῆ[ν]. Καὶ πάντες ὁμοῦ εἰπόντες τὸ ἀμὴν ἀπέδωκαν τὰς ψυχάς. Ὁ δὲ υἱὸς (10) ὁ παραινούμενος ὑπὸ τῆς μητρὸς ὀνόματι Μελίτων ἔτι ἐμπνέων ἦν· καὶ ἐκέλευσαν οἱ τύραννοι ἐνεχθῆν[αι] ἁμάξας καὶ ἐπιτεθῆναι τὰ σώματα τῶν ἁγίω[ν] καὶ ἤνεγκαν παρὰ τὸ χεῖλος τοῦ ποταμοῦ ἀφέντες τὸν νεώτερον, προσδοκῶν τες ζῆν αὐτόν. (15) Ἡ δὲ μήτηρ θεασαμένη τὸν υἱὸν αὐτῆς μόνον καταλειφθέντα ἀποδυσαμένη τὴν γυναικείαν ἀσθένειαν καὶ ἀναλαβοῦσα ἀνδρείαν φρόνησιν καὶ ἰσχὺν, ἀραμένη τὸν υἱὸν αὐτῆς ἐπὶ τῶν ὤμων γενναίως (20) ταῖς ἁμάξαις ἠκολούθει. Βασταζόμενος δὲ ὁ υἱὸς ὑπὸ τῆς μητρὸς

прѣдастъ дх҃ъ свои радоуѧ са• нес^{шн} же и
мт҃и ѥго поврꙑже и врьхоу ихъ• вьзгнѣ-
тивъше же огнь съжегоша тѣлеса ст҃ꙑн-
хъ• сьвѣтъ же сътворьша мѫунтелѣ
25 рекоста• сиѧ останькꙑ аште сице оста-
вимъ• вьзати ѧ имѫтъ крьстиꙗни•
и напльнити вьсь миръ• нъ придѣте
да ѧ въврьжемъ вь рѣкѫ• и събꙑравъше кости ст҃ꙑнхъ и пепелъ съметъше
30 бꙑсꙑпаша вь рѣкѫ• и нну'соже не [погоуб]
81 и рѣка ихъ• по трехъ же дьнехъ ꙗвиша
са ѥпискоупоу града того• именемь петрꙋ•
ꙗко сѫтъ съхранѥнꙑ кости наша семь мѣ-
стѣ• приди оубо вь ноштн и їзнеси нꙑ и-
5 з-д-рѣкꙑ• и поимъ ѥппъ клирикꙑ и мѫ-
жа вѣрьнꙑ• и пришедъ ста на брѣзѣ рѣ-
кꙑ• и се просвьтѣа са кости ст҃ꙑнхъ вь
водѣ• акꙑ и свѣтильннци• и аште кде о-
ставьѥна бꙑваꙗше кость свѣтомъ ꙗвь-
10 ꙗше са• и тако събꙑравъше кости ст҃ꙑнх'•

ἀπέδωκε τὴν ψυχὴν αὐτοῦ τῷ κυρίῳ χαίρων· ἐνέγκασα δὲ αὐτὸν ἔρριψεν αὐτὸν
ἐπάνω αὐτῶν καὶ ἀνάψαντες πυρὰν κατέκαυσαν τὰ σώματα τῶν ἁγίων καὶ
σκεψάμενοι πρὸς ἀλλήλους οἱ τύραννοι (25) εἶπον· ἐὰν ἐάσωμεν αὐτοὺς οὕτως,
ἐλθόντες οἱ χριστιανοὶ ἀροῦσι αὐτὰ καὶ πληρώσουσιν ὅλον τὸν κόσμον.
Σβέσαντες οὖν τὴν πυρὰν καὶ ἀναλεξάμενοι τὰ σώματα τῶν ἁγίων ἔρριψαν
εἰς τὸν ποταμὸν τὸν σύνεγγυς. Συνήχθη δὲ τὰ λείψανα τῶν (81.1) ἁγίων πρὸς
τὸν κρημνὸν καὶ οὐδὲν αὐτῶν ἐμείωσεν ὁ ποταμός. Μετὰ δὲ ἡμέρας τρεῖς
ἀπεκαλύφθη τῷ ἐπισκόπῳ· ὅτι εἰσὶν πεφυλαγμένα τὰ σώματα ἡμῶν ἐν τῷδε
τῷ τόπῳ· ἐλθὲ οὖν διὰ νυκτὸς καὶ ἔκβαλε ἡμᾶς. (5) Παραλαβὼν δὲ ὁ
ἐπίσκοπος, Πέτρος, ἄνδρας εὐλαβεῖς καὶ ἐλθόντες ἔστησαν παρὰ τὸ χεῖλος
τοῦ ποταμοῦ· καὶ ἰδοὺ ἔλαμψαν τὰ σώματα τῶν ἁγίων ὡς φωστῆρες καὶ, ὅπου
ὑπελείφθη λείψανον, διὰ τοῦ φέγγους κατεμηνύετο. (10) Καὶ οὕτως
ἀναλεξάμενοι τὰ σώματα τῶν ἁγίων

мѫченнкъ• положнша ѧ въ ракахъ• и сн-
це пострадавъше вѣньчанн бꙑша• и сн-
ꙗіѫтъ ꙗко и ѕвѣѕдꙑ въ вьсемь мнрѣ•
богоу вѣровавъше хѣа нсповѣдавъше•
15 стааго дха не отъврьгъше га. прославѣ́н-
нн бꙑвъше о хѣ• памѧть въ жнтнн семь
оставнша• на съпасеннѥ вьсѣмь вѣроуѭ-
штнїмъ• въ оцъ н снъ н стꙑн дхъ• ѧтн же
бꙑша стнн мѫченнцн на мѫченннѥ о хѣ•
20 прѣжде четꙑрь калан'дъ мар'та• снрѣчь
въ ꙅꙅ феѵроара• прѣдаша же своѧ доуша
господевн• прѣжде ꙁ дьнь марта• прн лн-
кннни самовластьцн• нам же цѣсарьствꙋ-
ѭштоу гоу нашемоу н боу н спсоу• н вла-
25 дꙑцѣ нашемоу їс хсоу• ѥмоуже ѥстъ сла-
ва н дрьжава н честь• нꙑнѣ н прнсно н въ
вѣкꙑ вѣкомъ• амннъ•:•

ἀπῆλθον. Οὕτως οὖν ἀθλήσαντες καὶ τελειωθέντες λάμπουσιν ὡς φωστῆρες ἐν κόσμῳ· θεὸν πιστεύσαντες. Χριστὸν ὁμολογήσαντες (15) καὶ ἅγιον πνεῦμα μὴ ἀρνησάμενοι συνεδοξάσθησαν τῷ Χριστῷ μνήμην τῷ βίῳ καταλιπόντες ἐπὶ σωτηρίᾳ πάντων τῶν πιστευόντων εἰς πατέρα καὶ υἱὸν καὶ ἅγιον πνεῦμα, ... (25) ᾧ ἡ δόξα καὶ τὸ κράτος εἰς τοὺς αἰῶνας τῶν αἰώνων. ἀμήν.

Sava Gospel 43v.1–44r.18: Matt. 18.23–35

23. ρεγε гь приτъγѫ снѫ. подобьно е
стъ црствне нбскоє. ѵлкоу црю.
иже изволи съвѣщати слово съ
рабъі своими. 24. ҙаѵънъшю же ємоу
сърнцати слово. привєдє са ємоу е
5 динъ длъжъникъ тьмѣ таланѣ
тъ. 25. и не имѫщю ємоу ѵто въздати.
повєлѣ ємоу гь продати са. и женѫ
и всє имѣнне єбоє.

23 Διὰ τοῦτο ὡμοιώθη ἡ βασιλεία τῶν οὐρανῶν ἀνθρώπῳ βασιλεῖ, ὃς ἠθέλησεν συνᾶραι λόγον μετὰ τῶν δούλων αὐτοῦ. 24 ἀρξαμένου δὲ αὐτοῦ συναίρειν προσηνέχθη εἷς αὐτῷ ὀφειλέτης μυρίων ταλάντων. 25 μὴ ἔχοντος δὲ αὐτοῦ ἀποδοῦναι ἐκέλευσεν αὐτὸν ὁ κύριος πραθῆναι καὶ τὴν γυναῖκα καὶ τὰ τέκνα καὶ πάντα ὅσα εἶχεν, καὶ ἀποδοθῆναι.

---

24 °add λογον p συναιρειν   °var αυτω εις   *25* °add αυτου p κ̅ς̅
°add αυτου p γυναικα

Marianus, 21v8-22r14	*Assem., 43b.13–*

Marianus, 21v8-22r14

23. sego radi upodobilo sn estъ
csr̄stvie nb̄skoe člv̄ku csr̄ü. ιže vъ
sxotě sъtnzati sn o slovesi. sъ ra
bъι svoimi.

24. načenъšü že emu sъtn
zati sn o slovesi. privěsn emu dlъ
žъnikъ edinъ. tъmoǫ talanъtъ.

25. ne imǫštü že emu vъzdati. pove
lě g̃ъ ego da prodadntъ ι i ženǫ ego
i čnda. ι vъse eliko iměaše. ι otъ
dati i.

Assem., 43b.13–

Reče g̃ъ prιtъčǫ
sιǫ. ūpodobi
sn crstvo nb̄sno
e. člku crü.
ιže vъsxotě
sъtnzati
sn ō slovesi.
sъ rabъι svo
ιmι. načenъšü
že emu sъtnza
tι sn ō slovesi.
Privěsn ēmu dlъ
žъnikъ ēdinъ.
dlъženъ tъmo
ǫ talanī̄ъ. ne
ιmǫψu že ēmu
česo vъ(z)dati.
[44c] Povelě g̃ъ ego
da prodadntъι. ϊ
ženǫ ēgo ϊ čnda.
ϊ vъse ēliko ϊ
měaše. ϊ ōtъda
tι ϊ.

26. ПАДЪ ЖЕ РАБЪ О́НЪ

КЛАНѦШЕ СѦ Е́МОУ. ГЛ҃Ѧ ГН҃ ПОТРѢПН

10   О́ МНѢ. Н̇ ВСЕ ТН ВЪ҇ДАМЬ. 27. МНЛОСРЬ

ДОВАВЪ ЖЕ ГЬ҃ РАБА ТОГО. О́ТЪПОУСТН І

Н̇ ДЛЪГЪ О́ТЪДАСТЪ Е́МОУ. 28. Н̇ ШѢДЪ

РАБЪ ТЪ[1] О́БРѢТЕ Е́ДННОГО ПОДРȢ

ГЪ СВОН̇ХЪ.[1] Н̇ЖЕ БѢ ДЛЪЖЪНЪ[2] Е̇

15   МОУ Р҃ МЪ ПѢНДҀЪ. Н̇ Н̇МЪ[2] Е̇ГО БНѦ

ШЕ. Н̇ ГЛ҃Ѧ. ВЪ҇ДАЖДЪ МН Н̇МЬЖЕ Е̇

СН ДЛЪЖЪНЪ. 29. ПАДЪ ЖЕ ПОДРОУГЪ О́НЪ

МОЛѢШЕ І ГЛ҃Ѧ. ПОТРЬПН О́ МНѢ Н̇ ВЪ

44   ҀДАМЪ ТН.

26 πεσὼν οὖν ὁ δοῦλος προσεκύνει αὐτῷ λέγων, Μακροθύμησον ἐπ᾽ ἐμοί, καὶ πάντα σοι ἀποδώσω.

27 σπλαγχνισθεὶς δὲ ὁ κύριος τοῦ δούλου ἐκείνου ἀπέλυσεν αὐτόν καὶ τὸ δάνειον ἀφῆκεν αὐτῷ.

28 ἐξελθὼν δὲ ὁ δοῦλος ἐκεῖνος εὗρεν ἕνα τῶν συνδούλων αὐτοῦ, ὃς ὤφειλεν αὐτῷ ἑκατὸν δηνάρια, καὶ κρατήσας αὐτὸν ἔπνιγεν λέγων, ᾿Απόδος εἴ τι ὀφείλεις.

29 πεσὼν οὖν ὁ σύνδουλος αὐτοῦ παρεκάλει αὐτὸν λέγων, Μακροθύμησον ἐπ᾽ ἐμοί, καὶ ἀποδώσω σοι.

Sav. *28* [1]протертый пергамент образует дыры в двух строках, между т и ъ слова тъ и между и у х слова своихъ. (Щ = Щепкин) [2]здесь дыра после длъ и и́мъ, между строками. (Щ) Gk. *26* °add εκεινος p δουλος °om αυτω °var αποδωσω σοι °δε⟧ ουν °εμε⟧ εμοι *28* °δος⟧ αποδος °add μοι p αποδος °add μοι p οφειλεις °om δε *29* °εκεινος⟧ αυτου °om αυτου °add παντα a αποδωσω °var σοι αποδωσω °δε⟧ ουν °εμε⟧ εμοι

26. padъ ubo rabotъ. klaněše
sɴ emu g͠ɪ̅ɴ. g̃i potrъpi na mьně i vъ
sě vъzdamъ ti.

27. milosr͡dvavъ
že g͡ъ raba togo. pusti i i dlъgъ o
tъpusti emu.

28. ⱅšьdъ že rabotъ.
obrěte edinogo otъ klevrětъ svoi
xъ. ⱅže bě dlъženъ emu sъtomъ
pěnɴꙁъ. ⱅ imъ davlěše i g͠ɪ̅ɴ. da
ždь mi imъže esi dlъženъ.

29. padъ
že klevrětъ molěše i g͠ɪ̅ɴ. potrъ
pi na mьně i vьse vъzdamъ ti.

Padъ že
ūbo rabotъ kla
něáše sɴ g͠ɪ̅ɴ. G̃i
potrъpi na mъ
ně ꙇ̄ vъse tⱅ vъ
zdamъ. Milo
srьdovavъ že
g͡ъ raba togo pu
stⱅ ꙇ̄ ꙇ̄ dlъgъ
ōtъpusti ēmu.
Ꙇ̄ šedъ že rabot
ǒbrěte ēdⱅnogo
oᵗ klevrětъ svo
ixъ. ꙇ̇že bě dlъ
ženъ ēmu. sъ
tomъ pěnɴꙁъ. Ꙇ̄
ēmъ ꙇ̇ davlěá
še g͠ɪ̅ɴ. da(ž)dъ
mi ꙇ̄imъže mi
ēsⱅ dlъženъ.
Padъ že klevrě
totъ molěāše i
g͠ɪ̅ɴ. Potrъpi [44d]
na mьně ꙇ̄ vъ
se ti vьzdam.

44   30. ѻнъ же не хотѣше. нъ ве

дъ і въгади въ тьмьницѫ. доньде

же въздастъ вcь длъгъ свои. 31. вн

дѣвъше же подроугꙑ его бꙑваіѫ

5   щаіѧ. сѫжалнша си ѕѣло. й прн

шъдъше съказаша гвн его. вса бꙑі

въшаіѧ. 32. тогда прнзъвавъ его. гь гла

емоу. рабе лѫкавꙑі. вьсь длъгъ тво

і ѻставнхъ тебѣ. понеже молн мѧ.

10   33. не подобаше лн й тебѣ помнловатн

подроуга своего. іакоже й азъ те

бе помнловахъ.

30 ὁ δὲ οὐκ ἤθελεν ἀλλὰ ἀπελθὼν ἔβαλεν αὐτὸν εἰς φυλακὴν ἕως
ἀποδῷ τὸ ὀφειλόμενον 31 ἰδόντες οὖν οἱ σύνδουλοι αὐτοῦ τὰ γενόμενα ἐλυπήθησαν σφόδρα
καὶ ἐλθόντες διεσάφησαν τῷ κυρίῳ ἑαυτῶν πάντα τὰ γενόμενα.
32 τότε προσκαλεσάμενος αὐτὸν ὁ κύριος αὐτοῦ λέγει αὐτῷ, Δοῦλε
πονηρέ, πᾶσαν τὴν ὀφειλὴν ἐκείνην ἀφῆκά σοι, ἐπεὶ παρεκάλεσάς
με·
33 οὐκ ἔδει καὶ σὲ ἐλεῆσαι τὸν σύνδουλόν σου, ὡς κἀγὼ σὲ ἠλέησα;

---

30 ᵒadd παν α το ᵒadd αυτω p οφειλ.   31 ᵒουν]] δε   ᵒom αυτου
ᵒγενομενα|

30. onъ že ne xotěše. nъ vedъ vъsadi i
vъ temъnicǫ. donъdeže vъzda
stъ emu vesъ dlъgъ.

31. viděvъ
še že ubo klevrěti (........)
bъivъša sъžališn si ʒělo. ι pri
šedъše sъkazašn g͡nu svoemu vъ
sě bъivъšaa.

32. tъgda prizъvavъ ι
g͡ь ego g͡la emu. rabe lǫkavъi. vъ
sъ dlъgъ tvoi otъpustixъ tebě.
poneže umoli mn.

33 ne podobaše li i
tebě pomilovati klevrěta tvoe
go. ěko i azъ tn pomilovaxъ ·:·

ōnъ že ne xotěā
šē. Nъ vedъ ῑ
vъsadι ῑ vъ
temъnicǫ.
donьdeže vъ
dastъ ēmu d
lъgъ vesь.
Vi
děvъše že kle
vrěti bъivъ
šaā sъžali
šn si ʒělo. ῑ
prιšedъsě sъ
kazašn gd͡nu
svoēmu vъsě
bъivъšaā.
togda prιzъ
vavъ ῑ g͡nъ ēgo.
G͡la ēmu rabe
lǫkavъiῑ.
vesь dlъgъ
tvoῑ ōtъpusti
xъ tebě. Pone
neže ūmoli mn.
Ne podobaāše lι
ῑ tebě. pom͡lva
tι klevrěta
tvoēgo. Ěko ῑ ā
[45a]zъ tn pom͡lvax:

112

34. и̂ прогнѣвавъ са гь̏
е́го. прѣдастъ і мжунтельмъ. до
15   ндеже въздастъ вcь длъгъ cвоі.
      35. такоже н̂ оц҃ь мои нбскъі. cтворн
      тъ вамъ [1]. аще не о́тъдаcте къждо
      братоу cвое́моу. о́тъ cр҃дць ваш(н)[2]
      хъ. прѣгрѣшеннı амннъ: —

34 καὶ ὀργισθεὶς ὁ κύριος αὐτοῦ παρέδωκεν αὐτὸν τοῖς βασανισταῖς
ἕως οὗ ἀποδῷ πᾶν τὸ ὀφειλόμενον αὐτῷ.
35 Οὕτως καὶ ὁ πατήρ μου ὁ οὐράνιος ποιήσει ὑμῖν, ἐὰν μὴ ἀφῆτε
ἕκαστος τῷ ἀδελφῷ αὐτοῦ ἀπὸ τῶν καρδιῶν ὑμῶν.

Sav. 35 [1]м слова вамъ писано самим писцом по разуре. (Щ) [2]край
строки оторван; от конечного и осталось одна левая половина.
(Щ) Gk. 34 °om αυτω 35 °add τα παραπτωματα αυτων ρ υμων

34. ı pro
gněvavъ sn g̃ь ego. prědastъ ı mǫ
čitelemъ. donьdeže vъzdastъ
vьsь dlъgъ svoi.

35. Tako i otecъ mo
i nb̅skъ sъtvoritъ vamъ. aψe ne
otъpuψaate kožьdo bratru svoe
mu otъ srd̅cъ vašixъ ·:· k͞c .

ı̅ progněvavъ
sn g̃ь ēgo prěda
stъ i mǫčıte
lemъ. donьde
že vъdastъ
dlъgъ vesь.
Tako ı̅ o̅cъ moı̅
nbs̅n̅ьi sъtvo
rıtъ vamъ.
āψe ne ōтъpuψa
ēte kožьdo bra
tu svoemu. ō
tъ srd̅cь vaši
xъ. prěgrěšenič
ı̅xъ ·.· —

Sava Gospel 124r.13–124v.13: Luke 1.41–48

41. и бꙑстъ ꙗко ѹслꙑ   uslъša (Mar.)
ша ѥлисавеѳь. цѣлованиѥ мариино.   ělisavьtь (Zog.)
вьзигра сѧ младеньць. радощами   mladъnesъ (Mar.)
вь ѹрѣвѣ ѥѧ. и испльни сѧ дхомь стꙑ   stъim (Zog.)
мъ елисавеѳь. 42. и вьзъпи гласомъ ве
лиѥмь и рече. благословена тꙑ въ
женахъ. и благословенъ плодъ
ѹрѣва твоѥго. 43. отъкѫдоу се мнѣ   ǫtrobъi tvoeę̇ (Mar.)
да придетъ мти га моѥго. 44. се бо ꙗ   otъkǫdǫ (Mar.)
ко бꙑстъ гласъ цѣлованиꙗ твоѥ   gī moego
го. въ оушню моѥю. вьзигра сѧ м   vъ nušiü (Mar.)
ладеньць. радощами в ѫтробѣ
моѥи. 45. и блажена ꙗже вѣ
рꙗ ѧтъ. ꙗко бѫдетъ съвръше
ниѥ гланꙑмъ ѥи отъ гн. 46. и рече ма   ǒtъ gě (Zog.)
риꙗ. велиунтъ дша моꙗ га. 47. и въз
драдова сѧ дхъ мои о бзѣ спсѣ моѥ   bzě (Zog.)
мь. 48. ꙗко призьрѣ на съмѣрениѥ ра
бꙑ своѥꙗ. се бо отъ селѣ блажатъ
мѧ вси роди.

NOTES

Assemanianus, Zographensis, Marianus: Luke 1

[v. 1] ♦ *poňeže*: V372 (§258) *ň* ~ *n* (in orthography: D144–45 (§55, Anm. 11), V59 (§35, par. 3). ♦ *mъnog-i₂* ↓ *mъnozi*: nom.pl.masc. (indef.) D212 (§100, Anm. 1) *mnozi, mnozi*: D103–6 (§29), V35–41 (§§22–24); D47 (§6, Anm. 39), 128 (§47, Anm. 2), 139 (§52), V62–63 (§37). ♦ *načьn-x-ę* ↓ *načęšę*: prod.aor. 3pl. *način-s-ę* ↓ *načęsę*: s-aor. 3pl. D240 (§114, Anm. 1), V234 (§153). ♦ *čini-ti*: inf. ♦ *pověst-ь*: acc.sg. ♦ *izvěstьn-yixъ*: loc.pl.def. ♦ *izvěst-ova-n-yxъ*: PPP loc.pl.def. -*ьiixъ*, -*ьixъ*, -*ьixъ*: D196 (§86, Anm. 14), 39–40 (§6, Anm. 17–18), 65 (§18, Anm. 2). ♦ *veψ-exъ, veštexъ*: loc.pl. D48 (§6, Anm. 42), V23 (§10, page-par. 1); but see also Durnovo 1929: 56ff.

[v. 2] ♦ *prěda-x-ę* ↓ *prědašę*: prod.aor. 3pl. ♦ *namъ*: dat.pl. D214 (§101), V147 (§97). ♦ *by-v-ъš-ei*: PAP nom.pl.masc.def. ♦ *samovidьc-i₂* ↓ *samovidьci*: nom.pl. ♦ *slug-y₂*. ↓ *slugy* nom.pl. ♦ *slov-es-e*: gen.sg. *slov-es-i*: gen. or dat.sg. D169–70 (§Anm. 2), V110 (§§72, 73), 180 (§120.a), 189 (§122).

[v. 3] ♦ *izvoli-x-ø* ↓ *izvoli*: prod.aor. 3sg. ♦ *sę*: acc. D213–14 (§101), V147 (§97), 172 (§114), 350 (§251). ♦ *mьně*: dat.sg. D213–14 (§101), V147 (§97). ♦ *xodi-ъš̌-u* ↓ *хоmьšŭ, хоždьšŭ*: PAP dat.sg.masc.indef. *хuždьšu* (Ass.). D100 (§27, Anm. 1). ♦ *prьv-a*: gen.sg.neut.indef. V219 (§142). ♦ *vьs-ě₂xъ* ↓ *vьsěxъ*: loc.pl. D208 (§92), V151 (§99.a), 204 (§128.e, page-par. 2). ♦ *istin-ǫ*: acc.sg. V199 (§128.a, page-par. 2). ♦ *rędu*: dat.sg. *rNdǫ* (Mar.): D99 (§26, Anm. 2), V204 (128.e, page-par. 1). ♦ *pьs-a-ti, pis-a-ti*: inf. D268 (§130, page-par. 3), V274 (§191). ♦ *tebě*: dat.sg. D213–14 (§101), V147 (§97). ♦ *slavьn-y*: voc.sg.masc.def. V123 (§81, par. 2). ♦ *teofil-e*: voc.sg. *t'*– (Zog.) D46 (§6, Anm. 31), V76 (§47).

[v. 4] ♦ *razumě-j-e-ši* ↓ *razuměeši*: non-past. 2sg. ♦ *n-j-ě₂xъ-že* ↓ *ňixъže*: loc.pl.post-prep(ositional) D126 (§46, Anm. 2), 207 (§91), V73 (§44, par. 2), 145–46 (§96). ♦ *nauči-l-ъ*: PerfAP masc.sg. ♦ *sę*: see v. 3. On passive meaning of "reflexive" see V352 (§252, 1°). ♦ *esi*: non-past (imperfective) 2.sg. D276 (§134), V311 (§221). ♦ *slov-es-exъ*: loc.pl.; antecedent incorporated into the relative clause. V358 (§256, par.1). ♦ *utvrьdi-e-n-ij-o* ↓ *utvrьмenie, utvrьždenie*: verbal subst. acc.sg.

[v. 5] ♦ *bystъ*: aor. 3sg. D276 (§134), 279 (Anm. 4), V312 (§221), 235 (§154). ♦ *dъn-i*: acc.pl. ♦ *irod-a*: gen.sg. ♦ *cěsaŕ-a* ↓ *cěsaŕě*: gen.sg. *cěsěrě* (Mar.): sic. ♦ *ijudej-ъsk-a* ↓ *iüdeiska*: gen.sg. masc. (indef.) V131 (§86, page-par. 3), 213 (§134). ♦ *ierej-ъ* ↓ *ierei*: nom.sg. ♦ *eter-ъ*: nom.sg.masc. (indef.) D211 (§98), V152 (§99.b). ♦ *edin-ъ*: nom.sg.masc. D206–7 (§90), V155–56 (§102). ♦ *im-en-etъ*: instr.sg. D173 (§74, Anm. 1), V108 (§72), 190 (§123, page-par. 1). ♦ *zaxarij-a* ↓ *zaxariě*: nom.sg. *zaxaria* (Ass.) D34 (§6, Anm. 15.3). ♦ *efimerij-y₂* ↓ *efimerię*: gen.sg. *efiměrię* (Mar.): D35 (§6, Anm. 15.3.c). ♦ *dъnevъn-y₂ę* ↓ *dъnevъnyę*: gen.sg.fem.def. ♦ *črěd-y₂* ↓ *črědy*: gen.sg. ♦ **avi(j)ań-y₂* ↓ *aviěńę, aviańę*: gen.sg.fem. (indef.) D33 (§6, Anm. 15.3), V131 (§86, page-par. 1), 132 (§87.b), 133–34 (§88). ♦ *žen-a*: nom.sg. ♦ *j-ogo* ↓ *ego*: gen.sg.masc. ♦ *žena emu* (Ass.): V189 (§122, page-par. 2), and compare the Greek. ♦ *dъ₩-er-ъ*: gen.pl. D178 (§82), V112–13 (§74). ♦ *aroń-ъ*: gen.pl. (indef.) D118 (§40, Anm. 8). ♦ *im-ę*: nom. sg. D173–74 (§74), 168 (§69), V108 (§72). Note *i* for *i i–* in Ass. and Zog. ♦ *j-oi* ↓ *ei*: dat.sg.fem. ♦ *elisavet-ъ*: nom.sg.

[v. 6] ♦ *bě-ax-e-te* ↓ *běašete*: impf. 3du. See v. 9. ♦ *ob-a*: nom.(du.)masc. D215 (§102), V156 (§102). ♦ *pravьdъn-a*: nom.du. masc. *pravьdъna, pravedъna*: D96–98 (§25), 101–3 (§28), 103–6 (§29), V35–41 (§§ 22–24). Cf., in this same verse, *vьsěхъ* (Ass.), *vsěхъ* (Zog.), and *vъsěхъ* (Mar.). ♦ *bog-otъ*: instr.sg. ♦ *xodi-ntj-a* ↓ *xodę₩ě* PrAP nom.du.masc.indef. ♦ *zapověd-exъ, -ьхъ*: loc.pl. ♦ *vьsěхъ*: see v. 3. ♦ *opravьda-n-ij-ě₂-хъ* ↓ *opravьdaniiхъ*: verbal subst. loc.pl. ♦ *gospodьń-ě₂хъ* ↓ *gospodьńiхъ*: loc.pl.neut. (indef.) V131 (§86, page-par. 1), 133 (§87.d). ♦ *porok-a*: gen.sg. *bes poroka*: D125 (§45), V65 (§40, par.1).

[v. 7] ♦ *bě-x-ø* ↓ *bě*: imperfect (aorist formation) 3sg. D279 (§134, Anm. 3), V312 (§221). ♦ *j-ě₂ma* ↓ *ima*: dat.du. V189 (§122, page-par. 2). ♦ *ne bě … čęda*: V354 (§ 253, par. 3). ♦ *čęd-a*: gen.sg. ♦ *elisavet-ъ*: nom.sg. See v. 24 (*elisavьtъ, elisaveθь*). ♦ *neplod-y*: nom.sg. D179 (§83), V112–13 (§74). ♦ *ob-a*: nom.(du.)masc. ♦ *zamatorě-v-ъš-a* ↓ *zamatorěvъšě*: PAP nom.du.masc.indef. ♦ *dъn-exъ*: loc.pl. ♦ *svoj-ě₂хъ* ↓ *svoiхъ*: loc.pl. D207 (§91), V138 (§92). ♦ *bě-ax-e-te* ↓ *běašete*: imperfect (imperfective formation) 3du. Cf. v. 6, where Ass. has contracted form *běšete*. Here, Ass. has the aorist

formation of the imperfective (cf. *bě* in this same verse) and the ending
-ta. See D228 (§108, Anm. 7), V228 (§147, page-par. 1).

[v. 8] ♦ *bystъ*: see v. 5. ♦ *služi-ntj-u* ↓ *služęψü*: PrAP dat.sg.
masc.indef. ♦ *j-omu* ↓ *emu*: dat.sg.masc. *emo* (Ass.): careless omission
of second half of glagolitic letter *u*; see the alphabet table in the
Grammar. D41 (§6, Anm. 20). *mu*: D208 (§91, Anm. 6), 115 (§36,
Anm. 10). ♦ *čin-u*: loc.sg. D156 (§62, Anm. 6), V91 (§58). ♦ *črědy*:
gen.sg. ♦ *svoj-oę* ↓ *svoeę*: gen.sg.fem. ♦ *bog-otъ*: instr.sg.

[v. 9] ♦ *obyčěj-u* ↓ *obyčěü*: dat.sg. V204 (§128.e, page-par. 1).
♦ *(i)erej-ъsk-umu* ↓ *(i)ereiskumu*: dat.sg.masc.def. V131 (§86, page-
par. 3). ♦ *kl'üči-x-ø* ↓ *kl'üči*: prod.aor. 3sg. ♦ *sę*: see v. 3. ♦ *j-omu* ↓
emu: dat.sg.masc. ♦ *pokadi-ti*: inf. ♦ *vъ-šъd-ъš-u* ↓ *vъšъdъšü*: PAP
dat.sg.masc.indef. D278–79 (§134, нтн), V303–4 (§214, ндɛ, нтн).
♦ *crъk-ъv-ъ*: acc.sg. D175 (§76), 179 (§83, Anm. 1.4), V112–14 (§74).
♦ *gospodъń-ǫ* ↓ *gospodъńǫ*: acc.sg.fem. (indef.). See v. 6 (*gospodъńixъ*).

[v. 10] ♦ *vъse*: nom.sg.neut. See v. 3 (*vъsěxъ*). ♦ *mъnožьstv-o*:
nom.sg. ♦ *l'üd-iji* ↓ *l'üdii*: gen.pl. D162 (§64, Anm. 6), V101 (§66). *bě*:
impf. 3sg. See v. 7. ♦ *molitv-ǫ*: acc.sg. ♦ *děj-j-y₂-ntj-ø* ↓ *děę*: PrAP
nom.sg.neut.indef. ♦ *god-ъ*: acc.sg. ♦ *tъmъěn-a*: gen.sg. On the
variations of the stem, see D28–29 (§6, Anm. 8), 38 (§6, Anm. 16),
V43 (§25).

[v. 11] ♦ *avi (ěvi)-x-ø* ↓ *avi, ěvi*: prod.aor. 3sg. *avi, ěvi*, ιᴀвн: D76–
77 (§20, Anm. 6.1), V34 (§ 21, page-par. 4). ♦ *sę*: see v. 3. ♦ *emu*: see
v. 9. ♦ *anиel-ъ:* nom.sg. ♦ *gospodъń-ъ* ↓ *gospodъńъ*: nom.sg.masc.
(indef.). See v. 6 (*gospodъńixъ*). ♦ *stoj-intj-ø* ↓ *stoę*: PrAP nom.sg.
masc.indef. ♦ *desn-ǫǫ̈*: acc.sg.fem.def. ♦ *o desnǫǫ̈*: V201 (§128.2,
page-par. 1); see also D104 (§29, Anm. 4) and V355 (§253, page-par.
1). ♦ *oltaŕ-a* ↓ *oltaŕě*: gen.sg. ♦ *kadilьn-aago, -aego*: gen.sg.masc.def.

[v. 12] ♦ *sъmęt-e-x-ø* ↓ *s ъmęte*: prod.aor. 3sg. ♦ *sę*: see v. 3.
♦ *zaxarij-a* ↓ *zaxariě*: nom.sg. ♦ *viдě-v-ъš-ø* ↓ *viдěvъ*: PAP nom.
sg.masc.indef. ♦ *strax-ъ*: nom.sg. ♦ *napad-e-x-ø* ↓ *napade*: prod.aor.
3sg. *n-j-ъ* ↓ *ń-ъ*: acc.sg.masc.post-prep. D208 (§91, Anm. 2), V146
(§96, page-par. 1 and 4).

[v. 13] ♦ *rek-e-x-ø* ↓ *reče*: prod.aor. 3sg. V236–37 (§155) ♦ *n-j-omu* ↓ *ńemu*: dat.sg.masc.post-prep. See v. 12 (*ń-ь*). ♦ *anжel-ъ*: nom.sg. ♦ *gospodьńь*: see v. 11. ♦ *boj-i-ø* ↓ *boi*: impv. 2sg. ♦ *sę*: see v. 3. ♦ *zaxarij-o* ↓ *zaxarie*: voc.sg. *zaxariě*: see v. 12. Both are here in vocative function. ♦ *uslyš-ě-n-a*: PPP nom.sg.fem.indef. ♦ *bystъ*: see v. 5. ♦ *molitv-a*: nom. sg. ♦ *tvoj-a* ↓ *tvoě*: nom.sg.fem. ♦ *žen-a*: nom.sg. ♦ *elisavet-ь*: nom.sg. See v. 24. ♦ *rodi-tъ*: non-past 3sg., perfective aspect. V323 (§231) and Dostál 1954: 86–88. ♦ *syn-ь*: acc.sg. D155–56 (§62, Anm. 4), V90 (§58). ♦ *tebě*: dat.sg. D213–14 (§101), V147 (§97). ♦ *narek-e-ši* ↓ *narečeši*: non-past 2sg. ♦ *im-ę*: acc.sg. See v. 5 (*imę*). ♦ *j-omu* ↓ *emu*: dat.sg.masc. ♦ *ioan(n)-ъ*: nom.sg. Nominative in "absolute" use. V174 (§116, par. 1).

[v. 14) ♦ *bǫd-e-tъ*: non-past (perfective) 3sg. ♦ *tebě*: see v. 13. *radost-ь*: nom.sg. ♦ *veselij-o* ↓ *veselie*: nom.sg. ♦ *velij-a* ↓ *veliě* (Ass.): nom.sg.fem. ♦ *mъnozi*: see v. 1. ♦ *rodьstv-ě₂* ↓ *rodьstvě*, *rodi-ьstv-ě₂* ↓ **roжьstvě*, *roždьstvě*: loc.sg. D131 (§49, Anm. 3). ♦ *j-ogo* ↓ *ego*: gen.sg. masc. ♦ *vъzdrad-uj-o-ntъ* ↓ *vъzdraduǫtъ*: non-past 3pl. D122 (§43, Anm. 2), V68 (§41, page-par. 2). ♦ *sę*: see v. 3.

[v. 15] ♦ *bǫdetъ*: see v. 14. ♦ *velij-ь* ↓ *velii*: nom.sg.masc.indef. *velei* (Mar.), *veli* (Ass.): D190 (§85, Anm. 3), V131 (§86, page-par. 1). ♦ *bog-otь*: instr.sg. ♦ *gospod-ьtь, -etь*: instr.sg. ♦ *vin-a* : gen.sg. ♦ *tvori-e-n-a* ↓ *tvoréna*: PPP gen.sg.masc.indef. *tvorena* (Zog.): D145–46 (§55, Anm. 13–15), V59 (§35, par. 3), 62 (§36, page-par. 1). ♦ *kvas-a*: gen.sg. ♦ *ima-tъ*: non-past 3sg. D278 (§134), V316 (§225). ♦ *pi-ti*: inf. ♦ *imatъ piti*: V342 (§245, page-par.2). ♦ *dux-otь*: instr.sg. ♦ *dux-a*: gen.sg. *dixotь ~ duxa*: V181 (§120.i) ♦ *svęt-y(i)mь*: instr.sg. masc.def. ♦ *svęta*: gen.sg.masc.indef. ♦ *svęt-aago*: gen.sg.masc.def. ♦ *isplьni-tъ*: non-past 3sg. ♦ *sę*: see v. 3. ♦ *črěv-a*: gen.sg. *i-črěva*, нцрѣва: V195 (§126 yz), 66 (§41 *šč*). ♦ *mat-er-e*: gen.sg. D175 (§76), 178 (§82), V112–13 (§74). ♦ *svoj-oę* ↓ *svoeę*: gen.sg.fem.

[v. 16] ♦ *mъnog-y₂* ↓ *mъnogy*: acc.pl.masc. (indef.) D212 (§100, Anm. 1) V154 (§100). ♦ *syn-ovъ*: gen.pl. D152 (§61), 156–57 (§62, Anm. 11), V90–91 (§58). ♦ *izdrailʼev-ъ*: gen.pl.masc. (indef.) V132 (§87.a), 131 (§ 86, page-par. 1) ♦ *obrati-tъ*: non-past 3sg. ♦ *g̃i, g̃u*: dat.sg. D162 (§64 Anm. 5), V102–3 (§66 господь), 60–61 (§ 36). ♦ *bog-u*: dat.sg. *b̃u~b̃v̄*: D41 (§6, Anm. 20). ♦ *j-ě₂xъ* ↓ *ixъ*: gen.pl.

[v. 17] ♦ *t-ь*: nom.sg.masc. ♦ *prědьid-e-tь*: non-past 3sg. ♦ *n-j-ě₂mь* ↓ *ńimь*: instr.sg.masc.post-prep. ♦ *dux-otь*: instr.sg. ♦ *sil-oǫ̈*: instr.sg. ♦ *ilij-ьn-oǫ̈* ↓ *iliinoǫ̈*: instr.sg.fem. (indef.) V131 (§86, page-par. 1), 133 (§87.c). Cf. declension of *izdrail'ev-* (see v. 16), also regularly indefinite. ♦ *obrati-ti*: inf. ♦ *srьdьc-a*: acc.pl. ♦ *otьc-otь* ↓ *otьcemь*: dat.pl. ♦ *otьc-ь* ↓ *otьcь*: gen.pl. ♦ *čęd-a*: acc.pl. ♦ *protivьn-y₂ę* ↓ *protivьnyę*: acc.pl.masc.def. ♦ *mǫdrost-ь*: acc.sg. ♦ *pravьdьn-y(i)xь*: gen.pl.def. On -*ьixь* (Zog.) see D65 (§18, Anm. 2). ♦ *ugot-ova-ti*: inf. ♦ *g͞vi*: dat.sg. See v. 16 (*g͞i, g͞ü*). ♦ *ľüd-i*: acc.pl. ♦ *sьvrьši-e-n-y₂* ↓ *sьvrьšeny*: PPP acc.pl.masc.indef.

[v. 18] ♦ *reče*: see v. 13. ♦ *zaxarič̈*: see v. 5. *anжel-u*: dat.sg. ♦ *česomu, čьsomu*: dat. D210 (§95), V142 (§94). ♦ *razumě-j-ǫ* ↓ *razuměǫ̈*: non-past 1sg. V324 (§232, page-par.1); Dostál 1954: 448–49. ♦ *azь*: nom.sg. D213 (§101), V147 (§97). ♦ *estь*: non-past (imperfective) 1sg. D276 (§134), V311 (§221) ♦ *star-ь*: nom.sg. masc.indef. ♦ *žen-a*: nom.sg. ♦ *moj-a* ↓ *moě*: nom.sg.fem. ♦ *zamatorě-v-ьš-i*: PAP nom.sg.fem.indef. ♦ *dьn-ьxь, dьn-exь*: loc.pl. ♦ *svoj-ěxь* ↓ *svoixь*: loc.pl.

[v. 19] ♦ *otъvěщě-v-ьš-ø* ↓ *o tъvěщěvь*: PAP nom.sg.masc.indef. ♦ *anжel-ь*: nom.sg. ♦ *reče*: see v. 13. ♦ *emu*: see v. 8. ♦ *azь*: see v. 18. ♦ *estь*: see v. 18. ♦ *gavriilь*: nom.sg. ♦ *prěstoj-i-ntj-ø* ↓ *prěstoę*, to which -*i* is added: PrAP nom.sg.masc.def. ♦ *bog-otь*: instr.sg. ♦ *posьl-a-n-ь*: PPP nom.sg.masc.indef. ♦ *glagol-a-ti*: inf. ♦ *tebě*: see v. 3. *(kь) tebě*: see V186 (§122). ♦ *blagověsti-ti*: inf. ♦ *se*: acc.sg.neut. D208–9 (§93), V139 (§93). ♦ *sii* (Ass.; cf. ταῦτα in the Greek): acc.pl.neut. D209 (§93, Anm. 1), V140 (§93, page-par.1).

[v. 20] ♦ *bǫd-e-ši*: non-past (perfective) 2sg. ♦ *mlьč-i-ntj-ø* ↓ *mlьčę*: PrAP nom.sg.masc.indef. ♦ *mog-y₂-ntj-ø* ↓ *mogy*: PrAP nom.sg. masc.indef. ♦ *proglagol-a-ti*: inf. ♦ *n-j-ogo-že* ↓ *ńegože*: gen.sg.masc. post-prep. See v. 4 (*ńixьže*) and V358 (§ 256, par. 1). ♦ *dьn-e*: gen.sg. ♦ *bǫd-e-tь*: non-past (perfective) 3sg. ♦ *bǫd-o-ntь* ↓ *bǫdǫtь*: non-past (perfective) 3pl. ♦ *se*: nom.sg.neut.; *sii*: nom.pl.neut. See v. 19, *se, sii*. ♦ *věr-ova-x-ø* ↓ *věrova*: aor. 2sg. ♦ *slov-es-emь*: dat.pl. D171 (§71, Anm. 14), V110 (§73). ♦ *moj-ě₂mь* ↓ *moimь*: dat.pl. D207–8 (§91), V138 (§92). ♦ *j-a-že* ↓ *ěže*: nom.pl.neut. ♦ *sьbǫd-o-ntь* ↓ *sьbǫdǫtь*: non-past 3pl. ♦ *sę*: see v. 3. ♦ *vrěm-ę*: acc.sg. D173–74 (§74), V108–9 (§72) ♦ *svoj-o* ↓ *svoe*: acc.sg.neut. *svoę* (Zog.): sic.

122

[v. 21] ♦ *bě-x-ę* ↓ *běšę*: impf. (aor. formation) 3pl. D279 (§134, Anm. 3), V312 (§221), 244 (§158, page-par. 2–3). ♦ *ľüd-ije* ↓ *ľüdie*: nom.pl. ♦ *žid-o-ntj-e* ↓ *židǫʉe*: PrAP nom.pl.masc.indef. ♦ *zaxarij-y₂* ↓ *zaxarię*: gen.sg. V182 (§120.i, page-par. 1). ♦ *čüdi-ě-ax-ǫ* ↓ **čüʍěaxǫ, čüžděaxǫ*: impf. 3pl. ♦ *sę*: see v. 3. ♦ *eže*: conjunction, V367–68 (§258). ♦ *mǫdi-ě-ax-e-ø* ↓ **mǫʍěaše, mǫžděaše*: impf. 3sg. *muždaaše* (Ass.): D98 (§26), V45 (§262). ♦ *crьk-ьv-e, crьk-ьv-i*: loc.sg. D175 (§ 76), 179 (§83, Anm. 5), V112 (§74).

[v. 22] ♦ Note omission in Zog., and observe the last words of v. 21. ♦ *išьd-ьš-ø* ↓ *išьd ъ*: PAP nom.sg.masc.indef. (infinitive: *iziti*). D136 (§51, Anm. 4), V65–66 (§41). ♦ *mog-ěax-e-ø* ↓ *možěaše*: impf. 3sg. ♦ *glagol-a-ti*: inf. ♦ *n-j-ě₂mъ* ↓ *ńimъ*: dat.pl.post-prep. ♦ *ľüd-emъ*: dat.pl. ♦ *razumě-x-ę* ↓ *razuměšę*: prod.aor. 3pl. ♦ *vidě-n-ij-o* ↓ *viděnie*: verbal subst. acc.sg. ♦ *vid-ě-x-ø* ↓ *vidě*: prod.aor. 3sg. ♦ *crьkъvi*: loc.sg. See v. 21. ♦ *t-ъ*: nom.sg.masc. ♦ *bě-x-ø* ↓ *bě*: impf. (aor. formation) 3sg. ♦ *pomava-j-y₂-ntj-ø* ↓ *pomavaę*: PrAP nom.sg.masc. indef. ♦ *j-ě₂mъ* ↓ *imъ*: dat.pl. ♦ *prěbyva-ax-e-ø* ↓ *prěbyvaaše*: impf. 3sg. ♦ *něm-ъ*: nom.sg.masc.indef.

[v. 23] ♦ *bystъ*: see v. 9. ♦ *isplьni-x-ę* ↓ *isplьnišę*: prod. aor. 3pl. ♦ *sę*: see v. 3. ♦ *dьn-ije* ↓ *dьnie*: nom.pl. *dьnьe ~ denьe ~ denie*: D65 (§ 18, Anm. 3–4), V41 (§ 25). ♦ *služьb-y₂* ↓ *služьby*: gen.sg. ♦ *ego*: see v. 14. ♦ *id-e-x-ø* ↓ *ide*: prod.aor. 3sg. On the aspect of *iti*, see Dostál 1954: 119–25. ♦ *dom-ъ*: acc. sg. ♦ *svoj-ь* ↓ *svoi*: acc.sg.masc.

[v. 24] ♦ *sixъ*: loc.pl. D209 (§94), V139 (§93). ♦ *dьn-exъ, dьnьxъ*: loc.pl. ♦ *začętъ*: aor. 3sg. D249 (§121, Anm. 4), V305–6 (§216). *z̄č̄*: *začęlo* 'beginning [of a Gospel lection]'. ♦ *elisavet-ь*: nom.sg. D181 (§84, Anm. 7), V101 (§65). *elisavьtь* (Zog.): D102 (§28, Anm. 3). *elisaveθь* (Ass.): D45–46 (§6, Anm. 31). ♦ *žen-a*: nom.sg. ♦ *ego*: see v. 5. ♦ *taji-ě-ax-e-ø* ↓ *taěaše. taěše* (Zog., Mar.) impf. 3sg.: see D114 (§36, Anm. 5), V55 (§32, par. 1). ♦ *pętь*: acc. V176 (§118, page-par. 2). ♦ *d̄*: letter used as numeral. See the alphabet tables in the Grammar. ♦ *měsęc-ъ* ↓ *měsęcь*: gen.pl. V157 (§102, page-par. 2). ♦ *glagol-j-o-ntj-i* ↓ *glagoľǫʉi*: PrAP nom.sg.fem.indef.

[v. 25] ♦ *sъtvori-x-ø* ↓ *s ъtvori*: prod.aor. 3sg. ♦ *mьně*: dat.sg. D213–14 (§101), V147 (§97). ♦ *gospod-ь* : nom.sg. *gospodь* (Mar.) D162 (§64, Anm. 5), V102–3. ♦ *dьn-i*: acc.pl. ♦ *n-j-y₂-že* ↓ *ńęže*:

acc.pl.masc.post-prep. ♦ *prizъr-ě-x-ø* ↓ *prizъrě*: prod.aor. 3sg. ♦ *otъm-ti* ↓ *otęti*: inf. *otъęti*: D88–89 (§22, Anm. 6), V339 (§243). ♦ *ponosi-e-n-ij-o* ↓ *ponošenie*: verbal subst. acc.sg. ♦ *moj-o* ↓ *moe*: acc.sg.neut. ♦ *člověk-ě₂xъ* ↓ *člověcěxъ*: loc.pl. V94 (§60, par.3). *otъ čkъ* (Zog.): error of transparent origin.

[v. 26] ♦ *šest-y*: acc.sg.masc.def. ♦ *měsęc-ъ* ↓ *měsęcь*: acc.sg. *vъ ... měsęcь*: V199 (§128.a, page-par. 1). ♦ *posъl-a-n-ъ*: PPP nom.sg. masc.indef. ♦ *bystъ*: see v. 5. ♦ *anжel-ъ*: nom.sg. See v. 28. *gav(ъ)ri(i)lъ*: nom.sg. ♦ *bog-a*: gen.sg. ♦ *grad-ъ*: acc.sg. ♦ *galilej-ъsk-ъ* ↓ *galileiskъ*: acc.sg.masc. (indef.) V131 (§86, page-par. 3). ♦ *j-omu-(že)* ↓ *emu(že)*: dat.sg.masc. ♦ *imę*: see v. 5. (Note that in Ass. *imę* presumably represents *i imę*.) ♦ *nazaret-ъ*: nom.sg. D181 (§84, Anm. 6), *–θ* (Ass.) D45–46 (§6, Anm. 31), V76 (§47, page-par. 1). ♦ *emuže imę nazaretъ*: V354–55 (§253) on "phrase nominale".

[v. 27] ♦ *děv-ě₂* ↓ *děvě*: dat.sg. ♦ *obrǫči-e-n-ě₂* ↓ *obrǫčeně*: PPP dat.sg.fem.indef. ♦ *mǫž-u* ↓ *mǫžü*, *mǫž-ovi* ↓ *mǫževi*: dat.sg. D155 (§62. Anm. 3), 159 (§63, Anm. 2), V93–94 (§59). ♦ *emuže imę*: see v. 26. *iosif-ъ*: nom.sg. ♦ *dom-u*: gen.sg. D154–55 (§62, Anm. 2), V91 (§58). ♦ *david-ov-a*: gen.sg.masc. (indef.) V132 (§87.a), 133 (§88), 131 (§86, page-par. 1). ♦ *(i) imę*: see vv. 5 and 26. ♦ *marij-a* ↓ *mariě*: nom.sg.

[v. 28] ♦ *vъ-šъd-ъš-ø* ↓ *vъšъdъ*: PAP nom.sg.masc.indef. See v. 9 (*vъšъdъšü*). ♦ *n-j-oi* ↓ *ńei*: dat.sg.fem.post-prep. See v. 4 (*ńixъže*). ♦ *anжel-ъ*: nom.sg. D48–49 (§6, Anm. 47). ♦ *reče*: see v. 13. ♦ *rad-uj-i₂-ø* ↓ *radui*: impv. 2sg. ♦ *blagodětъn-aě*, *blagodatъn-aě*: voc.sg. fem. (def.) V123 (§81). ♦ *gospod-ъ, -ъ*: nom.sg. D162 (§64), V102–3 (§66). ♦ *toboǫ̈*: instr.sg. D213–14 (§101), V147 (§97). ♦ *blagosloven-a*: PPP nom.sg.fem.indef. D132 (§49, Anm. 7), V259 (§176, page-par. 2). ♦ *ty*: nom.sg. ♦ *žen-axъ*: loc.pl.

[v. 29] ♦ *on-a*: nom.sg.fem. D206 (§90), V138 (§92). ♦ *slyš-ěv-ъš-i*, *vid-ě-v-ъš-i*: PAP nom.sg.fem.indef. ♦ *sъmęte sę*: see v. 12. ♦ *slov-es-i*: loc.sg. D170 (§71, Anm. 3), V110 (§73). ♦ *ego*: see v. 5. ♦ *pomyšľě-a-x-e-ø* ↓ impf. 3sg. ♦ *sebě*: loc.sg. D213 (§101), V147–48 (§97), 172 (§114). ♦ *kak-o, kakov-o*: nom.sg.neut. ♦ *se*: nom.sg.neut. See v. 19. ♦ *bǫd-e-tъ*: non-past (perfective) 3sg. ♦ *cěl-ova-n-ij-o* ↓ *cělovanie*: verbal subst. nom.sg.

[v. 30] ♦ *rek-e-x-ø.* ♦ *j-oi.* ♦ *anᴊᴇl-ъ.* ♦ *boj-i-ø.* ♦ *marij-o.*
♦ *obrět-e-x-ø.* ♦ *blagodět-ь, blagodat-ь.* ♦ *bog-a.*

[v. 31] ♦ *začьn-e-ši.* ♦ *črěv-ě₂.* ♦ *rodi-ši*: see v. 13 (*rodi-tъ*).
♦ *syn-ъ*: see v. 13. ♦ *narek-e-ši.* ♦ *im-ę.* ♦ *j-omu.* ♦ *isus-ъ*: see v. 13
(*ioan(n)-ъ*).

[v. 32] ♦ *sь*: see v. 19 (*se*). ♦ *bǫd-e-tъ.* ♦ *velij-ь.* ♦ *syn-ъ*:
nom.sg. V174 (§116, par. 2). ♦ *vyšьń-aago.* ♦ *narek-e-tъ sę.* ♦ *dad-tъ*:
non-past 3sg. D277 (§134), V313 (§222). ♦ *j-omu.* ♦ *gospod-ь, -ъ*: see
v. 25. ♦ *bog-ъ.* ♦ *prěstol-ъ.* ♦ *david-a.* ♦ *otьc-a.* ♦ *j-ogo.*

[v. 33] ♦ *vъcěsaŕi-tъ sę.* ♦ *dom-u*: loc.sg. D156 (§62, Anm. 4),
V91 (§58). ♦ *ijakovľě₂.* ♦ *věk-y₂.* ♦ *cěsaŕьstv-u, cěsaŕьstvij-u.* ♦ *j-ogo.*
♦ *bǫd-e-tъ* ♦ *konьc-a*: V184 (§ 120.i, page-par. 1).

[v. 34] ♦ *rek-e-x-ø.* ♦ *marij-a.* ♦ *anᴊᴇl-u.* ♦ *bǫd-e-tъ.* ♦ *se.*
♦ *mǫž-a.* ♦ *zna-j-ǫ.*

[v. 35] ♦ *otъvěᴊᴇ̌-v-ъš-ø.* ♦ *anᴊᴇl-ъ.* ♦ *rek-e-x-ø.* ♦ *j-oi.* ♦ *dux-ь.*
♦ *svęt-y.* ♦ *naid-e-tъ.* ♦ *tę.* ♦ *sil-a.* ♦ *vyšьń-aago.* ♦ *osěni-tъ.* ♦ *těmь*
že: V373 (§258). ♦ *j-o-že.* ♦ *roditъ sę.* ♦ *eže roditъ sę*: renders
participle with definite article of the Greek text. ♦ *svęt-o.* ♦ *narek-e-tъ.*
♦ *syn-ъ.* ♦ *božij-ъ.*

[v. 36] ♦ *elisavet-ь, elisavъt-ъ*: D39 (§6, Anm. 16). *elisave θ-ъ*:
D45-46 (§6, Anm. 31), V76 (§47, page-par. 1). ♦ *ǫžik-a.* ♦ *tvoj-a.*
♦ *t-a.* ♦ *začętъ*: see v. 24. *začьn-e-tъ* (Zog.): another error of
transparent origin. ♦ *starost-ь.* ♦ *svoj-ǫ.* ♦ *sь*: nom.sg.masc. D208–9
(§93), V139–40 (§93). Note *se* (Ass.). ♦ *měsęc-ъ.* ♦ *šest-y.* ♦ *estъ*:
non-past (imperfective) 3sg. D276 (§134), 279 (§134, Anm. 2),
V311–12 (§222). ♦ *j-oi.* ♦ *narica-j-om-ě₂i.* ♦ *neplod-ъv-i*: see v. 7
(*neplod-y*).

[v. 37] ♦ *iznemog-e-tъ.* ♦ *bog-a.* ♦ *vьsěk-ъ*: D143 (§55, Anm. 8),
205 (§88, Anm. 2), 207 (§90, Anm. 1), V150 (§99.a). ♦ *glagol-ъ.*

[v. 38] ♦ *rek-e-x-ø.* ♦ *marij-a.* ♦ *rab-a.* ♦ *gospodьń-a.* ♦ *bǫd-i₂-*
ø: imperative 3sg. V232–33 (§150). ♦ *mьně*: see v. 25. ♦ *glagol-u.*
♦ *tvoj-omu.* ♦ *otid-e-x-ø.* ♦ *n-j-oę.* ♦ *anᴊᴇl-ъ.* ♦ *k̄c̄: konьcь* 'end' [of a
Gospel lection].

[v. 39] ♦ *vъz-sta-v-ъš̌-i.* ♦ *marij-a.* ♦ *t-y₂.* ♦ *dъn-i.* ♦ *id-e-x-ø.*
♦ *gor-q.* ♦ *podъgorij-o.* ♦ *tъ̋̋-n-ij-otъ.* ♦ *grad-ъ.* ♦ *ijudov-ъ.*

[v. 40] ♦ *vъnid-e-x-ø.* ♦ *dom-ъ.* ♦ *zaxarij-in-ъ.* ♦ *cĕl-ova-x-ø.*
♦ *elisavet-ъ*: see v. 24.

[v. 41] ♦ *bystъ*: see v. 5. ♦ *uslyš̌-ĕx-ø* ↓ *uslyš̌a. uslъ̌š̌a* (Mar.):
D95 (§24, Anm. 2), 93 (§23, Anm. 3), 40 (§6, Anm. 17). ♦ *elisavet-ъ*:
see v. 24. ♦ *cĕl-ova-n-ij-o.* ♦ *marij-in-o.* ♦ *vъzigra-x-ø sę.*
♦ *mladъnъc-ъ.* ♦ *radoяami.* ♦ *črĕv-ĕ₂.* ♦ *qtrob-ĕ₂.* ♦ *j-oę.* ♦ *isplъn-i-x-
ø sę.* ♦ *dъx-otъ*: cf. v. 15 (*dъxotъ ~ dъxa*). ♦ *svęt-y(i)тъ.*

[v. 42] ♦ *vъzъpi-x-ø.* ♦ *glas-otъ.* ♦ *velij-otъ.* ♦ *rek-e-x-ø.*
♦ *blagosloven-a.* ♦ *ty*: D213 (§101), V147 (§97). ♦ *žen-axъ.*
♦ *blagosloven-ъ.* ♦ *plod-ъ.* ♦ *črĕv-a.* ♦ *qtrob-y₂.* ♦ *tvoj-ogo.* ♦ *tvoj-oę.*

[v. 43] ♦ *se*: nom.sg.neut. See v. 19 (*se*). ♦ *prid-e-tъ*: perfective
non-past 3sg. V341 (§245, par. 2). See also Dostál 1954: 283. ♦ *mat-i.*
♦ *gospod-i, gospod-a.* ♦ *moj-ogo.* ♦ *mъnĕ*: see v. 3.

[v. 44] ♦ *bystъ*: see v. 5. ♦ *glas-ъ.* ♦ *cĕl-ova-n-ij-a.* ♦ *tvoj-ogo.*
♦ *uš̌iü, uš̌ьü*: loc.du. D171–72 (§71, Anm. 17), V112 (§73). ♦ *vъ nuš̌iü*
(Mar.): D126–27 (§46, Anm. 3), V174 (§ 44, page-par. 1). ♦ *moj-oü.*
♦ *vъzigra-x-ø sę.* ♦ *mladъnъc-ъ.* ♦ *mladĕniя-ъ.* ♦ *radoяa-mi.* ♦ *črĕv-
ĕ₂.* ♦ *qtrob-ĕ₂.* ♦ *moj-otъ.* ♦ *moj-oi.*

[v. 45] ♦ *blaži-e-n-a.* ♦ *j-aže.* ♦ *vĕr-q.* ♦ *ętъ*: aor. 3sg. D246
(§121, Anm. 1–2), 240 (§114, Anm. 2), V305–6 (§216). ♦ *bqd-e-tъ.*
♦ *sъvrъš̌i-e-n-ij-o.* ♦ *glagol-a-n-ytъ.* ♦ *gospod-a, -ĕ, -i*: see v. 15
(g̃i, g̃ü).

[v. 46] ♦ *rek-e-x-ø.* ♦ *marij-a.* ♦ *velič̌i-tъ.* ♦ *duš̌-a.* ♦ *moj-a.*
♦ *gospod-a, -ĕ*: see vv. 45 and 15.

[v. 47] ♦ *vъzdrad-ova-x-ø sę*: see v. 14 (*vъzdraduętъ*). ♦ *dъx-ъ.*
♦ *moj-ъ.* ♦ *bog-ĕ₂.* ♦ *sъpas-ĕ₂.* ♦ *moj-otъ.*

[v. 48] ♦ *prizъr-ĕ-x-ø.* ♦ *sъmĕri-e-n-ij-o* ↓ *s ъmĕŕenie.* ♦ *rab-y₂.*
♦ *svoj-oę.* ♦ *otъ selĕ*: cf. *otъ kqdu* (v. 43). V219 (§142). ♦ *blažętъ*
(*blaži-ntъ*): imperfective, although rendering a Greek future tense.
V342 (§245, page-par. 1). See also Dostál 1954: 208–9. ♦ *mę*:
D213–14 (§101), V147 (§97). ♦ *vьsi*: D208 (§92), V150–51 (§99.a).
♦ *rod-i₂.*

126

[v. 49] ♦ sъtvori-x-∅. ♦ mьně: see v. 3. ♦ veličij-o. ♦ veličij-a ↓ veličiě (cf. Greek μεγαλεῖα). ♦ silьn-y. ♦ svęt-o. ♦ im-ę: see v. 5 (imenemъ). ♦ j-ogo.

[v. 50] ♦ milost-ь. ♦ j-ogo. ♦ rod-y₂ ι rod-ъ (Zog., cf. γενεᾶς καὶ γενεῶν); rod-ъ i rod-ъ (Mar., cf. γενεάν καὶ γενεάν). ♦ boj-i-ntj-yimъ sę. ♦ j-ogo.

[v. 51] ♦ sъtvori-x-∅. ♦ drъžěv-ǫ. ♦ myšьc-oǫ̈. ♦ svoj-oǫ̈. ♦ rastoči-x-∅; rastači (Mar): sic. ♦ grъd-y₂ę. ♦ mysl-ijǫ: V190 (§ 123, page-par. 1). ♦ srъdьc-a: V168 (§ 111, page-par. 2). ♦ j-ě₂xъ.

[v. 52] ♦ nizъloži-x-∅. ♦ silьn-y₂ę. ♦ prěstol-ъ. ♦ vъznes-e-x-∅. ♦ sъměri-e-n-y₂ę ↓ sъměřenyę.

[v. 53] ♦ lak-j-o-ntj-y₂ę, alk-j-o-ntj-y₂ę: D60 (§14, Anm. 3), V72 (§ 43). ♦ isplьni-x-∅. ♦ blag-ъ: V181 (§120.i). ♦ bogati-ntj-y₂ę sę. ♦ otъpusti-x-∅. ♦ tъʉ-y₂.

[v. 54] ♦ prętъ: see v. 45 (ętъ). ♦ izdrail'-a: V176 (§119). ♦ otrok-a. ♦ svoj-ogo. ♦ pomě-nǫ-ti. ♦ milost-ь.

[v. 55] ♦ glagol-a-x-∅. ♦ otьc-otъ. ♦ naš-ě₂mъ. ♦ avram-u: D118 (§40, Anm. 8). ♦ sěm-en-i: D168 (§69), V108–9 (§72), sěmene (Zog.): sic. ♦ j-ogo. ♦ věk-a.

[v. 56] ♦ prěbystъ: see v. 5 (bystъ). ♦ marij-a. ♦ n-j-oǫ̈. ♦ tri: acc., agreeing with měsęcę. D215 (§102), V157 (§102, page-par 1). ♦ měsęc-y₂. ♦ vъzvrati-x-∅ sę. ♦ dom-ъ. ♦ svoj-ъ. ♦ k̅o̅: see v. 38. The lection that ends here, with v. 56, begins with v. 39 (not marked in Mar.).

[v. 57] ♦ elisavet-i: dat. ♦ isplьni-x-ę sę. ♦ dьn-ije. ♦ isplьni-x-∅. ♦ vrěm-ę: nom.sg. See v. 20 (vrěmę). ♦ rodi-ti. ♦ j-oi: dat. V361 (§257, par. 2). ♦ rodi-x-∅. ♦ syn-ъ: see v. 13.

[v. 58] ♦ slyš-ě-x-ę. ♦ živ-o-ntj-ei: PrAP nom.pl.masc.def. D250 (§121, Anm. 8), 125 (§43, Anm. 17), V303 (§214). *roženij-o, roždenie. ♦ j-oę. ♦ vъzveliči-l-ъ estъ: perfect 3sg.masc. D242 (§116), V253–54 (§170), 346–47 (§ 249). ♦ gospod-ь, -ъ. ♦ milost-ь. ♦ svoj-ǫ. ♦ n-j-oǫ̈. ♦ rad-ova-ax-ǫ. Note omission in Zog.

[v. 59] ♦ *bystъ*: aor. 3sg. See v. 5. ♦ *osm-y, osmы* (Zog.): sic.
D39 (§6, Anm. 17). ♦ *dъn-ь.* ♦ *prid-q*: simple aor. 3pl. D238 (§114),
V238–39 (§156). ♦ *obrěza-tъ*: supine. V349-50 (§250). ♦ *otroč-ęt-e*:
D168 (§69), 174 (§75), V108–9 (§72). Genitive, direct object of
supine: V181 (§120.h). ♦ *narica-ax-q*: V345 (§247). ♦ *j-o.* ♦ *im-en-*
emь. ♦ *otьc-a.* ♦ *svoj-ogo.* ♦ *zaxarij-a* ↓ *zaxarič:* nom. "absolute".
V174 (§116, par. 1). ♦ *zaxarij-y₂* ↓ *zaxarię*: gen., in apposition to
otьca.

[v. 60] ♦ *otъvěщě-v-ъš-i.* ♦ *mat-i.* ♦ *j-ogo.* ♦ *re-ke-x-φ.* ♦ *re*
(Ass.): sic. ♦ *narek-e-tъ sę.* ♦ *da narečetъ sę*: V233 (§150). ♦ *ioan-ъ.*

[v. 61] *rěk-s-ę*: s-aor. 3pl. ♦ *(n)-j-oj.* ♦ *nikъtоže.* ♦ *estъ.*
♦ **roменij-a, roždeniě.* ♦ *tvoj-ogo.* ♦ *j-ъ-že.* ♦ *narica-j-e-tъ sę.*
naricaatъ (Mar.): D274 (§132, Anm. 2). ♦ *im-en-emь.* ♦ *t-ě₂mь.*

[v. 62] ♦ *pomava-ax-q.* ♦ *otьc-u.* ♦ *pomavaaše ... otьcъ*: another
"improvement" in the text of Zog.! ♦ *j-ogo.* ♦ *bi* D276 (§134). ♦ *xot-ě-*
l-ъ: cond. 3sg.masc. ♦ *narek-ti* ♦ *j-o.*

[v. 63] ♦ *isprosi-ъš-φ.* ♦ *dъщic-q.* ♦ *napьs-a-x-φ, napis-a-x-φ.*
♦ *glagol-j-y₂-ntj-φ.* ♦ *ioan-ъ.* ♦ *estъ.* ♦ *im-ę.* ♦ *j-omu.* ♦ *čüdi-x-ę sę.*
♦ *vьsi.*

[v. 64] ♦ *otvrěz-s-ę.* ♦ *otvrьz-o-x-ę sę.* ♦ *ust-a.* ♦ *j-ogo.* ♦ *ęzyk-ъ.*
♦ *glagola-ax-e-φ.* ♦ *blagoslov(estv)i-ntj-φ*; *b̄lvǫ* (Ass.): sic. D107 (§30,
Anm. 2), V47 (§26.c). ♦ *bog-a.*

[v. 65] ♦ *bystъ*: see v. 5. ♦ *vьs-ě₂xъ.* ♦ *strax-ъ.* ♦ *živ-o-ntj-yixъ.*
♦ *j-ě₂xъ.* ♦ *vьsei.* Note haplography in Zog. ♦ *stran-ě₂, strěně* (Zog.):
D33 (§6, Anm. 15.1), V54 (§31, page-par. 2). ♦ *ijudej-, ijuděj-ьsk-ě₂i*:
D136–37 (§51, Anm. 5), V67 (§41). ♦ *pověda-j-o-m-i₂.* ♦ *bě-ax-q.*
♦ *povědaemi běaxǫ*: V352 (§252, 2°). ♦ *vьs-i₂.* ♦ *glagol-i₂.* ♦ *sii, sι*
(Ass.): nom.pl.masc. D209 (§93, Anm. 1), V140 (§93, page-par. 3).

[v. 66] ♦ *položi-x-ę.* ♦ *vьsi.* ♦ *slyš-ě-v-ъš-ei.* ♦ *srьdьc-ě₂xъ.*
♦ *svoj-ě₂xъ.* ♦ *glagol-j-ontj-e.* ♦ *slyš-i-ntj-ei.* ♦ *čьto.* ♦ *otroč-ę.* ♦ *se.*
♦ *bǫd-e-tъ.* ♦ *rǫk-a.* ♦ *gospodьń-a.* ♦ *bě-x-φ.* ♦ *n-j-ě₂mь.*

[v. 67] ♦ *zaxarij-a.* ♦ *otьc-ъ.* ♦ *j-ogo.* ♦ *isplьni-x-φ sę.* ♦ *dux-*
omь. ♦ *svęty(i)mь.* ♦ *proročьstv-ova-x-φ.* ♦ *glagol-j-y₂-ntj-φ.*

128

[v. 68] ♦ *blagosloven-ъ.* ♦ *gospod-ь, -ъ.* ♦ *izdrail'-ev-ъ.* ♦ *posěti-x-∅.* ♦ *sъtvori-x-∅.* ♦ *izbavi-e-n-ij-o.* ♦ *l'üdemъ, -ьmъ.* ♦ *svoj-ě₂mъ.*

[v. 69] ♦ *vъzdvig-e-x-∅.* ♦ *rog-ъ.* ♦ *sъpas-e-n-ij-a.* ♦ *naš-ogo.* ♦ *dom-u.* ♦ *david-ov-ě₂.* ♦ *david-a.* ♦ *otrok-a:* V134 (§88, page-par.2). ♦ *svoj-ogo.*

[v. 70] ♦ *glagol-a-x-∅.* ♦ *ust-y.* ♦ *svęt-y(i)xъ.* ♦ *s-o-ntj-yixъ.* ♦ *věk-a.* ♦ *prorok-ъ:* gen.pl. ♦ *j-ogo.*

[v. 71] ♦ *sъpas-e-n-ij-o.* ♦ *vrag-ъ.* ♦ *naš-ě₂xъ.* ♦ *rǫk-y₂, -ъ.* ♦ *izdrǫk-* (with scribal error in Mar.): D122 (§43, Anm. 2), V68 (§41, page-par. 2). ♦ *vьs-ě₂xъ.* ♦ *nenavid-i-ntj-y(i)xъ.* ♦ *nasъ.*

[v. 72] ♦ *sъtvori-ti.* ♦ *milost-ь.* ♦ *otьc-y.* ♦ *naš-ě₂mi.* ♦ *poměnǫ-, pomęnǫ-ti:* D58 (§13, Anm. 9), V46 (§26.b). ♦ *zavět-ъ.* ♦ *svętoi:* D144 (§86, Anm. 3), V121 (§80). ♦ *svoj-ъ.*

[v. 73] ♦ *klętv-ǫ, klętv-oǫ̈:* cf. *slovesexъ* (v. 4). ♦ *j-oǫ̈-že:* V191 (§123, page-par. 2) ♦ *klętъ:* D227 (§108, Anm. 3), V234–36 (§154). ♦ *avra(a)m-u:* D118 (§40, Anm. 8). ♦ *o tьc-u.* ♦ *naš-omu.* ♦ *da-ti.* ♦ *namъ.*

[v. 74] ♦ *bez strax-a.* ♦ *izdrǫky:* see v. 71. ♦ *vrag-ъ.* ♦ *naš-ě₂xъ.* ♦ *izbavi-ъ̌-omъ sę:* dat.pl.masc. in agreement with *namъ* (v. 73). ♦ *služi-ti.* ♦ *j-omu.*

[v. 75] ♦ *prěpodobij-omъ.* ♦ *pravьd-oǫ̈.* ♦ *n-j-ě₂mъ.* ♦ *vьsę.* ♦ *dьn-i.* ♦ *život-a.* ♦ *naš-ogo.*

[v. 76] ♦ *ty.* ♦ *otroč-ę.* ♦ *prorok-ъ.* ♦ *vyšьň-a(a)go.* ♦ *narek-e-ši sę.* ♦ *prědъid-e-ši.* ♦ *lic-omъ.* ♦ *gospodьň-omъ.* ♦ *ugot-ova-ti.* ♦ *pǫt-i, pǫtь* (Zog.) D66 (§18, Anm. 4). ♦ *j-ogo.*

[v. 77] ♦ *da-ti.* ♦ *razum-ъ.* ♦ *sъpas-e-n-ij-a.* ♦ *l'üd-emъ.* ♦ *j-ogo.* ♦ *otъpusti-e-n-ij-o.* ♦ *ostavi-e-n-ij-o.* ♦ Note introduction of marginal gloss into text of Zog. ♦ *grěx-ъ, grěx-ovъ:* D156–57 (§62, Anm. 11). ♦ *naš-ě₂xъ.*

[v. 78] ♦ *milosrьdij-ь.* ♦ *milosrьdы, -dei:* D173 (§73, Anm. 1), V95 (§61). ♦ *bog-a.* ♦ *naš-ogo.* ♦ *n-j-ě₂xъ-že.* ♦ *posěti-x-∅, posěti-l-ъ estъ:* V346–47 (§249). ♦ *nasъ.* ♦ *vъstok-ъ.* ♦ *sъ vyše:* V219 (§142, par. 1).

129

[v. 79] ♦ *prosvěti-ti*. ♦ *sěd-i-ntj-y₂ę̧*. ♦ *tьm-ě₂*. ♦ *sěn-i*. ♦ *sъmrь-tьn-ě₂, -ě₂i*. ♦ *napravi-ti*. ♦ *nog-y₂*. ♦ *naš-y₂*. ♦ *pǫt-ь*. ♦ *mirьn-ъ*.

[v. 80] ♦ *otroč-ę̧*. ♦ *rast-ě-ax-e-ø̧*. ♦ *krěpi-ě-ax-e-ø̧ sę̧*. ♦ *dux-omь*. ♦ *bě-x-ø̧*. ♦ *pustyń-axъ*. ♦ *dьn-e*. ♦ *(j)avi-e-n-ij-a*. ♦ *svoj-ogo*. ♦ *izdrai-l'-u*. ♦ *k̄ᶜ, k̄o̅ᶜ: konьc-ъ*. See v. 38.

Zographensis 242v.6–245r.23: John 6.35–71.

♦ [v. 35] *grNdꙗı̄*: cf. *sꙗı̄* (v. 46), *ědꙗı̄* (v. 54), *ědыı* (vv. 56, 57), *ědꙗı̄* (v. 58), *vědыı* (v. 61), *sыı* (v. 71). D31 (§6, Anm. 14), 125 (§47, Anm. 5), 233 (§111, Anm. 3), V30 (§16, 6°, page-par. 2), 127 (§83, page-par. 2). ♦ [v. 39] *ę̧*: sic. ♦ [v. 40] *syna*: D155–56 (§62, Anm. 4), V90 (§ 58), 178 (§119). ♦ *vъskrěšǫ ι*: ἀναστήσω αὐτόν. Cf. v. 44: *vъskrěšǫ ego*, also translating ἀναστῆσω αὐτόν. V146 (§96, page-par. 4). ♦ [v. 45]*bogomь*: V189 (§123, par. 1). ♦ *kъ mьně*: cf. *vъ mę̧* (v. 47). D214 (§101, Anm. 1). ♦ [v. 47] *imatь života*: V183 (§120.i). ♦ [v. 49] *ěšę̧*: D280 (§134, Anm. 8), V238 (§ 155). ♦ [v. 51] *živъ bǫdetь*: ζήσει. So also in vv. 57 and 58. ♦ [v. 53]*pieti*: sic. On the aspect of the verb, see Dostál 1954: 126–27, and cf. V342 (§245, page-par. 2). ♦ [v. 56] *prěby* (!): cf. *prěbyvaatъ* in Mar. ♦ [v. 60]*otъ učenikъ*: V195 (§126). ♦ *ego slušati*: V182 (§120.i). ♦ [v. 63]*živ(e)tъ*: Jagić notes, "*lit. inclusam in* жнвєтъ *emend. cyrill. delevit atque* н *superposuit, pro* жнвєтъ *ut* жнвнтъ *legeres*". (Jagić's edition of Zog. is in Cyrillic transcription). ♦ [v. 67]*oběma na desę̧te*: definite. Contrast *dъva na desę̧te* (v. 70). ♦ [v. 71] *glagolaaše*: 'spoke of'.

Marianus 71v.29–72r.26: Mark 14.41–52.

♦ [v. 41] *rǫcě*: dual. V169–70 (§ 111, page-par. 2). ♦ [v. 43] *glagol'ǫ̈ü*: dative absolute. V362 (§257, page-par. 2). *oboǫ̈*: sic. D98–99 (§ 26, Anm. 1 and 2), V45–46 (§26.a). ♦ *starecъ*: D101 (§28), V36–37 (§23). ♦ [v. 44] *ego, egože, i* (after *iměte*): V179 (§119). ♦ *egože ašte*: V364 (§258, s.v. aŝte). ♦ [v. 45] *pristǫpь*: D131 (§49, Anm. 4, 5), V63–64 (§39). Cf. *ostavьše*. ♦ [v. 50] *ostavь*: see v. 52. ♦ [v. 51] *edinъ ... eterъ*: D211 (§98, Anm. 1), V152 (§99.b). ♦ *oděnъ vъ plaštanicǫ*: V199 (§128.a, page-par. 2).

130

Clozianus

1. Clozianus 4r.34–5r.12 (II.111–172). On avarice.

4r. ♦ 34–35. Cf. Matthew 26.15. ♦ 36. *sętъ*: D281 (§134, Anm. 27), V306–7 (§216). ♦ 37–38. *vɪnъi*: read *vinǫ*. ♦ 38. *prědaše*: read *prědaeši*. ♦ 39. *imьže*: V370 (§ 258).

4v. ♦ 3–4. *čüdesa*: D171 (§ 71, Anm. 12), V110–11 (§ 73). ♦ 4. *tvoriti*: read *tvoriši*. ♦ 7. *pače*: D200 (§ 87, Anm. 1), V219 (§141, par. 1), 137 (§91). ♦ 8. *vьse se zъloe*: acc. ♦ *to*: nom. ♦ 9. *to*: acc. ♦ *vъzlübь*: D138 (§ 51, Anm. 11), V65 (§ 40, par. 5); and see note on *pristǫpь* (John 6.45 in Zog. above). ♦ 11. *běsa*: V137 (§90, page-par. 1). ♦ *gorьi* (= *goŕii*): D199 (§87), V135 (§ 89.a). ♦ 12. *vьsę*: acc.pl.masc. D208 (§92), V151 (§99). ♦ *ɪskrъnixъ = i iskrъńixъ*. ♦ 13. *tělesъnago obъičaě*: sic. Seems to be an act of desperation on the translator's part. ♦ 16. *oslěpi*: read *oslěpь* (= *oslěpl´ъ*), and see note on *pristǫpь* (John 6.45 above). ♦ 19. *vɪždъ ɪ*: perhaps for *viždi*: see D262 (§126, Anm. 2), V262 (§180, par. 2). ♦ *vъšedъ* (= *vъšьdъ*): nom.sg.neut.indef. ♦ 20. *ɪüdov. ɪ*: read *ɪüdovъi* (= *iüdovy*). ♦ 21. *eže*: corresponds to Greek definite article before adnominal prepositional phrase (τὴν ἐν τραπέζῃ). V358–59. Cf. *otьcь vašь iže vъ nebesexъ* 'our Father which is in Heaven' (Mark 11.26): ὁ Πατὴρ ὑμῶν ὁ ἐν τοῖς οὐρανοῖς. ♦ 23. *vьse to*: acc. ♦ *sъrebrolübьstvьe*: nom. ♦ 24. *pravy*: adverb. V218 (§140, page-par. 2). ♦ 26–27: cf. 1 Timothy 6.10. ♦ 32–33. *vьsěčьskaa*: D194 (§26, Anm. 4), V121 (§80, page-par. 4). ♦ 34. *mɪru*: sic. Read *moŕü* (= τῇ θαλάττῃ). ♦ 36. *povelěnьmь* (= *povelěniemь*). ♦ 37. *bezumьe go*: D115 (§36, Anm. 10). ♦ 39–40. *prědanъü*: adnominal dative. V189 (§122, page-par. 2). ♦ 40. *prɪdǫ*: simple aorist. ♦ *orǫžɪ i* (= *orǫžii i*): D113 (§36).

5r. ♦ 2. *znaxǫ*: imperfect, contracted form; cf. *možaše* (ll. 3–4), *nošaxǫ* (l. 9), *stoěše* (l. 10). D236–37 (§113, Anm. 4), V243 (§158). ♦ 6–7. *světilьnikomь ... tolikamъ*: datives absolute. ♦ 8. *světilьnikъi* (= *světilьnikъ ɪ*). ♦ 10. *rekъi*: PAP nom.sg.masc.def. ♦ 11–12. *prědamɪ i* (= *prědamъ i*).

2. *Clozianus 12r32–12v36 (I.752—792): The Entombment*

12r. ♦ 33. *pogrebeni* (= *pogrebenii*). ♦ *těla*: D169–72 (§71), V104 (§68). *gně*: adjective, gen.sg.masc. ♦ *ba͞*: noun, gen.sg. V133 (§87.d), 133–34 (§88), 131 (§86, page-par. 1). ♦ 34. *iže*: see note on *eže* (p. 81, 4v21), and cf. τὸν 'Ιωσὴφ τὸν ἀπὸ 'Αριμαθαίας. ♦ *arimetěę̜*: D45–46 (§6, Anm. 31), 34–35 (§ 6, Anm. 15, 3b), V76 (§47, page-par. 1), 52 (§29, page-par. 1). ♦ 34–35. *sъnii*: read *sъnitii.* ♦ 35. *mycě*: read *mucě* (D41, §6, Anm. 20), for *mǫcě*; see D99 (§26, Anm. 2), V45–46 (§26). ♦ 36. *bъivъšü*: perhaps a dangling part of a dative absolute construction. Cf. in Mar., Luke 12.4: *ne uboite sę otъ ubivaǫ̑ŵiixъ tělo i po tomь ne mogǫŵemъ lixa česo sъtvoriti* (but in the Greek: μὴ φοβηθῆτε ἀπὸ τῶν ἀποτεινόντων τὸ σῶμα καὶ μετὰ ταῦτα μὴ ἐχόντων περισσότερόν τι ποιῆσαι).

12v. ♦ 2. *zemi* (= *zeml'i*). ♦ 5. Cf. Ps. 76.8 (Septuagint 75.10). ♦ 5–6. *plъtьǫ̜*: V190 (§123, page-par. 1). ♦ *umrětъ*: D249 (§121, Anm. 4, par. 6), V235 (§154, page-par. 1). ♦ 7. *vъ malě*: V219 (§142, par. 2). ♦ 8. *adama*: read *ada*, as in the parallel text in Suprasliensis (448.8), отъ ада въскрѣсн). ♦ 13. *čєsare*: D167 (§68, Anm. 2), V108 (§71, page-par. 1). ♦ 14. *osǫždenьię̜*: note fem. form, commonly found in adjectives modifying plural forms of second-declension masculine nouns. ♦ 15–16. *beštislъni*: original reading probably *beštinьnii* (= ἄτακτοι). ♦ 18–20. Cf. Ps. 2.1. ♦ 20–21. Read *akrogoniei.* Cf. Ps. 118.22 (Septuagint 117.22) and Luke 20.17–18. ♦ *vъ ... kamenь*: note different construction (in l. 24) with *potъkǫ sę.* ♦ 21. *xъ̑*: accusative [!] in apposition to *kamenь.* ♦ 23. *pěny*: acc.pl. ♦ *vlъny*: nom.pl. ♦ 25. *vъzněsę*: s-aorist. ♦ 26. *sъšedъ* (= *sъšьdъ*): referring to *kamenь.* ♦ 27. *s(m)pssa*: read *sampsona.* ♦ 27–28. *slъnьca*: acc.sg. [!], personification. Cf. Hebrew *šimšôn* 'Samson', *šémeš* 'sun'. ♦ 28. *razdrěšъ* = *razdrěšь* (PAP). ♦ 31–32. *prěmračьnǫǫ̜*: *-nǫ* might have been expected, since there is no article in the Greek.

3. *Clozianus 2r.28–2v.21 (I.108–142): On adultery*

2r. ♦ 28–29. *vъ...krъštenьe*: see V199 (§128, page-par. 2). ♦ 33–34. *imenuetъ*: 3sg. See V355 (§253, page-par. 2). ♦ 35. *slъišitъ*: emend to *lъstitъ* (*lъsti-* (vi) 'deceive').

132

2v. ♦ 1. *crk̄ve*: acc. D179 (§83, Anm.4), V114 (§74, page-par. 1).
♦ 3–4. *nesьmьislьnъ poxotiιmъ*: sic. ♦ 8. *e*: non-past (imperfective)
3sg. of *byti*. See D279 (§134, Anm. 2), 227 (§108, Anm. 3), V227
(§147). ♦ 11–12. *prělübъι*: acc.sg. See D179 (§83, Anm. 4), V114
(§74, page-par. 3). ♦ 14. *fropιtu*: sic. See D45 (§6, Anm. 26).

Psalterium Sinaiticum

1. 2b.14–21, 3a.1–19: Psalm 3.

♦ 1. *běgaše*: imperfect, contracted form. ♦ *lic-a-veseluma = lica
aveseluma*. ♦ 2. *umьnožιšę*: note use of *ę* (not *ν*) after consonants in
this ms. See D30–31 (§6, Anm. 12.5), V29–30 (§16). ♦ *Mnoзιι* ...: note
dittography. ♦ 3. *glǫtъ = glagol´ǫtъ*. ♦ 4. *vьznese*: a conjunction and
participle might have been expected (cf. καὶ ὑψῶν). ♦ 5. *glasьmъ =
glasъmь* (but -*ьmь* is not a common ending in this ms.). Read footnote
3, and reconstruct what was erased. ♦ 8. *vιažьdυǫ̈ęę = vražьduǫ̈štęę*.

2. 30a.13–21, 30b.1–20, 31a.1-7: Psalm 25.

♦ 1. *moǫ̈*: instr.sg.fem. See D208 (§91, Anm. 5), V150 (§98). ♦ 3.
vъι-istιně = vъ istιně. See D67 (§18, Anm. 5). ♦ 4. *sědъ*: simple aorist
1sg. ♦ 6. *nepovιnъιхъ = nepovιnьnъιхъ*. See D103–6 (§29), V38–41
(§24). ♦ 7. *ispověmъ = i ispověmъ*. ♦ 9. *krьvъι = krъvii* (αἱματῶν is
gen.pl.). But see D180 (§83, Anm. 10), V115 (§74). ♦ 10. *nιхъže*:
gen.pl.post-prep. Note that it is adnominal to *rǫku*, not governed by *vъ*,
which governs *rǫku*. See V73 (§44, par. 2), 192–93 (§124).
bezakonenъě: bezakonь-niě. See D66 (§18, Anm. 4).

3. 172a.13–25, 172b.1-7: Psalm 129.

♦ 2. *vьneml¹ǫ̈šte*: sic. On the gender of *uši* and *oči* see D172 (§71,
Anm. 17) and V112 (§73). ♦ 3. *bezakonenιě*: cf. *bezakonenъě* in Ps.
25.10. ♦ 6. *milost-ι = milosti i*. ♦ *bezakonьnъιхъ*: sic. Read
bezakonьnii (ἐκ πασῶν τῶν ἀνομιῶν).

4. 35a.18–37b.13. Psalm 30.

♦ 1. ḋavъ = davidovъ ♦ 2. pravъdǫǫ̈: read pravъdoǫ̈. D175 (§77, Anm. 1), V98 (§62). ♦ ızъmı = i izъmi. ♦ 3. ko = kъ. D103 (§28, Anm. 7), V36–37 (§23). ♦ zaštıtıtelъ: acc.sg. V178 (§119). ♦ 4. imenı: i imeni ♦ 5. esę̇: read seę̇ (gen.sg.fem.). ♦ 8. vъzraduǫ̈: contrast vъzdradova (Luke 1.47 above) and vъzdraduǫ̈tъ (Luke 1.14 above). D122 (§43, Anm. 2), V68 (§41, page-par. 2). ♦ vъzveselǫ: vъzvesel´ǫ̈ (cf. skrъblǫ in v. 10). D145 (§55, Anm. 12). ♦ 10. ǫtrǫba: read ǫtroba. ♦ 11. oskodě: read oskǫdě. ♦ vъzdъıxanъı = -nii (instr.pl.). ♦ sъmęšę̇: aor. 3pl. See D240 (§114, Anm. 1), V298 (§211 s.v. ᴍᴀᴛᴇ-, ᴍᴀᴄᴛʜ), 237 (§155.a, s.v. ᴍᴀᴛж, ᴍᴀᴄᴛʜ). ♦ 12. moı: read moixъ. ♦ ponošenъ̈ı: see V188 (§122, page-par. 1). ♦ mne = mene. D214 (§101, Anm. 2), V148 (§97, page-par. 2). ♦ 14. mnogo: -gъ might have been expected (= πολλῶν). ♦ egoᵈᵃ: read egda. ♦ 16. žrěbъı: renders alternate Gk. reading κλῆροι (instead of καιροί). ♦ otъ: i otъ might have been expected (καὶ ἐκ). ♦ 17. tvoǫ̈ = tvoeǫ̈. ♦ 18. postъždǫ: read postъ̈ždǫ. ♦ nečъstıvı-i = -vii i (οἱ ἀσεβεῖς καὶ). ♦ 19. bezakonenъe: cf. Ps. 25.10 and Ps. 129.3. ♦ 20. sъkъı: read sъkrъı. ♦ 22. g̃ı = gospodь (before Vꟳ ě). ♦ ostoěnъě = ostoěniě. Cf. bezzakonenъě (Ps. 25.10). ♦ 23. vozъ-vaxъ: cf. ko (Ps. 30.3). ♦ 24. prěpodobınıi = -bьnii. ♦ grъdъınǫ = -ńǫ̈: see D145 (§55, Anm. 11).

5. 27a.16–27b.18: Psalm 22.

♦ 3. nastavılъ mę esı: nastavi would have been expected (aorist 3sg. nastavi mę rendering ὡδήγησέν με). ♦ stъзǫ: read stъзę. D107 (§30, Anm. 2), V47 (§26.c). ♦ 4. ˢo mnoǫ̈ = sъ mъnoǫ̈. Cf. Ps. 30.3 (ko). ♦ tvo-ı = tvoi i. ♦ 6. vъselǫ: cf. Ps. 30.8 (vъzveselǫ).

Kiev Missal. 1v–7v23.

1v. ♦ 1. ı̃v: numeral '23'. Supply "of November". ♦ 2. b̃ъ: nominative instead of expected vocative; cf. Latin Deus. ♦ nъı: accusative; note use of digraph ъı in this text. ♦ lěta ogrędǫcě: may be taken as genitive, adnominal to čъstьǫ̈ (l. 5). Note use of ę (not ɴ) in this text, and actualization of tj as c, dj as z. Cf. podazь in ll. 5–6. ♦ 5–6. podazь: note z in this text corresponding to žd in other texts.

♦ 6. *mɪlostɪvꞓî*: cf. Latin adjective *propitius*. ♦ *egože*: might be taken as having as its antecedent either an unexpressed object of *naslěduemъ* or (if *siloǫ̈* is considered an error for *silǫ*) of *ego* in l. 8. ♦ *siloö*: conceivably reflects a misunderstanding of *virtutem* written *virtutē* and so confused with ablative *virtute*. ♦ 9. *g͞mь = per Dominum [nostrum Iesum Christum Filium tuum, qui tecum vivit et regnat in unitate Spiritus Sancti, Deus, per omnia saecula saeculorum]* 'through our Lord Jesus Christ, Thy Son, Who liveth and reigneth with Thee in the unity of the Holy Ghost, [one] God, world without end'. ♦ *oplatmь = oplatъmь* (inst.sg. ending -*ъmь* is normal for this text). ♦ 10. *rovanię*: ? ♦ 11. *xodataęcü*: cf. note on *ogredǫcě* in l. 2; in dative absolute construction with *klimentu* (cf. Latin ablative absolute: *intercedente beato Clemente*). ♦ 14. *nꞓi*: accusative (cf. l. 2), direct object of *očisti*. ♦ 14–15. *grěxъ ... naštxъ*: adnominal to *skvrьnostiι*? Note odd word order. ♦ 16. *do věčьnꞑ b͞že*: perhaps = '[Read the regular beginning of the Preface] up to [the words] "O eternal God" [and then continue as follows]'. But *DO* might be intended as an abbreviation of *dostoino*, corresponding to the Latin *UD* taken as representing the beginning of the Preface, '*uere dignum ....*' ♦ 19. *čьstęce*: presumably nom.pl. masc.indef. of PrAP (cf. ll. 2 and 11) agreeing with a 1pl. pronoun (expressed or unexpressed) in the here omitted beginning of the Preface. ♦ *ιže*: the antecedent is *klimenta*.

2r. ♦ 3. *x͞mь g͞mь naštmь* (= *našimь*): *per Christum Dominum nostrum ....* ♦ 6. *krъve*: gen., adnominal to *vъlitič̌*. ♦ *naplьneni*: agrees with unexpressed subject of *prosimъ*. ♦ 8–10. *da eže ... obъmetъ*: perhaps to be construed so as to yield "that that which we bear as ... we may embrace as ...." But compare accusatives *oběčěnič̌, izdrěšenič̌* and ablatives *devotione, redemptione*. Perhaps, also, compare Latin *devotio* and *votum*. ♦ 11. *tъze*: see note on *podazь* (1v5–6), and cf. *toęze* (2r16), *takoze* (4v.4). ♦ 17 *zaščιtι*: note use of *šč̌* in this text as Cˢ corresponding to Cᵛ *sk* (and to Vᴺ *st*). Cf. *щ, št* of other texts. D136–37 (§51, Anm. 2, 9), V63 (§38). ndъ opl = *nadъ oplatъmь*. ♦ 19. Supply, perhaps, *ęže* (or, by attraction, *ixъže*) and construe: ♦ *čьstьǫ̈*: adverbial to *sъtvorι*. ♦ *svętъix*: adnominal to *čьstьǫ̈* and antecedent of *ęže*. ♦ *ęže*: direct object of *čьstimъ*. ♦ *nꞓi* (l. 20): subject of *čьstimъ*. ♦ *nꞓi* (l. 21):

direct object of *sьtvorı*. On nominative *nьi*, see D214 (§101, Anm. 6), V148 (§97, page-par. 4).

2v. ♦ 10. *bъ̃*: see note on 1v.2. ♦ 15. *namъ*: governed by *vьsxotěvъ*. V187 (§122, page-par. 3).

3r. ♦ 7. *podasь*: read *podazь*, and cf. 1v.5–6. ♦ 8. *ımъ*: part of a concluding formula; cf. 5r.11, 3v.16–17. ♦ 12. *prıemlǫce*: see note on *ogrędǫcě* (1v2). ♦ 13. *očıščenıě*: see note on 2r.17. Perhaps, also, compare Latin *perceptio* and *purificatio*. ♦ 21. *sušętъ*: compare, perhaps, Latin *affligo* and (when written with long ∫'s) *assicco*. Contrast 4r2. ♦ 23. *našı* = *našımъ*: see note on 1v.9. Cf. 3v.4.

3v. ♦ 1. *sьı*: acc.sg.masc. of *s*- 'this'; cf. alternate form *sь* (4r9). D208–9, V139–40. ♦ 11. *oběcělъ*: see note on *ogrędǫcě* (1v.2). ♦ 21. *očıstitъ*: compare, perhaps, Latin *exuo* and *eluo*.

4r. ♦ 6. *očıstı*: note here and elsewhere imperative, although the clause is introduced by *da*. 12. *dazь*: see notes on 1v.2 and 1v.5–6. Cf. 4v.2, 10.

4v. ♦ 4. *pıcę*: cf. *ogrędǫcě* (1v.2), *oběcělь* (3v.11), etc. ♦ 6. *utvrьdı*: cf. *očısti* (4r.6). ♦ 8. *(c)ěsarьstvě*: loc., governed by *prızьrı*. See V186 (§121.c). Compare, perhaps, Latin *rego* and *regnum*. ♦ 10–11. *tuzımъ*: cf. *podazь*, etc. ♦ 15. *svętъimъ*: supply *duxъmъ* (... *qui regnat cum Patre et cum Spiritu Sancto* ...). ♦ 17–18. *zaščıtı*: imperative 3sg. See note on 2r17. ♦ 19–20. Compare, perhaps, Latin *simul* and *similis*.

5r. ♦ 2 *sı*: nom.pl.fem., perhaps in error for *się*. D209 (§93, Anm. 1), V140 (§93, page-par. 3). Cf. below, 7r15, reading *si ixъ̃*. ♦ *ěkъıže*: cf. 5v.2 and Latin *quia* and *qualis*. ♦ 16. *bǫdǫ*: imperative 3pl. V311 (§221). ♦ 17. Note *c* in *pomocьö*.

5v. ♦ 8. *vъrěsnı* .... 10. *bǫdı* .... 17. *utvrьdı*: imperative 3sg. 11–14: Compare, perhaps, Latin *noxius* and *nox, mundanus* and *mundus, clades* and *claudo, dignanter* and *dignus, digne*.

6r. ♦ 2. *prınesenъı* : *prınosımъ* might have been expected. ♦ 14–15. *bež negože*: ideal *bez-n-j-ogo-že*); perhaps better spaced as *bež nego že* (with intensive, not relativizing, *že*). Note that the object of the preposition is *milosti*. ♦ 22. *vъsǫda*: genitive governed by *nasъiceni* (ideal *nasyti-e-n-i₂*). See V181 (§120.j).

6v. ♦ 7–8. *nebesъskuǫ̈* (or *-skǫǫ*): *nebesъskoǫ̈*. ♦ 15. *prispěi*: imperative 3sg. ♦ 19. *zapovědъi*. Cf., perhaps, Latin *perceptio* and *praeceptio*.

7r. ♦ 2. *pomlimъ*: read *pomolimъ* imperative 1 pl. ♦ 3. *bъ̃*: cf. 1v.2, 2v.10. ♦ *iže*: subject of *vъzveselilъ esi* (ll. 12–13). ♦ *molitvъi*: gen., object of *radi*. ♦ 4–5. *blaženъię*. ♦ *bcę̃* ... *marię*: gen., adnominal to *molitvъi*. ♦ 5–6. *blaženъixъ* ... *anжelъ*: gen., appears as object of interposed *radi*. ♦ 7–8. *silaxъ*: read *silъ*? Cf. 7v.8. Note that in both instances the two preceding words are ambiguously genitive or locative. ♦ 10. *vъsěxъ*: note unexpected back jer (ъ) in first syllable. Cf. l. 22, and contrast ll. 21, 7v.7, 8. ♦ 15. *silxъ*: probably better spaced *si ixъ*. See note on 5r2.

7v. ♦ 1–2, 4. *hǫdi, otъplati*: imperative 3sg., (subject is *Darъ*, 7r.20). ♦ 10–12. *vъsǫdъmь simь vъzętъimь*: cf. Latin constructions with PPP, such as *ab Urbe condita* 'from the founding of the City.' ♦ 13. *na = našimь* ....

Euchologium Sinaiticum

Excerpt 1. 45a.16–46a.18: Against fever

45a. ♦ 16. *molitva nadъ vъsěmь tręsomomь tręsaviceǫ̈*. ♦ 17. *zaprěжaetъ*: read *zaprěжǫ̈*. The error probably stems from the fact that other exorcisms in Euch.Sin. begin with the formula *zaprěжaetъ ti gь̃*. ♦ 19. *ęze*: Euch.Sin. does not have the letter ӡ. D47 (§6, Anm. 39), V623 (§37). ♦ 21. *vsн tvoę*: supply *tręsavicę*. Cf. 45b.10–11, below. ♦ 22–23. *mǫdrostei ... krěpostei*: note gen.pl. ending *-ei* for third-declension nouns in this text. D178 (§81, Anm. 1), V100 (§64).

45b. ♦ 1. *posъlaniě*: read *poslušaniě*. ♦ 3. *vъ buesti*: read simply *buesti*; cf. *mǫdrostei, krěpostei, mǫžьstva, ženъstva, posl[uš]aniě*, all genitives. ♦ *emłetъ*: read *emľete*. (Diels, Part II, p. 34, heartlessly suggests emending to imperative *emľite* or *emľěte*.) ♦ 11. *prětъikanei*: cf. note on 45a, 22–23, and *postrašenei* (45b. 13). ♦ 14. *kričнже*: on "gerundive" use of active participial forms in *-e*, see V252–53 (§169). ♦ 17. *imeni*: gen.sg. D168 (§69), 173 (§74, Anm. 2). ♦ 18. *egože*: gen., governed by *trepeψǫtъ*. V183 (§120, page-par. 1). ♦ 20–23. The Seraphim are missing from the nine choirs of angels: Cherubim, Seraphim, Thrones; Dominations, Virtues, Powers; Principalities, Archangels, Angels. ♦ 22. *mnogorazličъnii*: read *mъnogoočitii* (constant epithet of the Cherubim). ♦ 25. *pače v̄sěxъ*: genitive with *pače*. D200 (§87, Anm. 1), V137 (§90).

46a. ♦ 1. *ιsego = iz sego*. ♦ 5. *bǫdi*: imperative 3sg. ♦ 5–6. *imeni*: gen. V184 (§120.i). ♦ 6. *tebě*: read *tebe*. ♦ 8–10. *časъ ... godinъ ... vrěmenъ*: gen., governed by *vъzbrańěti*, which also governs the dative *ti*, in l. 8. V183 (§120, page-par. 1), 187 (§122, page-par. 2). ♦ 10. *em^lǫψiixъ*: supply *tręsavicь*. ♦ 15. *vo nъ = vъ ńь*. ♦ 16–17. *imeni tvoemu*: read *imeni svoemu* (cf. *imN tvoe* in l. 18). ♦ 17. *v̄s̄*: *vъzglašenie* (ἐκφώνησις). The voice is to be raised for the concluding doxology. ♦ 18. *o͡ca i s͡na ι s͡taago [duxa]*: see note on 77.4 of Suprasliensis.

Excerpt 2. 59a5–59b.14: Against pests
59a. ♦ 5. *molitva svętaago Trofona o vьsemь* .... On Trofona, see D28 (§6, Anm. 8,3). ♦ 6. *gubNψiimь*: loc.sg.masc.def. D195 (§86, Anm. 8), V122 (§80, page-par. 2). ♦ 9–10. *sъlězъ*: read, perhaps, *sъlěze*. D217 (§102, Anm. 4). ♦ 12. *g͡a*: perhaps originally the numeral *ḡi* (14). ♦ 18ff.: clearly corrupt. For *osuša eǫ̈ i*, read, perhaps, *osušaęi*, but other difficulties remain. ♦ 23. *ti*: see V373 (§258).

59b ♦ 2. *vъι*: dative. D214 (§101, Anm. 1), V148 (§97). Cf. accusatives *vы* (l. 7) and *vasъ* (ll. 3–4). ♦ 8. *niνъι*: read, perhaps, *niνъ* [gen.pl.] *i*. ♦ 9. *mne = mene*. D214 (§101, Anm. 2), V148 (§97, page-par. 2). ♦ 10. *c͡lskъιę*: ! Read *nebesъskъιę*. ♦ 14. *vъ vě[kъι věkomъ]*.

Excerpt 3. 72a.1–73a.1: Confessional prayer
72a ♦ 1. *vъlězěte*: imperative 3du. The implied subjects are the confessor and the penitent. ♦ 9. *v̄semogъι*: on final *-ъι* see D193 (§86, Anm. 3). ♦ 7. *sego*: read *vъsego*. ♦ 8. Supply *lixo* before *izḡlaxъ*. For *i lixo* read, probably, *ili lixo* (so also on next line). ♦ 21. *da tъι mi račilъ*: expected *bi* may have been lost in copying. ♦ 22–24. Cf. Ps. 25.2 (Septuagint 24.2).

72b. ♦ 11. *grěšьnikъ*: gen., governed by *izbavitъ* (supine). ♦ 12. *s[ъ]p[a]sъi* : would appear on comparison with *podavъi* (l. 6), to be PAP nom.sg.masc.def. *izbavi* = *i izbavi*. ♦ 13. *б̃e*: read *б̃ii*. ♦ 19. *ěkože*: read *i ěkože*. ♦ 16. *ei*: read *g̃i*. ♦ 21–25. *i moi životъ … avi*: Frček proposes reading *i moi životъ i moě slovesa i moe dělo. okonьčai, g̃i, tvoǫ milostь vъ mьně grěšьně rabě tvoemь* (*otъloži* might, according to Vondrák's (1894) suggestion, have arisen as a corruption of *i tělo že*; this could have entailed the insertion of *moę grěxъi* to supply an object for *otloži*; *moě slovesa i moe dělo* could have then have been reinterpreted as objects of *okonьčai*; finally, *avi* could have been added to provide a verb to govern *milostь*.) ♦ 25. *tvoimь*: read *tvoemь*. D208 (§91, Anm. 7).

Excerpt 4. 102a.5–102b.5: On penitence

102a. ♦ 7. Evidently the numeral *ã* '1' has been lost from this line. ♦ 8. *ĩ*: numeral '10'. So also in l. 21 and in 102b, 15. ♦ 11–12. *pokaalб̃*: *pokaalъ sę*. D82–83 (§21, Anm. 3.g), V276 (§193). ♦ 13. *epĩspъ* = *episkupъ* (cf. 102b, 14). *р̃pove* = *popove*. D156 (§62, Anm. 10), V93 (§59). ♦ 15–16. *l̃ĩ … pokaalб̃*: note repeated *sę*. ♦ 17. (right margin) *б̃*: numeral '2'. ♦ 18. *д̃*: numeral '5'. So also in 102b, 2 and 7. ♦ 19, 20. *ṽ* numeral '3'. So also in l. 22 and in 102b, 3, 8, 11, 13. ♦ 23. *g̃*: numeral '4'. So also in 102b, 12.

102b. ♦ 1. *ž̃*: numeral '7'. So also in following line. ♦ 4. *ẽ*: numeral '6', placed one line too low in the ms. This line should have the numeral *ž̃* '7'. ♦ 7. This line should have the numeral *ʒ̃* '8'. ♦ 9. *ž̃*: numeral '9', repeated in the margin at l. 12 and l. 14. ♦ 15. *daᵖ kaetб̃* = *da pokaetъ sę*.

Codex Suprasliensis. 75.29–81.27: The Forty Martyrs

76, ♦ 6–7. агрнколлү: read *agrikolau*. Diels refers to §6, Anm. 8.20, §19, Anm. 6, §84, Anm. 33. ♦ 8. съвлзлвъше: on the "gerundives" (adverbial forms of active participles), see D233 (§111, Anm. 2), 241 (§115, Anm. 1), V252–53 (§169). ♦ 16. воннъи: acc.pl., in apposition to *stražę*. ♦ 26. отъплдъше: corrupt text. The meaning required is "seeing him to have deserted and have thus expired."

♦ 27–30. ѥда въ рѣкахъ ... оустрѣмьѥнне твоѥ: cf. Habakkuk 3.8. ♦ 30. нꙗже бо отлꙗꙗ унвъ сꙗ : "for the one who ...." Note construction, in which нꙗже is used like the Greek definite article with a participle.

77. ♦ 1–2. акъ вода ...: cf. Ps. 22.14 (Septuagint 21.15). ♦ 2–4. мꙑ же ...: cf. Ps. 80.18 (Septuagint 79.19). ♦ 4. ѥгоже: personal masc.acc.sg.; antecedent may be considered to be the 2sg. personal pronoun implied in the possessive твоѥ. ♦ 5–7. ꙁмнѥвѥ ...: cf. Ps. 148.7–8. ♦ 8–9. свердпꙑнмъ влънамъ: the accusative might have been expected. Cf. verbs listed in V187 (§122). ♦ 10–11. нꙗже оуслꙑшавъ: ὁ ἐπακούσας. See note on 76.30. ♦ 11. н далꙗшта: read далꙗшта to make sense. ♦ 13. раздѣлѣꙗ: present active participle, nom.sg.masc.indef. Correct rendering of the Greek would have required the participle to refer to Moses. The confusion in the text may be explained by the preceding ходан (ll. 7–8) and кротан (l. 10). ♦ 14. настав ...: the original ending was erased and replaced by нвън, which, again, fails to render the expected meaning. ♦ 19–20. да не потопнтъ ...: cf. Ps. 69.15 (Septuagint 68.16). ♦ 21–22. ꙗко обннштахомъ ꙃѣло: cf. Ps. 79.8–9 (Septuagint 78.8–9). ♦ 23. мору: cf. агрнколау (76.6–7). ♦ 27. Cf. Ps. 22.5 (Septuagint 21.6).

78. ♦ 2–3. съдръжнмн бѣахѫ: see V352 (§252, 2°). ♦ 5. нꙗже прнбѣгъ: cf. нꙗже ... отлꙗкунвъ сꙗ (76.30). ♦ 7. снн: read снн (sii). ♦ 9. свѣтъ: V182–84 (§120). ♦ 12. л͞ѳ: Cyrillic numerals '39'. ♦ 13. уетꙑре (adj., nom.) десꙗте (noun, nom.pl.) нхъ (gen.pl.). ♦ 15. прнбѣгꙑн: contrast нꙗже прнбѣгъ (78.5); in both instances, Gk. ὁ προσφυγών.

79. ♦ 6–7. Cf. Ps. 77.13–14 (Septuagint 76.14–15). ♦ 10. ньн = ny. ♦ 22–23. нꙁвꙁладавъшѥ: Diels suggests "für съвꙁладавъшѥ, Versehen?" Cf. note to 76.8. ♦ 25 нхъ: locative. On the use of the locative with pri- and other preverbs, see V186 (§121.c). ♦ 26. юнѣн: comparative. D198ff. (§87), V134ff. (§89). ♦ вьсѣхъ: gen. V137 (§90).

80. ♦ 4ff. Cf. Ps. 124.7–8 (Septuagint 123.7–8). ♦ 6. нꙁбавьѥнн: cf. оустрѣмьѥннѥ (76.29–30). D131 (§49, Anm. 4–5), V63–64 (§39). ♦ 7. сътворьшаꙗго: cf. construction of ѥгоже at 77.4. ♦ 14. оставьшѥ: cf. preceding note and, in Mar., *ostavъše, ostavъ*, and *pristǫpъ* (Mark 14.45 above). Note also оставьѥнъ, ꙗвьꙗшѥ, etc. below. ♦ 14–15. ѥмоу жнвоу бꙑтн: see V188 (§122, last page-par.). ♦ 15–16. тъ ѥдннъ оставьѥнъ: see V179 (§119, page-par. 1). ♦ 21. несъшн: несъшн PAP

140

nom.sg.fem.indef. ♦ 26. вьζати ѧ нмѫтъ: see V342 (§245, page-par. 2). ♦ 80.30–81.1. н нну'соже не [...]н: a corrector has replaced the erased portion with погоуб.

81. ♦ 3–4. семь мѣстѣ: as the text stands, a locative used without preposition. See V185–86 (§121.b). ♦ 4–5. нζ-ᴧ-рѫкъı: D122 (§43, Anm. 2), V68 (§41, page-par. 2). ♦ 16. о хѣ̄: "in Christ". V200–1 (§128 s.v. о). ♦ 18. о͞цъ ... с͞нъ ... с͞тъıн а͞хъ ...: accusatives. V178 (§119). See particularly Meillet (1897). ♦ 20. = *ante diem quartum Kalendas Martias* 'the fourth [by our reckoning, the third] day before the Calends of March'. ♦ 21. к͞ѕ: '26'. D25 (§6, page-par. 1), V23 (§12). ♦ 22. = *ante diem septimum [Idus] Martias* 'the seventh (i.e. the sixth) day before the Ides of March' = March 9. ♦ 23–25. цѣсарьствоуѭштоу го͞у ... бо͞у ... сп͞соу ... влаᴧъıцѣ ... і͞с х͞соу: dative absolute.

[There are no notes on the remaining texts.]

VOCABULARY

A

a but, and, while. V363–64.

abije immediately. V218, 40–41, D66, 76.

ad- m-1. Hell (ᾅδης). V94, 177, D155.

adam- m-1. Adam ('Αδάμ).

agrikola(j)- m-1. Agrikolaos ('Αγρικόλαος). D184, 159.

*akrogoniej- adj. (ἀκρογωνιαῖος). ◆ kam-en- ~ cornerstone.

aky as, like. V364, 34, 50, D77, 93.

*alk-a- vi. hunger. V272, 72–73, 181, D59–60.

*amin(ъ) amen (ἀμήν). D117.

*anꙉel- m-1. angel (ἄγγελος). V178, D147, 156.

apostol- m-1. apostle (ἀπόστολος). V93, D157.

arimatěj- f-2. Arimathea ('Αριμαθαία). V117–18, D182.

aroń- adj. of Aaron ('Ααρών). V132, D118.

*arxanꙉel- m-1. archangel (ἀρχάγγελος). D147.

*arxiepiskup- m-1. archbishop (ἀρχιεπίσκοπος). V31, D118.

*arxierej- m-1. high priest (ἀρχιερεύς). V118, D34, 159, 186.

*arxiereov- adj. of the high priest. V132.

ašte if. V364, 34, 143, D76, 204.

avesulum- m-1. Absalom ('Αβεσσαλώμ). V31, D118, 146.

avi- vp. manifest. ◆ ~ sę appear. V323, 34, D32, 73, 76–77.

*avi(j)ań- adj. of Abia ('Αβιά). V132.

avl'enij- n-1. manifestation. V251–52, D243.

avr(a)am- m-1. Abraham ('Αβραάμ,"Αβραμ). V115, D118.

azъ pron. I. V147–48, 179, D213–14, 76–77.

B

b- See by-.

balьstv- n-1. medicament. V209.

bań- f-2. bath.

besěd- f-2. conversation.

bestudij- n-1. shamelessness. V208, 79.

beštislьn- adj. without number. V212–15, 66–67, D136.

bez prep. + G. without. V194, D86, 125.

bezakonьn- adj. lawless. V212–13, 215.

bezakonьnij- n-1. lawlessness. V208.

bezdъnij-, bezdьnij- n-1. abyss. V208, D110.

bezmlъvij- *n-1.* silence. V208.
bezumij- *n-1.* madness. V208.
bě- See **by-**.
běd- *f-2.* misery.
bědьn- *adj.* poor. V212–13.
běga-j- *vi.* flee. V181.
běs- *m-1.* evil spirit, demon. V93, 178, D156.
běž-ě- *vip.* flee. V181.
bi- See **by-**.
bi-j- *vi.* beat. V28, 42, 280, D254–55, 56.
blag- *adj.* good.
blagodat- *f-3.* grace. V208.
blagodatьn- *adj.* graced. V212–13, 214.
blagodět- *f-3.* grace. V208.
blagodětьn- *adj.* graced. V212–13, 214.
blagosloven- See **blagoslovi-**. V258–59, D132.
blagoslovesti- *v(i)p.* bless. V258–59.
blagoslovestvi- *vip.* bless. **blagoslovestven-** PPP. V84, 258–59, D138.
blagoslovesьstv-ova- *vip.* bless.
blagosloveštvenij- *n-1.* blessing.
blagoslovi- *vip.* bless. **blagosloven-** PPP. V258–59, D132.
blagost- *f-3.* goodness. V208.
blagověsti- *vip.* announce good tidings of.
blazni- *vi.* scandalize. D138.
blaži- *vi.* pronounce happy, bless.
blažьn- *adj.* blessèd. V212–13.
blęd- *f-3.* error. V207–8, 78.
blizъ *adv.*, *prep.* + G, D. near. V197.
blǫd- *m-1.* fornication. V78, 206.
bo *enclitic.* for, because. V364, 377–78.
bog- *m-1.* God, god. V93.
bogati-sę *vi* be(come) rich.
bogorodic- *f-2.* Mother of God (Θεοτόκος). V211.
boj-ě-sę *vi.* fear. V183.
bolězn- *f-3.* misery, illness. V209, 96, D178.
bol'ij-, bol'ьš- *adj.* better, larger. V123–25, 135, D199–200.
božij- *adj.* of God. V172, 213, 119, 133, D189, 198.

bǫd- See **by-**.

brašьn- *n-1*. food.

brat(r)- *m-1*. brother. V75, 94, 167, D140, 158.

brĕg- *m-1*. shore, hill, slope, crag.

bridъk- *adj*. sharp, bitter. V213.

buest- *f-3*. folly. V208.

buj- *adj*. foolish. D159.

buŕ- *f-2*. storm.

buŕьn- *adj*. of the storm. V212–13.

by- *v*. be, happen, become. **b-:** Cond. 3pl. **bǫ, bĕ-:** Aor. (*i*.), Impf. D279. **bi-:** Cond. (sg. **bimь, bi, bi**, pl. **bimъ, biste, bišę**). D280. **bǫd-:** Non-past (*p*.), Impv., PrAP (*p*.). D227. **by-:** Aor. (*p*.) (2-3sg. **by(stъ)**). D279, 235. Cond. (2-3sg. **by;** elsewhere like Aor. (*p*.)), PAP, PfAP, Inf., Sup. **es-:** Non-past. (*i*.) (sg. **esmь, esi, estъ**, pl. **esmъ, este, –,** du. **esvĕ, esta, este**). D89, 227. **s-:** Non-past. (*i*.) 3pl. **sǫtъ**, PrAP. D89. V310–12, 184, 321, D276, 279–80.

bytij- *n-1*. being. V208.

byva-j- *vi*. be, take place. V332, 318, 320.

bъd-ĕ- *vi*. be awake. V53.

C

cĕl-ova- *vi*. greet. V269–70.

cĕsari- *vi*. reign.

cĕsaŕ- *m-1, 4*. king. V108, D129, 167, 159.

cĕsaŕьstv- *n-1*. kingdom. V208–9.

cĕsaŕьstvij- *n-1*. kingdom. V208–9.

cĕsaŕьstv-ova- *vi*. reign. V269.

*cirkъn- *adj*. of the church.

*cirk-ъv- See **crьk-ъv-**. V51, D63.

crьk-ъv- *f-4*. church, the Sanctuary. V112–14, D38, 129, 179–80, 175.

Č

čemu, čemь, česo(go), česomu See **čьto**.

četyr- *num*. four. V156–57, D217.

čĕj-a- *vi*. expect. V277, 182, D83, 272.

čĕs- *m-1*. time, hour. V185.

146

čěš- *f-2.* cup, goblet. V61.

čęd- *n-1.* child.

čimь See **čьto.**

čin- *m-1.* order, succession, rank. V91, D154, 156–57.

čini- *vi.* compose.

čisl- *n-1.* number. V210.

čist- *adj.* clean, pure.

člověč- *adj.* of man. V213.

člověčьsk- *adj.* of man. V213, 133–34.

člověk- *m-1.* man. V94, 178.

črěd- *f-2.* course, (daily) turn (of priests).

črěv- *n-1.* womb. V111.

črьnьc- *m-1.* monk. V210.

črьven- *adj.* red. D132.

čüd-es- *n-1, 4.* wonder. V110–11, D169–71.

čüdi- sę *vi.* wonder at. V187.

čьso, čьsomu See **čьto.**

čьst- *f-3.* festival, solemnity; honor.

čьsti- *vi.* celebrate.

čьstьn- *adj.* venerable. V221–23.

čьto *pron.* what, why, how. V139, 142–43, D210, 204.

D

da that, in order that; let; and. V364–66, 50, D93.

da- *vp.* give, grant. **da-:** Aor. (2–3sg.) **da(stъ)),** PAP, PfAP, PPP, Inf., Sup. **dad-:** Non-past. (sg. **damь, dasi, dastъ,** pl. **damъ, daste, dadętъ,** du. –, **dasta, daste**), PrAP, Impf. V312–13, 183, 321, D277, 280. **dadi-** Impv. (2-3sg. **daždь**). D280, 231.

daj-a- *vi.* give. V276–77, 332, 94, D82–83.

dalьń- *adj.* far, beyond.

dar- *m-1.* gift. V92–93, 94, D156, 157.

davi- *vi.* throttle, choke.

david- *m-1.* David (Δαυίδ). V33, D29.

davidov- *adj.* of David. V213, 132.

desęt- *m-f-4.* ten. V157–58, 159–60, D217–18. ♦ **dъv- na ~e** twelve. V158, 160. ♦ **ob- na ~e** the twelve. V158.

desn- *adj.* right. D104–5. ♦ **o ~ǫǫ** at, in the right hand.

desnic- *f-2.* right hand.

děj-a- *vi.* do, make. V277–78, 321–22, D271–72, 278, 281.
  ♦ **molitvǫ ~** offer prayer.
děl-es- *n-1, 4.* deed, action. V111, 210, D169–71.
dětel-, dětěl- *f-3.* deed. V209.
děv- *f-2.* virgin. D176.
děvic- *f-2.* girl, virgin. V211.
***diěk-** *m-1.* deacon (διάκονος, διάκων). D34.
***diěpsalma** selah (διάψαλμα).
***diěvol-** *m-1.* devil (διάβολος). D33–34.
divьn- *adj.* miraculous. V212–13. ♦ **divьno** miraculously,
  wondrously.
dlъg- *m-1.* debt. V92, D154.
dlъžьn- *adj.* owing, obliged. V212.
dlъžьnik- *m-1.* debtor. V211.
dlьgot- *f-2.* length. V33, 208.
do *prep.* + G. until, up to. V194–95. ♦ **~ věka** for evermore.
dobr- *adj.* good. D112.
dobr- *n-1.* piece of goods. V170.
dom- *m-1.* house. V91–92, 94, D154–57.
dońьdeže until. V366, 60, 73, D126.
doselě till now. V222.
dostoj-ě- *vi.* behoove. V324.
dostojьn- *adj.* fitting, worthy. V212–13, 188.
dovьlě-j- sę *vi.* be content.
drag- *adj.* precious.
drěv-es- *n-1, 4.* tree. V111, D169–71.
drug- *m-1.* friend. V152.
drug- *adj.* other, else. V152, 154, 162, 174, D203, 212, 213.
  ♦ **drugъ druga** one another. V174, 152–53.
družьb- *f-2.* friendship. V209.
drьkol- *m-1, 3.* club. D162.
drьzost- *f-3.* audacity, rashness. V208.
drьž-ě- *vi.* hold. V324. ♦ **~ sę** cleave to. V183, 186.
drьžěv- *f-2.* power, (display of) might. V209.
drьžěvьn- *adj.* powerful, most excellent. V212.
duš- *f-2.* soul. V208, D176.
dux- *m-1.* spirit. V93, 178, D156. ♦ **svęt- ~** Holy Ghost, Spirit.
dvьr- *f-3 pl.* door. V166, 168, D178.

148

dyx-a-, dyxa-j- vi. breathe. V273, 275.

dъšt-er- f-4. daughter. V113, D178, 85, 109.

dъštic- f-2. tablet. V211, D136.

dъv- num. two. V156, 160, 138–39, D215, 217, 109. ◆ ~ na desęte twelve.

dьn- m-4. day. V105–6, 100, D153, 163–64.

dьnevьn- adj. daily. V212–13.

dьnьn- adj. daily. V212–13.

dьnьsь today. V219, D163.

E

e See j-.

eda interrogative particle. lest, can it be that …. V367.

edin- num., adj. one, (a) certain, alone. V155–56, 138, 158, 152, D215, 217, 218, 207.

edьn- See edin-.

edьnodušьn- adj. like-minded. V212–13.

eę See j-.

efimerij-, efimĕrij- f-2. course, daily turn of priests (ἐφημερία). V117.

egda when. V366, 221, D123.

ego See j-.

egʊpt- m-1. Egypt (Αἴγυπτος). V32, D28, 39, 49.

ei See j-.

eliko howsoever much, howsoever many. V153, D204, 212, 221.

elisavet- f-3. Elizabeth (Ἐλισάβετ). V101, 118, D181.

emľ- vi. seize, take. 2: ima-. V273–74.

emu, emь, eǫ See j-.

epifanij- m-1. Epiphanius (Ἐπιφάνιος). V116, D184.

episkop-, episkup- m-1. bishop (ἐπίσκοπος). V31, 52, D118.

erĕjьsk- See ierejьsk-.

es- See by-.

ešte (že) still. V219.

eter- adj. (a) certain. V152, D211, 75.

eü See j-.

*evanℵelist- m-1. evangelist (εὐαγγελιστής). D29.

ezer- n-1. lake. V166, D75.

eže as to the fact that. V367–68.

Ě

ě See j-.

ě- See **ěd-**.

ěd- *vi.* eat. **ě-:** Aor. (sg. **ěxъ/ěsъ, ěstъ, ěstъ**, pl. **ěxomъ/ěsomъ, ěste, ěšę/ěsę**, du. **ěxově/ěsově, ěsta, ěste**). **ěd-:** Non-past (sg. **ěmь, ěsi, ěstъ**, pl. **ěmъ, ěste, ědętъ**, du. –, **ěsta, ěste**), PrAp, PrPP, PAP, PfAP, Inf., Sup., PPP, Impf. **ědi-:** Impv. (2–3sg. **ědi-ь ↓ ěždь**). V313–14, D276–77, 280.

ědenij- *n-1.* eating. V251–52.

ěk- *že adj.* (Lat. *qualis*), of whatever sort, kind.

ěko that; as, when; for; about, approximately. V374–75, 34, D77.
◆ ~ **da** so that. ◆ ~ **(i)** about, approximately. ◆ ~**i** even as.

ěkože as. V375–76, D77.

ěkyže as. V375.

ěrost- *f-3.* rage. V208.

ěšte See **ašte**.

ěvi- See **avi-**. D76.

Ę

ę See j-.

ęzyk- *m-1.* tongue. V176.

ęз- *f-2.* illness. D134.

F

faraon- *m-1.* Pharaoh (Φαραώ). V117, D187.

felicit- *f-2.* Felicitas.

fevroar- *m-1.* February (Φεβρουάριος). V116, D29, 184.

filos- See **psilos-**.

fropit- *m-1.* prophet (προφήτης).

G

gad- *m-1.* reptile, vermin. V93, D156.

galilejьsk-, galilějьsk- *adj.* of Galilee (Γαλιλαία). V213.

***gavriil-, gavъril-** *m-1.* Gabriel (Γαβριήλ). D117, 29.

glagol- *m-1.* word.

glagol-a- *vi.* speak, say. V270–71, 321, 326.

glas- *m-1.* voice. V92.

glav- *f-2.* head.

150

glavьn- *adj.* important. V212–13.
glǫbin- *f-2.* depths. V209.
gněv- *m-1.* wrath.
god- *m-1.* hour.
godin- *f-2.* hour.
golěn- *f-3.* shinbone.
goni- *vi.* drive, persecute, pursue. V325.
gor- *f-2.* mountain, hill country.
gorьń- *adj.* mountainous. V214.
goŕij-, goŕьš- *adj.comp.* worse. V135, 123–25, D199.
gospod- *m-3, 1.* the Lord. V61, 102–4, D162.
gospodin- *m-1.* master. V102–3, 167, D166, 162.
gospodьń- *adj.* of the Lord. V214, 133.
gospodьsk- *adj.* of the Lord. V213.
gospodьstvij- *n-1.* Domination. V209.
govor- *m-1.* clamor, uproar.
grad- *m-1.* city; hail. V93, D156, 59.
grěšьn- *adj.* sinful. V212–13.
grěšьnik- *m-1.* sinner. V211.
grěx- *m-1.* sin. V93, D156–57.
gręd- *vi.* go, come. V297–98.
grobьn- *adj.* of the grave. V212–13. ♦ **sъnitij-** ~ the descent into Hell.
grozd- *m-1.* grape. D156–57.
grъd- *adj.* proud.
grъdyń- *f-2.* arrogance, pride, vainglory. Nom.sg. -i. V209–10.
gubi- *vi.* destroy.

I

i and; too, also; even. ♦ ~ ... ~ both ... and. V368.
i See **j-**.
i- See **iz-**.
i- *vip.* go. **i-**: Inf. **id-**: Non-past, Impv., PrAP, Aor I, II, Impf. **šьd-**: PAP, PfAP. V303–4, 318, 325, 184, D278–79, 281, 74.
iakov- *m-1.* Jacob ('Ιακώβ). V34, D33.
iakovľ- *adj.* of Jacob. V132.
ibo for, even.
id- See **i-**.

ide since. V369.

ideže where.

ierejьsk-, ierějьsk- *adj.* of the priesthood.

ierej-, ierěj- *m-1.* priest (ἱερεύς). V116, D34, 186.

ili or. V370–71.

iliin- *adj.* of Elias ('Ηλίας). V133.

ilos- *m-1.* ichneumon fly (ὕλλος). D28, II-34.

im- *vp.* take. V321, 329, D246. ◆ **věrǫ ~** come to believe. V326.

im- See **imě-**.

ima See **j-**.

ima- *vi.* seize, take. 1: **eml′-**. V273–74, 321, 329, D268–69, 73.

ima See **imě-**.

im-en- *n-4.* name. V108–9, D173–74.

imen-ova- sę *vi.* to be mentioned.

imě- *vi.* have, be to; (fut. aux.). **im-:** Non-past 3pl. **imǫtъ**, PrAP. **ima-:** Non-past (sg. **imamь, imaši, imatъ**, pl. **imamъ, imate**, –, du. **imavě, imata, imate**). **imě-:** Aor, PAP, PfAP, Inf, Sup. **iměj-:** Non-past 3pl. **iměǫtъ**, Impv., PrAP. V316–17, 183, 319, 342, D278, 281.

iměnij- *n-1.* property. V251–52.

imę See **im-en-**.

imьže because. V370, 220.

in- *pron.* (an)other. V138, 150, 152, 179, D203, 94.

inokost- *f-3.* peregrination. V208.

inoplemenьnik- *m-1.* alien, stranger. V211.

ioan- *m-1.* John ('Ιωάννης). V116, D182–83.

iosif- *m-1.* Joseph ('Ιωσήφ). V115, 93.

iosifov- *adj.* of Joseph. V132.

irod- *m-1.* Herod ('Ηρῴδης). V116, D182–83.

isaavov- *adj.* of Esau ('Ησαῦ). V132, 75, D29.

isk-a- *vi.* seek. V182–83, 272, D267, 269.

iskariot- *m-1.* Iscariot ('Ισκαριώτης). V167, 116, D182–83, 166.

iskoni from the beginning. V219.

iskrьń- *adj.* near, neighboring. V214.

iskusi- *vp.* try, tempt.

iskušenij- *n-1.* trial, test. V251–52.

isplьni- *vp.* fill, fulfill. V181.

152

ispověd- *f-3.* confession.

ispověda-j- sę *vi.* confess. V326.

ispovědě- *vp.* confess, acknowledge. For conjugation, see **vědě-**. V314–16, D278, 280–81.

ispovědьn- *adj.* confessed. V212–13.

ispravi- *vp.* correct.

isprosi- *vp.* request.

isprьva from the first. V219.

ispytanij- *n-1.* inquiry, investigation, examination.

istin- *f-2.* truth. ◆ **vъ ~ǫ** accurately. D67.

istinьn- *adj.* true. V212–13.

isus- *m-1.* Jesus ('Ιησοῦς).

isuxrьst- *m-1.* Jesus Christ ('Ιησοῦς Χριστός). V115, 117, 31.

išьd- See **izi-**.

iüd- *m-2.* Judas ('Ιούδας). V116, D43, 183.

iüdejьsk- *adj.* of Judaea ('Ιουδαία). D34, 43.

iüde(j)-, iüdě(j)- *m-1.* Jew ('Ιουδαῖος). V116, D34, 43, 159.

iüdějьsk- *adj.* of Judaea ('Ιουδαία). D34, 43.

iüdov- *adj.* of Juda, of Judas ('Ιούδας).

ixъ See **j-**.

iz *prep.* + G. from. V195, D86–87. ◆ **is prьva** from the beginning. V219.

izbavi- *vp.* save.

izbavľenij- *n-1.* salvation. V251–52.

izber- *vp.* choose. 2: **izbьra-**.

izběga-j- *vi.* flee.

izběg-nǫ- *vp.* flee.

izbьra- *vp* choose. 1: **izber-**.

izdraiľ- *m-1.* Israel ('Ισραήλ). V68, 115, D146–47, 180–81.

izdraiľev- *adj.* of Israel. V132, D180.

izdrěšenij- *n-1.* redemption. V68, D121–22.

izdrǫky = iz rǫky. V68, D122.

izěd- *vp.* devour. For conjugation, see **ěd-**. V313–14, D276–77, 280.

izglagola- *vp.* utter. V326.

izgъna- *vp.* drive out. 1: **izden-**. V310, 82, 325, D136.

izi- *vp.* go out. For conjugation, see **i-**. V304.

izlixa *adv.* exceedingly, in full measure, excessively, immediately. (cf. **lix-**). V219.

izmьr- *vp.* die. **izm(ь)rě-**: Aor., Inf., Sup. V305, D247.

iznemog- *vp.* be impossible; weaken. V301, 299, D249.

iznes- *vp.* carry out. V281–83, D244.

izved- *vp.* lead out. V297, D249.

izvěst-ova- *vi.* establish as certain.

izvěstьn- *adj.* established as certain (πεπληροφορημένος). V212–13.

izvęz-a- *vp.* unbind.

izvlěk- *vp.* drag out. **izvlьk-**: PfAP, also PAP, PPP. V300, D247–48.

izvoli- *vp.* deign. ♦ ~ sę seem good.

izvrьg- *vp.* depose. **izvrěg-**: Inf., Sup. V300, D247.

izъ See **iz**. D86.

izьm- *vp.* take away, deliver. V306.

ižde since. V369.

ižden- *vp.* drive out. 2: **izgъna-**. V310, 82, 325.

J

j- anaphoric pronoun. V145–47, 73, 138–39, 179, D207–8, 74–75, 77, 126, 203.

j- že relative pronoun. V145–46, 138, 179–80, D207–8, 74–75, 77, 94, 126, 203, 205.

K

kadilьn- *adj.* of the burning of incense. V210, 212–13.

kak- *pron. adj.* of what sort. V150, D206–7.

kako how; in some way.

kakov- *adj.* of what sort. V153, D211.

*kaland- *f-2 pl.* calends (καλάνδαι).

kam-en- *m-4.* stone. V106, 168, D163–64. ♦ ~ **akrogoniej-** cornerstone (ἀκρογωνιαῖος).

kaperъnaum- *m-1.* Capharnaum (Καπερναούμ). V115, D181.

kapiklarij- *m-1.* jailer (καπικλάριος). V116, D184.

*karъkinos- *m-1.* [plant disease] (καρκίνος)?.

kataaros- *m-1.* (κάνθαρος) scarab.

klańě-j- sę *vi.* bow down, humble oneself. V328, 331.

154

klevetьnik- *m-1.* slanderer.
klevrět- *m-1.* fellow servant.
klętv- *f-2.* oath. V209.
*kliment- *m-1.* Clement (Κλημέντ-).
klirik- *m-1.* priest, clergyman (κληρικός).
klьn- sę *vip.* swear. V191, D246.
kľ üči- sę *vi/p?* fall by lot. V323.
kol- *n-1, pl.* cart, wagon. V111, 168, D169–71.
kolěn- *n-1.* knee. V166, 170.
kolik- *adj.* how much. V153, D213, 221.
koližьdo ...-soever. V220, D204.
kolь how, to what degree. V222.
kolьmi *m-1.* how much. V218, 222.
konьc- *m-1.* end.
konьčin- *f-2.* end. V209.
kor-en- *m-4.* root. V105–6, 166, D163–64.
kost- *f-3.* bone.
kotor- *adj.* which; any. V145, 152, D204–5, 212, 93.
kov- *m-1.* ambush, snare, riot, insult.
kǫdu where, whence. ✦ otъ ~ whence. V221.
kraj- *m-1.* edge, bank, end, country. ✦ vъs krai near.
krasot- *f-2.* beauty. V208.
krěpi- sę *vi.* grow strong.
krěpost- *f-3.* power, strength. V208.
krěpъk- *adj.* powerful. V213. ✦ krěpъko *adv.* strongly. V216.
krič-ě- *vi.* shriek.
kroti- *vi.* tame.
krov- *m-1.* roof, pavilion, tabernacle.
krъv- *f-4.* blood. V114–15, D179–80, 61, 98, 102–3.
krьsti- *vp.* baptize.
krьstijan- *m-1.* Christian. V170, 167, D165, 34, 103.
krьštenij- *n-1.* baptism.
kup- *m-1.* heap. ✦ vъ ~ě together.
kupьno together. V216.
kυprьsk- *adj.* of Cyprus (Κύπρος).
*kυrion- *m-1.* (Κυρίων) Quirion.
kvas- *m-1.* leaven. ✦ ~ tvoŕen- strong drink.
kyi, koe, kaě *pron. adj.* what. V143–45, D210–11, 204–5, 141.

155

kъ *prep.* + D. to, towards. V197, 186. ✦ ~ **tomu ne** no longer. V220.

kъde where. V370, 220. ✦ **ašte** ~ wherever. V364.

kъnęʒ- *m-1.* prince, ruler.

kъńig- *f-2 pl.* book, scripture.

kъńižьnik- *m-1.* scribe. V211.

kъsni- *vi.* delay.

kъto, kogo, ... *pron.* who; anyone. V142–43, 144, 138, D209–10, 204.

kъždo *pron. adj. sg.* everyone. V36, 146, 142, D203, 205, 207.

L

lak-a- *vi.* hunger. V72, D59–60.

led- *m-1.* ice. D156.

lĕt- *n-1.* year. V186.

lĕv- *adj.* left. ✦ **o ~ǫǫ** at, in the left hand.

li *interrogative particle.* whether; or. ✦ **a** ~ and if. V370–71.

lic-es- *n-1, 4.* face. ✦ **otъ lica** from before. V111, D172, 133.

*likinij- *m-1.* Licinius (Λικίνιος). V116, 59, D50, 184.

lišenij- *m-1.* deficiency. V181.

liši- *vip.* deprive, let want. V260.

lix- *adj.* excessive, evil. ✦ **iz lixa** excessively, immoderately, exceedingly, in full measure. V219.

lixoklętv- *f-2.* perjury.

lobъz-a- *vp.* kiss. V272.

lovi- *vi.* hunt.

lozij- *n-1.* vine. V208.

lǫkav- *adj.* wicked. V212–13.

lǫkavьn- *adj.* wicked. V212–13.

lǫkavьstv- *n-1.* wickedness. V209.

lъž- *f-2.* lie. V208.

lьstiv- *adj.* lying, deceitful. V213.

lьʒĕ *indecl.* permitted, possible.

L′

ľüb- *adj.* pleasing. D201.

ľübo or. V371.

ľübodĕanij- *n-1.* fornication, adultery.

156

ľ üboděanь n- *adj.* of adultery.
ľ übodě j- *m-1.* fornicator, adulterer.
ľ üb-ъ v- *f-4.* love, desire. V113–14, D179, 109.
ľ üd- *m-3, pl.* people. V101, 94, 167, D166, 162.
ľ üt- *adj.* cruel.
ľ ütost- *f-3.* harshness.

M

mal- *adj.* small. D213. ✦ vъ ~ě for a little time.
*malaxej- *m-1.* Malachi (Μαλαχίας).
malo a little. D221.
*mann- *f-2.* manna (μάννα). V186.
marij- *f-2.* Mary (Μαρία). V117, D34.
marijin- *adj.* of Mary. V133.
*mart- *m-1.* March (Μάρτιος). V116, D184.
mat-er- *f-4* mother. V112–13, D175, 178, 85.
mati See mat-er-.
meč- *m-1.* sword.
melit- *m-1.* Meliton (Μελίτων).
mene See azъ.
meta-j- *vi.* throw, cast. V307, 326, 299, 272, D136, 269.
meždü *prep.* + I. among. V198.
měsęc- *m-1.* month; moon.
měsęčьn- *adj.* of the moon. V212–13.
měst- *n-1.* place. V197, 185, 95, 192.
mę See azъ.
mękъk- *adj.* soft. V213.
mętež- *m-1.* tumult, confusion. V209.
mi See azъ.
milosrь dij- *n-1.* affection of the heart. V208.
milosrь d-ova- *vi.* feel pity. V269.
milost- *f-3.* mercy, grace. V208.
milostiv- *adj.* merciful. V213. ✦ milostivь no *adv.* mercifully.
V212–13, 216.
mir- *m-1.* world; peace. V93–94, 176, D154–56.
mirь n- *adj.* of peace. V212–13.
mixail- *m-1.* Michael (Μιχαήλ).
mladeništ- *m-1.* child.

mladьnьc- *m-1.* child. V50–51, D94.

mlъv- *f-2.* tumult.

mlьč-ě- *vi.* be silent, be dumb.

mog- *vi.* be able.

moj- *pron. adj.* my. V138, 149–50, D207–8.

mokr- *adj.* wet.

moli- *vi.* beg. ✦ ~ sę pray.

molitv- *f-2.* prayer. V209. ✦ ~ǫ děj-a- offer prayer.

moŕ- *n-1.* sea. V94, 96, 177, D172.

moʋsij- *m-1,2.* Moses (Μωϋσῆς). V116, D183.

mǫčenic- *f-2.* martyr. V211.

mǫčenij- *n-1.* martyrdom. V208, 251–52.

mǫčenik- *m-1.* martyr. V211.

mǫči- *vi.* torture.

mǫčiteľ- torturer, tormentor, tyrant. V210, 107–8, D166–67.

mǫdi- *vi.* delay. V45, D58.

mǫdr- *adj.* wise.

mǫdrost- *f-3.* wisdom, rightmindedness. V208.

mǫk- *f-2.* passion, suffering.

mǫž- *m-1.* man. V178, 93, D152.

mǫžě-j- sę *vi.* take courage. V267.

mǫžьsk- *adj.* of men, human. V133–34, 213.

mǫ̌žьstv- *n-1.* virility, masculinity. V209.

mraz- *m-1.* cold, frost.

mrьtv- *adj.* dead. V171.

my *pron.* we. V147–48, 179, D214.

mysl- *f-3.* thought.

mysli- *vi.* think. V323–24.

myšьc- *f-2.* arm. V211.

myt- *n-1.* gift.

mъnog- *pron. adj.* many, much. V153–54, 218, D212, 221.

mъnogoočit- *adj.* many-eyed. V215.

mъnogorazličьn- Emend to mъnogoočit-, which see.

mъnoǫ See azъ.

mъnožьstv- *n-1.* multitude. V209.

mьně See azъ.

mьš- *f-2.* mass.

mьzd- *f-2.* return, repayment, reward. V54.

158

N

na *prep.* + L, A. on; upon, to, against. V200. ◆ **dъv-** ~ **desęte** twelve. V158, D215, 218. ◆ **ob-** ~ **desęte** the twelve. V158, D215, 218.

načьn- *vp.* undertake, begin. V306, D249.

nadъ *prep.* + I, A. over. V201.

nag- *adj.* naked.

nai- *vp.* come upon. For conjugation, see i-. V303–4, D278–79, 281.

nakazanij- *n-1.* admonition, trial, instruction. V251–52.

nakoval- *n-1.* anvil. V210.

namĕstьnik- *m-1.* vicar, successor. V211.

napad- *vp.* fall upon. V298, D249.

napada-j- *vi.* fall upon. V186, 327.

napis-a- *vp.* write. V274, D268.

naplьni- *vp.* fill.

napravi- *vp.* direct.

napьsa- *vp.* write. 1: **napisj-.** V274.

narek- *vp.* call, name. V301.

narica-j- *vi.* call, name. V328, 81.

narod- *m-1.* nation, people; pl. also: crowd.

naslĕd-ova- *vp.* (**naslĕdьstv-ova-** *vi.*) inherit; follow, imitate.

naslĕdьnik- *m-1.* follower. V211.

nastavi- *vp.* guide, teach.

nasyti- *vp.* fill. V181.

naš- *pron. adj.* our. V138, 149, D207.

nauči- *vp.* instruct, teach. V187.

navyk-nǫ- *vp.* learn.

nazaret- *m-1.* Nazareth (Ναζαρέτ, Ναζαρέθ). V31, 76, D181, 35, 45–46.

nazьr-ĕ- *vp.* look upon, consider. V324.

ne not. ◆ **kъ tomu** ~ no longer. V220.

neb-es- *n-1, 4.* heaven. V108–10, 177, D169–71.

nebesьn- *adj.* heavenly. V212.

nebesьsk- *adj.* of the sky, heavenly. V213.

nebytij- *n-1.* non-being. V208.

nečist- *adj.* unclean.

nečistot- *f-2.* uncleanliness, unclean thing.

nečüvьstvij- *n-1.* heartlessness. V208, 209.

nečьstij- *n-1.* wickedness.

nečьstiv- *adj.* ungodly, godless. V213.

nedobrě badly. V216–17.

nedǫžьn- *adj.* ill. V212–13.

neistovьstv- *n-1.* rage, madness. V209.

nemošt- *f-3.* weakness. V208.

nenavid-ě- *vi.* hate. V185, 324.

neplod-ъv- *f-4.* barren woman. V113–14, D179.

neplodьn- *adj.* not bearing fruit. V212–13.

nepobědim- *adj.* unconquerable. V214.

neposlušьliv- *adj.* disobedient. V213.

neposramľen- *adj.* unashamed. V215.

nepovinьn- *adj.* innocent. V212–13.

nepravьdьn- *adj.* unrighteous, iniquitous. V212–13.

neprijěznin- *adj.* of the Devil. V133.

nesъmyslьn- *adj.* senseless, foolish.

nevěždьstvij- *n-1.* ignorance. V208–9.

nevidim- *adj.* invisible. V214.

nezъlob- *f-2.* innocence. V209.

něm- *adj.* dumb.

něstъ (= ne + estъ). V311.

ni nay. V356, 372. ♦ ~ ... ~ neither ... nor.

nicь prostrate. D191.

ničьtože *pron.* nothing. V356–57, 143, D210.

ničьže See ničьtоže.

nikak- že *pron. adj.* no. V356–57, 150, D206–7.

nikodim- *m-1.* Nicodemus (Νικόδημος).

nikogdaže never. V221.

nikъtоže *pron.* no one. V356–57, 143, D209–10.

ništet- *f-2.* poverty, misery. V208.

nizъloži- *vp.* cast down.

nog- *f-2.* foot, leg. V169.

nosi- *vi.* carry, bring. V318, 325.

nošt- *f-3.* night.

nož- *m-1.* knife, sword. D158.

nǫdьmi under compulsion. V218, D58.

nǫžd- *f-2.* constraint, force. V45, D58.

ny *pron.* we. V147, D214.

nyně now. V219.

nъ but. V372.

Ń

ńiv- *f-2.* field.

O

o *prep.* + L, A. about, concerning; in; at; around; on. V200–1.

o O, oh.

ob- *num.* both, the two. V156, 139, D215. ◆ ~ **na desęte** the twelve. V158, D215, 218.

oběcě-j- *vip.* promise. V63, D131.

oběcěnij- *n-1.* promise. V63, D131.

obět- *m-1.* promise.

obi- *vp.* go round. For conjugation, see **i-**.

obid-ě- *vp.* harm. V324.

obidьliv- *adj.* unjust, unrighteous.

oblast- *f-3.* district; power, authority. V208.

oblobyza-j- *vi.* kiss. V272.

oblьgъči- *vp.* lighten.

obniště-j- *vp.* become poor.

obrati- *vp.* bring back, return.

obraz- *m-1.* form, likeness.

obrět- *vp.* find. 1: **obrętj-**. V302, D252, 236.

obrěta-j- *vi.* find.

obrěz-a- *vp.* circumcise.

obrętj- *vp.* find. 2: **obrět-**. V302, D252, 236.

obrǫči- *vp.* betroth.

obyčěj- *m-1.* custom.

obьm- *vp.* embrace.

obьštenij- *n-1.* communion, fellowship.

ocěštenij- *n-1.* cleansing, purification. V84.

oč(es)- See **ok-es-**.

očisti- *vp.* cleanse.

očiště-j- *vi.* cleanse.

odě-j- *vp.* dress. V285, 277–78, D278, 281.

odrъž-ě- *vi.* contain. V324.

ogń- *m-1, 3.* fire. V103, D161–62, 145, 129.

ogręd- *vi.?* go round. V297, D246. ♦ lěta ~qcě of each year, annual.

ok-es- *n-1, 4.* eye. V111–12, 169, D171–72. oč-: Fem.du.: NAV oči, GL očiü, DI očima.

okonьčě-j- *vp.* complete, accomplish.

okrьstь round about. V196. ♦ ~ živ- live near, be a neighbor.

olěj- *m-1.* oil. V35, D35, 82.

*ol(ъ)tař- *m-1.* altar. V31.

on- *pron. adj.* that, he, she, it, they. V138, 140–41, D203, 206.

oplat- *m-1.* oblation.

opravьdanij- *n-1.* ordinance. V251–52.

orǫžij- *n-1.* weapon, arm. V166.

osěni- *vp.* overshadow, obumbrate.

oskǫdě-j- *vp.* be exhausted.

oslěpi- *vp.* blind.

osm- *adj.* eighth. V162, D219.

osǫdi- *vp.* condemn.

ostanъk- *m-1.* remnant. V209.

ostatъk- *m-1.* remnant. V209.

ostavi- *vp.* remit, leave.

ostoěnij- *n-1.* ♦ gradъ ostoěniě fortified town.

osušě-j- *vi.* dry up.

oti- *vp.* depart. For conjugation, see i-. V304, D278–79.

otroč-ęt- *n-4.* infant. V108–9, D168, 174.

otrok- *m-1.* servant.

otvrěz- See otvrьz-.

otvrьz- *vp.* open. otvrěz-: Inf., Sup., s-Aor. V296, D247.

otъ *prep.* + G. from, from among, of, by. V195. ♦ ~ kǫdu whence. V221. ♦ ~ selě henceforth. V222. ♦ ~ věka from the beginning of time, from the ages.

otъda- *vp.* give over, give up, render up. For conjugation see da-. V313, D277.

otъgъna- *vp.* drive off. 1: otъžen-. V310, D266.

otъim- *vp.* take away, free. V306, D249.

otъkǫdu whence. V221.

otъloži- *vp.* remit.

otъlǫči- sę *vp.* separate.

162

otъpad- *vp.* fall away. V298, D249.
otъplati- *vp.* requite.
otъpusti- *vp.* send away, dismiss, remit.
otъpuště-j- *vi.* forgive.
otъrek- *vp.* deny, reject; answer.
otъstǫpi- *vp.* withdraw.
otъved- *vp.* lead away. V297, D249.
otъvěstě-j- *vip.* answer. V327, D281.
otъvrěg- (sę) See otъvrьg- (sę).
otъvrьg- *vp.* cast away, drive off. otъvrěg-: Inf., Sup.
otъvrьg- sę *vp.* recant, deny. otъvrěg- sę: Inf., Sup. V299–300, D247, 249.
otъxodi- *vi.* depart. V325.
otъžen- *vp.* drive off. 2: otъgъna-. V310, D266.
otьc- *m-1.* father.
otьčьstv- *n-1.* homeland, family. V209.
otьm- *vp.* take away, free. V306, D246.
otьnǫdь quite.
oživi- *vp.* make live.

Q

qtrob- *f-2.* womb. loins, inmost parts. V209.
qz- *f-2.* bond.
qžik- *f-2.* kinswoman. V166.

P

pače more, rather. V136.
pad- *vp.* fall. V205, 321, 298, D249.
pakost- *f-3.* harm. V208.
pakostьnik- *m-1.* wrongdoer, tyrant. V211.
paky again. V205.
palic- *f-2.* staff. V211.
pamęt- *f-3.* memory. D173.
papež- *m-1.* pope.
pas- *vi.* feed, pasture, shepherd. V297, D246.
pastvinьn- *adj.* of pasture. V212.
pavьl- *m-1.* Paul (Παῦλος). V29, 39.
pepel- *m-1.* ash. V49, D93.

petr- *m-1.* Peter (Πέτρος).
pě- *vip.* sing. 1: **poj-**. Impf. on stem **poj-**. V284, D255–56, 55.
pěn- *f-2.* foam, froth.
pěnęʒ- *m-1.* coin, denarius, penny. V61, 89, D58, 160.
pěsn- *f-3.* song. V209.
pęt- *f-3.* five. V157, D217.
pi-j- *vip.* drink. V281.
pic- *f-2.* food. V63, 208.
pis-a- *vi.* write. V274, D268.
pišt- *f-2.* food. V208.
pitij- *n-1.* drinking. V251.
piv- *n-1.* drink. V209.
plaštanic- *f-2.* linen cloth. V211.
plěn- *m-1.* captivity.
plod- *m-1.* fruit. V93, D157.
plъt- *f-3.* flesh.
po *prep.* + D, L, A. according to, in virtue of, after, over, for.
V203–4. ◆ ~ **ńeže** since, because, inasmuch as. V372–73, 220.
◆ ~ **rędu** in order. ◆ ~ **srědě** in the middle. V197. ◆ ~ **suxu** on
dry land. ◆ **xodi-** ~ trace, follow.
pobědi- *vp.* overcome, conquer.
počiva-j- *vi.* rest. V332.
poda- *vp.* grant. For conjugation, see **da-**. V313, D277.
podoba-j- *vi.* be fitting.
podobьn- *adj.* similar. V188, 212.
podrug- *m-1.* companion.
podviʒa-j- *sę* *vi.* bestir oneself, fight. V330.
podъ *prep.* + I, A. beneath, under. V201.
podъgorij- *n-1.* hill country. V208, 215.
podъkopa-j- *vp.* undermine.
poganьsk- *adj.* pagan. V31, D118.
pogrebenij- *n-1.* burial. V251–52.
pogubi- *vp.* lose, destroy.
pogъna- *vp.* follow. 1: **požen-**. V310.
poi- *vp.* go. For conjugation, see **i-**. V303–4.
poim- *vp.* take. V306, D246.
poj- *vip.* sing. 2: **pě-**; Impf. on stem **poj-**. V284, D255–56, 55.
pokadi- *vp.* burn incense.

164

pokaj-a- sę *vp.* repent.
pokojьn- *adj.* peaceful. V212.
pokry-j- *vp.* conceal, cover, shelter. V282.
položi- *vp.* lay up, lay. V205, 317, 259.
polьȝ- *f-2.* benefit, profit.
pomaěnij- *n-1.* sign. V251–52.
pomaga-j- *vi.* help. V328.
pomaj-a- *vi.* make signs. V277, D272.
pomava-j- *vi.* make signs. V332.
pomě-nǫ-, pomę-nǫ- *vp.* remember. V324, D58.
pomil-ova- *vp.* have mercy on.
pomoc- *f-3.* help. V63, 208, D131.
pomog- *vp.* help, come in aid. V187, D246.
pomoli- sę *vp.* pray.
pomošt- *f-3.* help. V208, D173.
pomoštьnik- *m-1.* helper. V211.
pomysli- *vp.* think. V324.
pomyšľě-j- *vi.* ponder. V331.
pomьn-ě- *vi.* remember, think of.
ponošenij- *n-1.* reproach. V251–52.
poňeže since, because, inasmuch as. V372–73, 220.
pop- *m-1.* priest. V93, D156.
porazi- *vp.* smite.
porok- *m-1.* fault.
posěti- *vp.* visit.
poslědь finally. V220.
poslědьň- *adj.* last. V154.
poslušě-j- *vip.* obey, listen. V182, 327.
poslušьliv- *adj.* obedient. V213.
poslušьstv-ova- *vip.* witness.
posǫdi- *vp.* judge.
posrědě *adv., prep.* + G. in the midst. V219.
postavi- *vp.* place. V205.
postoj-ě- *vp.* stand.
postrad-a- *vp.* suffer. V272, 181.
postrašenij- *n-1.* threat.
postyd-ě- sę *vp.* be confounded, be put to shame.
posъl-a- *vp.* send. V271.

poštenij- *n-1.* fasting.
potopi- *vp.* submerge, drown.
potrъp-ě- *vp.* await, submit to.
potъk-nǫ- sę *vp.* stumble. V290, D260.
potьpěg- *f-2.* repudiated woman.
pouči- sę *vp.* learn, study.
povel-ě- *vp.* command.
povelěva-j- *vi.* command. V333.
pověda-j- *vi.* tell. V326.
pověst- *f-3.* narration, relation, history. V208.
povrěg- See **povrьg-**.
povrьg- *vp.* throw. **povrěg-:** Inf., Sup. V300, D247.
poxot- *f-3.* desire. V207.
pozna-j- *vp.* know, perceive.
požen- *vp.* follow. 2: **pogъna-.** V310.
požrě- See **požьr-**.
požьr- *vp.* swallow. **požrě:** Inf., Sup., Aor. V304-5, D247.
pǫt- *m-3.* way. V99-101, 103-4, D162.
prav- *adj.* right, of righteousness. V218. ◆ **pravy** rightly, truly.
V218.
pravьd- *f-2.* rectitude, virtue. V209.
pravьdьn- *adj.* righteous, just. V212-13.
prěbiva-j- *vi.* break. V332.
prěby- *vp.* remain. For conjugation, see **by-**. V312, D276, 279.
prěbyva-j- *vi.* remain, continue. V332.
prěda- *vp.* deliver, betray, commit, give up. For conjugation, see
da-. V312-13, D277, 280.
prědaj-a- *vi.* deliver, betray, commit, give up. V332.
prědrag- *adj.* most precious.
prědъ *prep.* + I, A. before, in the sight of. V201-2.
prědъi- *vp.* go before, precede. For conjugation, see **i-**. V303-4,
D278-79, 281.
prědъstoj-ě *vi.* stand by. V324, 340.
prěfacij- *f-2.* preface (Lat. *praefatio*).
prěgrěšenij- *n-1.* transgression. V215, 208.
prěľüb-ъv- *f-4.* adultery.
prěměni- *vp.* change.
prěmračьn- *adj.* darkest. V212-13.

166

prěpitě-j- *vp.* maintain, nourish, bring up. V265–66.
prěpodobij- *n-1.* piety, holiness. V208.
prěpodobьn- *adj.* holy. V137.
prěrěka-j- *vi.* quarrel, contradict. V328.
prěstavľenij- *n-1.* transposition (death). V251–52.
prěstoj-ě- *vi.* stand in attendance, attend. V324, 340.
prěstol- *m-1.* throne.
prětrьp-ě- *vp.* hold out.
prětyka-j- *vi.* oppose. V328.
prětykanij- *n-1.* obstacle. V251–52.
prěvez- *vp.* transport. V296.
prěžde before. V196.
pri- *vp.* come. For conjugation, see **i-**. D113.
priběg-nǫ- *vp.* take refuge. V290, D257.
priběž-ě- *vp.* take refuge.
priběžišt- *n-1.* refuge. V210.
približi-sę *vp.* approach.
pričęstьn- *adj.* associate, partaking. V212–13.
pričit- See **pričьt-**.
pričьt- *vp.* count among. **pričit-:** Inf., Sup., s-Aor. V298.
pričьtьnik- *m-1.* cleric. V211.
prijemľ- See **prijima-**.
prijima- *vi.* receive. 1: **prijemľ-**. V273, D268–69.
prijьm- *vp.* receive, accept, take. V55, 183, D113–14.
prikloni- *vp.* incline.
prikos-nǫ-sę *vp.* touch. V186, 289, D259.
prilež-ě- *vi.* tend. V186.
prilěpľ ě-j-sę *vi.* attach oneself to.
prines- *vp.* bring, offer.
prinos- *m-1.* offering. V206.
prinosi- *vi.* bring, offer.
prisno forever, ever. V216, D105.
prispě-j- *vp.* come.
pristavi- *vp.* place over.
pristǫpi- *vp.* come up.
prišьd- See **pri-**. V303, D278–79.
pritъč- *f-2.* parable. V27.
prived- *vp.* lead, bring up. V297, D249.

privlěk- *vp.* draw. V300, D247.

privrěg- See privrьg-.

privrьg- *vp.* cast against. privrěg-: Inf., Sup. V299–300, D247.

prizov- See prizъva-.

prizъva- *vp.* call on. 1: prizov-. V310, D266–67.

prizьr-ě- *vp.* look upon (with favor).

pročij- *adj.* other, remaining. ✦ pročee on, further, for the remaining time. V152, D203.

proda- *vp.* sell. For conjugation, see da-. V313, D277.

proglagol-a- *vp.* (begin to) speak. V270–71, 339.

progněva-j- sę *vp.* become angry.

prokažen- *adj.* leprous.

proklina-j- sę *vi.* perjure oneself.

proročьstv-ova- *vi.* prophesy.

prorok- *m-1.* prophet. V207.

prosi- *vip.* ask, beg. V182–83.

proslavi- *vp.* glorify, exalt.

proslavľ ě-j- *vi.* glorify, exalt. V330–31.

prosvěti- *vp.* give light to, enlighten.

prostran- *adj.* wide, vast. ✦ na ~ě in a spacious place.

prosvьt-ě- sę *vp.* light up, (make) shine.

protivi- sę *vip.* oppose. V323.

protivьn- *adj.* contumacious. V212–13.

prozьr-ě- *vp.* see. V336.

prǫg- *m-1.* locust.

prьv- *adj.* first. V154, 162, D219, 201. ✦ is ~ a from the beginning.

*psalm- *m-1.* psalm (ψαλμός). V115, 177, D39, 45, 184.

*psilos- *m-1.* aphid (ψύλλος).

pust- *adj.* deserted.

pusti- *vp.* let go. V258.

pustoš- *f-3.* vanity. V208.

pustyń- *f-2.* desert. Nom.sg. -i. V98, D175–76.

puště-j- *vi.* send away, let go.

pъsalъm- *m-1.* psalm (ψαλμός). V115, 17, D39, 45, 184.

pъtic- *f-2.* bird.

pьř-ě- sę *vi.* dispute.

pьsa- *vi.* write. 1: pisj-. V274, D268.

168

R

rab- *m-1.* servant. V49, 180, D60.

rab- *f-2.* handmaiden. V208.

rači- *vi.* deign.

radi *postp.* + G. because of, for the sake of. V193, 197.

radost- *f-3.* joy. V208.

radostьn- *adj.* joyful. V212–13.

radošt- *f-2.* exultation. V218.

rad-ova- sę *vi.* rejoice. V187.

rafail- *m-1.* Raphael ('Ραφαήλ).

rak- *f-2.* shrine.

ram- *n-1.* shoulder.

raspada-j- sę *vi.* fall apart. V327.

rast- *vi.* grow. V298, D246.

rastače-j- *vi.* disperse, scatter. V331.

rastaj-a- sę *vp.* melt away. V277, D271.

rasti- sę *vi.* grow. V298, D246.

rastoči- *vp.* disperse, scatter.

*ravvi *indecl.* rabbi, master (ῥαββί).

razboj- *m-1.* murder.

razbojьnik- *m-1.* robber, murderer. V211.

razděľě-j- *vi.* divide. V330–31.

razdrěšenij- *n-1.* absolution. V251–52, 68, D122.

razdrěši- *vp.* loose. V68, D122.

razgněva-j- sę *vp.* become angry.

razi- sę *vp.* be broken up. For conjugation, see i-.

razlěj- sę *vp.* stream away. 2: razlija-. V279–80, D271, 273.

razlija- sę *vp.* stream away. 1: razlěj-. V279–80, D271, 273.

razlǫčě-j- sę *vi.* be separated, put asunder.

razum- *m-1.* knowledge.

razumě-j- *vip.* know, perceive, understand. V182, 187, 324, 327.

razvě *prep.* + G. except.

razvrati- *vp.* pervert.

raždeg-, raždьg- *vp.* inflame, heat up. V300, 82, D248, 136.

rek- *vp.* say. V301, 321, 326, D246, 248.

rěk- *f-2.* river.

rěsnot- *f-2.* truth. V208, D105.

rěsnotivьn- *adj.* true, certain. V212.

ręd- *m-1.* order. V91, D154, 156. ♦ po ~u in order.

riz- *f-2.* garment.

rod- *m-1.* generation, relationship, family. V92–93, D154, 157.

rodi- *vp.* bear. V323. ~ sę be born.

rodьstv- *n-1.* birth. V209, D131.

rog- *m-1.* horn.

rovanij- *f-2?* gift.

roždenij- *n-1.* birth, family. V209.

roždьstv- *n-1.* birth.

rǫg- *m-1.* mockery.

rǫk- *f-2.* hand. V169–70.

rǫženij- *n-1.* censure, slander. V251–52.

rъpъt-a- *vi.* murmur. V272, D110.

S.

s- See by-.

s- *pron. adj.* this. V139–41, 99, 168, D208–9.

sam- *pron. adj.* self. V138, 150, D207, 203.

samovidьc- *m-1.* eyewitness. V210.

samovlastьc- *m-1.* autocrat. V210.

*sampson- *m-1.* Samson (Σαμψών).

san- *m-1.* office. V92, D157.

se behold. V220.

sedm- *f-3.* seven. V157, 160, D217.

selě ♦ otъ ~ henceforth. V222.

sevastij- *f-2.* Sebaste (Σεβαστεία).

sěd- *vp.* sit down. 1: sęd-. V205, 321, D246, 249.

sěd-ě- *vi.* sit. V325.

sěm-en- *n-4.* seed. V109, D168, 173–74.

sěn- *f-3.* shadow. V103.

sět- *f-3.* net.

sę *refl. pron.* V147–49, 172–73, 184–85, D213–14.

sęd- *vp.* sit down. 2: sěd-. V205, 321, D246, 249.

sętъ he says. V306–7, D279, 281.

sice thus, in this way. V222.

sijě-j- *vi.* shine. V280.

*sikera *f. indecl.* strong drink (σίκερα). V118–19.

sil- *f-2.* power, strength, virtue.

silьn- *adj.* powerful, mighty. V212.

simon- *m-1.* Simon (Σίμων).

simonov- *adj.* (son) of Simon. V132.

sirěčь that is to say. V253.

skot- *m-1.* cattle.

skozě *prep.* + A. through. V194.

skrъb-ě- *vi.* be distressed, be sad. V262.

skrъbьn- *adj.* sorrowful. V212.

skvrьnost- *f-3.* stain. V208.

slab- *adj.* weak.

sladъk- *adj.* sweet. V213.

slan- *f-2.* hoarfrost.

slav- *f-2.* glory.

slavi- *vi.* glorify.

slavьn- *adj.* noble, glorious. V212–13.

slěd- *m-1.* trace, track. ♦ **vъ** ~**ъ** after. V197.

slěp- *adj.* blind. V171.

slov-es- *n-1, 4.* word; homily; case. V96, 110, D169–71.

slug- *m-2.* servant, minister. V165.

slušě-j- *vi.* listen to. V182, 325.

služi- *vi.* officiate as priest. serve.

služb- *f-2.* ministry, service. V209.

slyš-ě- *vip.* hear. V261, D93, 95.

slyšitъ Cloz. 2r35. Emend to *lьstitъ*: **lьsti-** *vi.* deceive.

slъnьc- *n-1.* sun. V177.

sněg- *m-1.* snow.

sodomьsk- *adj.* of Sodom (Σόδομα). V213.

sǫdi- *vip.* judge. V187.

sǫdij- *m-2.* judge. Nom.sg.: -**i.** V97–99, 165, 208, D176–77.

sǫsěd- *m-1.* neighbor.

srěd- *f-2.* middle. ♦ **po** ~**ě** in the middle. V197.

srьdьc- *n-1.* heart. V211, 95.

sta- *vp.* stand up. 1: **stan-**. V288, D278, 281.

stan- *vp.* stand up. 2: **sta-**. V288, D278, 281.

star- *adj.* old.

starost- *f-3.* old age. V208.

starьc- *m-1.* elder. V210, 89, D160.

stepenьn- *adj.* of degrees, of ascents. V212–13.

stoj-ě- *vi.* stand. V324.
stran- *f-2.* country, region.
straši- *vi.* threaten.
strax- *m-1.* fear.
straž- *f-2.* watch.
strěg- *vi.* guard. V301, D246, 248.
studen- *adj.* cold.
studen- *f-3.* cold. V207.
stьʒ- *f-2.* path.
suetьn- *adj.* vain, idle. V212–13.
suši- *vi.* dry.
sux- *adj.* dry. ✦ po ~u on dry land.
sverěp- *adj.* wild.
svěšt- *f-2.* torch. V208.
svět- *m-1.* world, light. V176–77.
světilьnik- *m-1.* lantern. V211.
svęt- *adj.* holy, saint. V154, 171. ✦ ~ dux- Holy Ghost, Spirit.
svęti- *vi.* sanctify, bless. V323.
svoj- *refl. poss. pron.* V138, 149–50, 173, D207–8.
syn- *m-1.* son. V90–91, 178, D152–57.
sъ *prep.* + G, I. from; with. V202. ✦ ~ vyše from on high. V193, 219.
sъber- *vp.* gather. 2: sъbьra-. V309, D266.
sъbira-j- *vip.* gather.
sъblȗd- *vp.* keep, observe. V297.
sъbǫd- sę See sъby- sę. V311–12, D276.
sъby- sę *vp.* be fulfilled. For conjugation, see by-. V311–12, D276.
sъbьra- *vp.* gather. 1: sъber-. V309, D266.
sъdravij- *n-1.* health, healing. V208.
sъdrъž-ě- *vi.* hold fast. V324.
sъgrěšě-j- *vi.* sin. V330–31.
sъgrěši- *vp.* sin.
sъizvěst-ova- *vi.* testify together with.
sъkaza-j- *vi.* show. V327.
sъklěště-j- sę *vi.* press together. V330–31.
sъkruši- *vp.* shatter, break.
sъkry-j- *vp.* conceal. V282.

172

sъlěz- *vp.* descend. V296, D246.
sъmet- *vp.* sweep up. V298, D246.
sъměrьn- *adj.* humble, lowly. V212–13.
sъmeŕen- *adj.* humble, lowly.
sъměŕenij- *n-1.* lowliness. V251–52.
sъmęt- sę *vp.* be troubled. V298, D246.
sъmrьtьn- *adj.* of death. V212–13.
sъmysl- *m-1.* mind, understanding, reason.
sъmyšľ ě-j- *vi.* think.
sъn- *m-1.* sleep.
sъněd- *vp.* eat, consume. For conjugation, see **ěd-**. V313–14, D277.
sъni- *vp.* come down. For conjugation, see **i-**. V303–4, D278–79.
sъnitij- *n-1.* descent. V251–52. ♦ ~ **grobьn-** the descent into Hell. V212–13.
sъnьm- *m-1.* congregation.
sъnьmišt- *n-1.* synagogue. V210.
sъpa- *vi.* sleep. 1: **sъpi-**. V263, D218.
sъpas- *m-1.* savior. V207.
sъpas- *vp.* save. V297, D246.
sъpasa-j- *vi.* save.
sъpasenij- *n-1.* salvation. V251–52.
sъpasьn- *adj.* saving. V212–13.
sъpi- *vi.* sleep. 2: **sъpa-**. V263, D278.
sъpodobi- *vp.* deem worthy, consider sth. (A) as requiring sth. (D).
sъrica-j- *vi.* ~ **slovo** settle accounts with. V328.
sъsǫd- *m-1.* vessel.
sъšьd- See **sъni-**.
sъt- *n-1.* hundred.
sъtęž-ě- *vp.* make trial of. V325.
sъtęza-j- *vp.* ~ **o slovesi** settle accounts.
sъtǫžě-j- *vi.* oppress, afflict.
sъtvori- *vp.* do, work, make. V318, 336, 320. ♦ ~ **sъvětъ** take counsel.
sъtьŕ-, sъtьr- *vp.* pulverize. **sъtrъ-**: Inf., Sup., PfAP. V284, 305, D253.
sъved- *vp.* join, bring together.
sъvědě- *vi.* be conscious. For conjugation, see **vedě-**. V323, D278.

sъvěst-ova- *vi.* acknowledge.
sъvěště-j- *vp.* deliberate, conspire. ♦ ~ slovo make reckoning with.
sъvět- *m-1.* council, counsel.
sъvęz-a- *vp.* bind. V272.
sъvrěg- See sъvrьg-.
sъvrьg- *vp.* cast off. sъvrěg-: Inf., Sup. V300, D247.
sъvrьši- *vp.* prepare, put in readiness, fulfill, make perfect.
sъxodi- *vi.* come down.
sъxrani- *vp.* preserve.
sъxranьno securely.
sъžeg- *vp.* burn up. Stem 1 also sъžьg-. V300, D298.
sъžěli- si *vp.* be distressed. V350.
sьrebrol´übl´enij- *n-1.* love of money. V251–52.
sьrebrol´übьstvij- *n-1.* love of money. V208–9.

Š

šest- *adj.* sixth. V161–62, D219.
šętanij- *n-1.* blustering, insolence. V251–52.
štedrot- *f-2.* mercy. V208.
šьd- See i-.

T

t- *pron. adj.* that, he, she, it, they. V138, 140–41, 171, D207.
♦ kъ ~omu ne no longer. V220. ♦ ~ěmь že therefore. V373.
t- že, t- ze (KM) *pron. adj.* the same. V141, D207, 203, 205.
taji- sę *vi.* conceal oneself (in retirement).
tajьn- *f-2.* secret, mystery. V212.
tak- *pron. adj.* such. V138, 159, 152, D207.
tako thus, so. V222.
takov- *pron. adj.* such. V153.
takožde, takoze (KM) likewise.
takože likewise. V63, 222.
takyže so.
*talant- *m-1.* talent (τάλαντον). D184.
tamo there.
teofil- *m-1.* Theophilus (Θεόφιλος).
těl-es- *n-1, 4.* body. V110, 96, 177, D169–71.
tělesьn- *adj.* of the body. V212–13.

těmь že therefore, likewise. V373.
tęgost- *f-3.* burden. V208.
tęʒ-a- *vip.* demand, ask. V273.
ti and, then. V373, 160, 162.
to then. V373.
togda then. V50, 221, D93, 106, 123.
toli then. V222.
tolik- *pron. adj.* so great, so much, so many. V153–54, D213.
tolьmi so much, to such a degree. V222.
topl- *adj.* warm. V50, D93.
toplot- *f-2.* warmth. V208, D93.
tr- *num.* three. V156, D217.
trapěz- *f-2.* table (τράπεζα).
trepet- *m-1.* trembling.
trepet-a- *vi.* tremble before. V272, 183.
tretij- *adj.* third. V161–62, D219.
tretijici for the third time. V223, D114, 220.
tręs- *vi.* shake, agitate. V297, D246.
tręsavic- *f-2.* fever. V211.
trofon- *m-1.* Tryphon (Τρύφων).
troic- *f-2.* trinity. V211.
trǫt- *m-1.* watch, guard.
tu there, here.
tuz- *adj.* of another, foreign. V63, D13, and see **tužd-**.
tužd- *adj.* of another, foreign. V75, 154, D213, 203–4, 140–41.
tvar- *f-3.* creation, creature. V207.
tvoj- *pron. adj.* thy. V138, 149–50, D207–8.
tvori- *vi.* do, make. V318, 320. ✦ **tvoŕen- kvas-** strong drink.
tvrьd- *f-3.* firmness. V207.
tvrьd- *adj.* solid, firm.
ty *pron.* thou. V147–48, 192, D213–14.
tьgda = **togda**.
tьkъmo unless.
tьšt- *adj.* empty. ✦ **za ~ee** See **xrani-**.
tьštetьn- *adj.* vain. V212–13.
tьšt-ě- sę *vi.* hasten.
tьm- *f-2.* darkness; myriad. V159, D218.

tьmьěn- *m-1*. (act of burning) incense (θυμίαμα). V32, 118, D28–29, 38, 46, 186.
tьmьn- *adj*. dark, of darkness. V212–13.
tьmьnic- *f-2*. prison. V211.

U

ubal-ova- *vp*. heal.
ubi-j- *vp*. kill. V280, D254.
ubo now, indeed, then. V373.
uboj-ě- sę *vp*. take fear. D262.
učenik- *m-1*. disciple. V211.
uči- *vi*. teach, counsel. V187.
učiteľ- *m-1*. teacher. V210.
udari- *vp*. strike.
udivi- *vp*. make wonderful, show marvelously.
uędri- *vp*. hurry, hasten.
ugodi- *vp*. take pleasure in. V187.
ugot-ova- *vp*. make ready, prepare.
ukori- *vp*. despise.
ukrad- *vp*. steal. V298, D246.
um- *m-1*. mind, understanding. V177.
umasti- *vp*. anoint.
umlьč-ě- *vp*. fall silent. D262.
umoli- *vp*. implore. V257–58.
umrě- See umьr-.
umrьtvi- *vp*. kill.
umy-j- *vp*. wash. D254.
umъnoži- *vp*. multiply.
umьr- *vp*. die. umrě-: Inf., Sup., Aor. V305, D246.
uničьženij- *m-1*. contempt, disdain. V251–52.
upaě-j- *vi*. intoxicate. V331.
upodobi- *vp*. liken, make like. V187.
upъva-j- *vip*. trust, hope. V191, 327.
upъvanij- *n-1*. hope. V251–52.
urěz-a- *vp*. cut off. V272.
uril- *m-1*. Uriel (Ούριήλ). V180–81.
uslyš-ě- *vp*. hear. V325, 261, D93, 95, 262.
uslъš-ě- *vp*. hear. V261, D93, 95, 262.

176

ust- *n-1. pl.* mouth. V166.
ustrьmľenij- *m-1.* violence, wrath. V251–52.
ustьn- *f-2.* lips. V169.
usъp-nǫ- *vp.* fall asleep. Aor. **usъnǫ-, usъp-.** Vb. subst.
  usъpenij-. PAP **usъpъš-.** V291, D257, 260.
uš- See **ux-es-.**
utěši- *vp.* comfort. V260.
utęg-nǫ- *vp.* be able. V290, D260.
utoli- *vp.* check.
utr- *n-1.* morning. V35, D78.
utrьń- *adj.* morning. V214.
utvrьdi- *vp.* strengthen.
utvrьždenij- *n-1.* certainty, confirmation. V251–52.
uvědě- *vp.* learn. For conjugation, see **vědě-.** V323, D278.
uvy alack! woe! V219.
ux-es- *n-1, 4.* ear. **uš-:** Du.: NAV **uši,** GL **ušiü,** DI **ušima.** V112,
  169, D169, 171–72.
uzьr-ě- *vp.* behold. V326.
užěs- *m-1.* fear, distress.

Ü

ün- *adj.* young. V78.
ünost- *f-3.* youth.
ünoš- *m-2.* youth. V165.
üže already. V35, 219, D43, 78.

V

va *pron.* you two. V147–49, D213–14.
vaš- *pron. adj.* your. V149, 138, D207.
večer- *m-1.* evening.
ved- *vip.* lead. V297, 318, 325, D249.
veliči- *vi.* magnify, extol.
veličij- *n-1.* great things, glory. V208.
veličьstv- *n-1.* glory. V209.
velij- *adj.* great. V131, 119–20, D190–91, 198.
velik- *adj.* great. V131.
velьmi greatly, very. V218.
veseli- *vi.* cause to rejoice. ~ **sę** rejoice.

veselij- *n-1.* exultation. V208.

vešt- *f-3.* fact, matter.

vě *pron.* we two. V147–48, 180, D213–14.

věčьn- *adj.* eternal. V212–13.

věd- See vědě-.

vědě- *vi.* know. věd-: Non-past (exc. 3pl.; sg. věmь/vědě, věsi, věstъ, du. věvě, věste, věsta, pl. věmъ, věste, vědętъ), PrAP, PrPP. vědi-: Non-past 3pl., Impv. (sg. věždь). V314–16, 323, D278, 280.

vědi- See vědě-.

věk- *m-1.* age. ✦ do ~a for evermore. ✦ otъ ~a from the beginning, from the ages. ✦ vъ ~y eternally. ✦ vъ ~ъ eternally.

věnik-? *m-1?* branch?

věnьc- *m-1.* wreath, crown. V210.

věnьčě-j- *vip.* crown. V322.

věr- *f-2.* belief, faith. ✦ ~ǫ im- *vp.* come to believe. V326.

věr-ova- *vi.* believe. V326.

věrьn- *adj.* faithful. V212–13.

vid-ě- *vip.* see. Impv. ending -ь in sg. V262, 182, 326, D262.

viděnij- *n-1.* vision. V251–52.

vidim- *adj.* visible. V247, D262.

vilitis- *m-1.* centipede? (φυλλίτης).

vin- *n-1.* wine; vine.

vin- *f-2.* fault.

vlad- *vi.* rule.

vladyk- *m-2.* lord, ruler. V165.

vlasteľ- *m-4.* principality. V210, 107, 167, D166–67.

vlьn- *f-2.* wave.

vod- *f-2.* water.

vodьn- *adj.* of water. V212–13.

voevod- *m-2.* commander. V165, 175.

voin- *m-1.* soldier. V167, D166.

voľ- *f-2.* will.

voz- *m-1.* wagon, cart.

vrag- *m-1.* enemy.

vražij- *adj.* hostile, of the enemy. V213, D190.

vražьd-ova- *vi.* be enemies (with).

vrěm-en- *n-4.* time, season, phase (of the moon). V108–9, D173–74.

vrěmę See **vrěm-en-**.

vrъxos- *m-1.* weevil? (βροῦχος).

vrьt- *m-1.* garden.

vrьtograd- *m-1.* garden.

vrьx- *m-1.* top. V91, D154, 156.

vrьxu *prep.* + G. on top of. V218, 196.

vy *pron.* you. V147–49, 179, D214.

vyj- *f-2.* neck.

vynes- *vp.* remove. V337, 297, D282.

vyše higher. V135. ✦ **sъ** ~ from on high. V219, 193.

vyšьń- *adj.* most high. V214.

vъ *prep.* + L, A, G. among, within, in, into, to, on, at. V198–200, D78, 126–27. ✦ ~ **istinǫ** accurately. ✦ ~ **malě** for a little time. ✦ ~ **slědъ** after. V197. ✦ ~ **věky** eternally. ✦ ~ **vekъ** eternally.

vъcěsaŕi-sę *vp.* reign.

vъčit- See **vъčьt-**.

vъčьt- *vp.* reckon in, include. **vъčit-:** Inf., Sup., s-Aor. V298, D247, 249.

vъkupě See **kup-**.

vъkupьn- *adj.* collective. V212–13.

vъlěz- *vp.* enter. V296, D249.

vъlitij- *n-1.* infusion. V208, 251–52.

vъnemľ- *vi.* attend to. 2: **vъnima-**. V273–74, D268–69.

vъnezaapǫ suddenly. D83, 113.

vъně *adv., prep.* + G. outside, without. V217–18, 196–97, D282.

vъni- *vp.* enter. For conjugation, see **i-**. V303–4, 73, D278–79, 281.

vъnima- *vi.* attend to. 1: **vъnemľ-**. V273–74, 73, D268–69.

vъnǫtrьń- *adj.* inner. V214, D126.

vъnъ *adv., prep.* + G. out, out of; away, outside. V53, 217–18, D78, 282.

vъnьm- *vp.* take. V73, 306, 187.

vъpi-j- *vi.* cry, shout. V33, 281, D78, 109, 254.

vъplъti- *vp.* incarnate.

vъprosi- *vp.* ask. V182.

vъrěsni-sę *vp.* become rooted.

vъsadi- *vp.* put into (prison). V205, 259.
vъseli- *vp.* take up abode, settle.
vъsěl'ě-j- *vi.* settle, establish. V331.
vъsijě-j- *vp.* shine forth.
vъsklad- *vp.* load. V298.
vъskoči- *vp.* jump in, up.
vъskrai See kraj-.
vъskrěsi- *vp.* raise up.
vъskrъs-nǫ- *vp.* arise. V289, D259.
vъsǫd- *m-l.* communion. V46.
vъsǫdьn- *adj.* communion. V212–13.
vъspętь back(wards). V219.
vъspitě-j- *vp.* nourish, raise, rear. V265–66.
vъspomę-nǫ- *vp.* recall, recollect. V287–88, 46, D58.
vъsprěštenij- *n-l.* threat, menace. V251–52.
vъsta- *vp.* arise, rise up. 1: vъstan-. V288, D278, 281.
vъstan- *vp.* arise. 2: vъsta-. V288, D278, 281.
vъstok- *m-l.* dawn.
vъstrepet-a- *vp.* set to trembling, begin to quake. V272.
vъsue idly, without reason, in vain. V219.
vъsxodi- *vi.* ascend.
vъsxot-ě- *vp.* conceive love for, love. For conjugation, see xot-ě-.
vъsyp-a- *vp.* scatter into. V330.
vъšьd- See vъni-.
vъved- *vp.* lead in. V297, D249.
vъvrěg- See vъvrъg-.
vъvrъg- *vp.* cast in. vъvrěg-: Inf., Sup. V300, 326, D247.
vъxodi- *vi.* enter.
vъxodьn- *adj.* of entrance. V212–13.
vъz *prep.* + A. for. V194, D78, 86. ♦ vъs krai near. V197.
vъzbrańě-j- *vi.* prohibit, forbid. V330–31.
vъzbudi- *vp.* awaken. V317.
vъzda- *vp.* give back. For conjugation, see da-. V337, 313.
vъzdaj-a- *vi.* give back. V332.
vъz(d)rad-ova- sę *vp.* rejoice. V68, D122.
vъzdrast- *vp.* grow. V68, 298, D122.
vъzdux- *m-l.* air.
vъzdyxa-j- *vi.* sigh. V275.

180

vъzdvig-nǫ- *vp.* raise. V289, D259.

vъzglašenij- *n-1.* part of prayer prounounced in a loud voice, ecphonesis. V251–52.

vъzgnĕti- *vp.* kindle.

vъzigra-j- sę *vp.* leap.

vъzira-j- *vi.* look at. V328.

vъziska-j- *vi.* search for. V182–83.

vъzlaga-j- *vi.* lay on.

vъzlak-a- sę *vp.* hunger. V272, D60.

vъzloži- *vp.* lay on. V259.

vъzľübi- *vp.* conceive love for, love, lust afer.

vъzmog- *vp.* be able, increase, grow. V301, D246.

vъznenavid-ĕ- *vp.* conceive hatred for.

vъznes- *vp.* exalt, raise. V297, D246.

vъzov- *vp.* cry out. 2: vъzъva-. V310, D266–67.

vъzveliči- *vp.* manifest wonderfully.

vъzveseli- *vp.* cause to rejoice.

vъzvrati- *vp.* return. ♦ ~ sę *vp.* return.

vъzъpi-j- *vp.* cry out. V281, D254.

vъzъva- *vp.* cry out. 1: vъzov-. V310, D266–67.

vъzъm- *vp.* receive, take on, take up. V306, D246.

vъzъr-ĕ- *vp.* look up.

vъždęd-a- sę *vp.* thirst. V272.

vъžľübi- *vp.* lust after, conceive love for, love.

vьčerašьń- *adj.* of yesterday. V214.

vьs- *pron. adj.* all, whole. V151–52, 168, 61–2, 179–80, D141–43, 205, 208, 133–35, 70.

vьsemog-ǫšt- *PrAP.* almighty.

vьsevladyk- *m-2.* lord of all. V165.

vьsĕčьsk- *adj.* of all kinds. D143, 205, 212.

vьsĕk- *pron. adj.* every. V61–62, 150–51, D141–43, 205.

X

*xerovim-, xi-, -ru- *m-1.* Cherubim (χερουβίμ). V32, D181, 41.

xlĕb- *m-1.* bread. V177.

xodatai- *vi.* intercede.

xodi- *vi.* go (in a course of life). V317–18, 325–26, D94. ♦ ~ po + L trace, follow.

xot-ě- vi. wish, desire. **xot-j-:** Non-past (exc. 3pl.), Impv. V262–63 183, 187, 50, D278, 281.

xot-j- See **xot-ě-**.

xrani- vi. hold, guard, keep. V258. ◆ ~ **suetь na za tь štee** "pay regard to vain idols" (Ps 30.7).

xrist- m-1. Christ (Χριστός). V53, 115, D38.

xudosilь n- adj. weak of body.

xudoumь n- adj. weak of mind.

xval- f-2. praise.

xvali- vi. praise.

Z

za prep.+ G, A, I. for, by. V202–3. ◆ ~ ńe inasmuch as. V220, 368–69.

zaby- vp.. forget. For conjugation, see **by-**. V311–12, 327, D276.

začęl- n-1. beginning.

začь n- vp. begin, conceive. V306, D246.

zai- vp. descend. For conjugation, see **i-**. V303–4, D278–79.

zaklep-nǫ- vp. close up, secure. V291, D257.

zaklina-j- vi. conjure. V328, 191.

zakon- m-1. law.

zakonoprěstǫpь n- adj. law-transgressing. V212–13.

zakonoprěstǫpь nik- m-1. transgressor of the law. V211.

zakonь nik- m-1. priest. V211.

zamatorě-j- vp. advance in years, mature. V50.

zamysl- m-1. intention.

zańe inasmuch as. V368–69, 220.

zapověd- f-3. commandment. V207.

zapověda-j- vi. instruct, command. V326.

zaprěště-j- vi. conjure. V330–31.

zastǫpi- vp. protect.

zastǫpь nik- m-1. protector, champion. V211.

zaščiti- vp. protect.

zaštititeľ- m-1. protector, defender. V210.

zatvařě-j- vi. close. V330–31.

zatvori- vp. shut, hand over. V338.

zavět- m-1. covenant.

zaxarij- m-2. Zacharias (Ζαχαρίας). V117.

182

zaxarijin- *adj.* of Zacharias. V133.
zemľ-, zemj- *f-2.* earth, ground. V63–64, D132.
zemľьsk-, zemьn- *adj.* of the earth. V213.
zmij- *m-1.* serpent. V93, 177, D160.
zna-j- *vi.* know.
znamenij- *n-1.* sign. V208.
zǫb- *m-1.* tooth.
zъl- *f-3.* wickedness. V207.
zъl- *n-1.* evil.
zъl- *adj.* evil, wicked.
zъlob- *f-2.* malignity, wickedness. V209, D178.
zьr-ě- *vi.* see. V182.

3

ʒělo very, very much.
ʒěluto (ʒělo ľüto) very cruel.
ʒvězd- *f-2.* star.

Ž

že *enclitic.* and, now, but. V368. ♦ **ešte že** still.
žen- *f-2.* wife, woman.
ženьsk- *adj.* of women. V213, 133–34.
ženьstv- *n-1.* femininity, muliebrity. V209.
žestok- *adj.* harsh. V213.
žęd-a-, žęda-j- *vi.* thirst. V272, 181.
žętv- *f-2.* harvest (time). V209.
žid-, žьd- *vi.* wait for. 2: **žьda-**. V310, 266–67.
ži- *vi.* live. 1: **živ-**. V303, 326, D248–50, 255, 125.
žitij- *n-1.* life. V208.
živ- *vi.* live. 2: **ži-**. V303, 326, D248–50, 255, 125. ♦ **okrъstь ~** be a neighbor.
živ- *adj.* alive, living. V154, 326.
živi- *vp.* give life.
život- *m-1.* life.
životьn- *adj.* of life. V211–13.
žrěbij- *m-1.* lot, fate. V208, 88, D159.
žьda- *vi.* wait for. 1: **žid-, žьd-**. V310, 182, D266–67.
žьzl- *m-1.* rod.

APPENDICES

APPENDIX A

PHONOLOGY

A. *Inventory and combination*

The largest unit in phonology is the WORD, which consists of one or more syllables.

A SYLLABLE contains a vowel as its final element, preceded by zero or more consonants.

A VOWEL (V) is the element necessarily present in final position in the syllable. The vowels of OCS are subdivided into two types on the basis of articulation, front or back (tongue position), and with one exception can be arranged as front-back pairs.

Back = V^B	*u*	*o*	*a*	*ъ*	*y*		*o*
Front = V^F	*ü*	*e*	*ě*	*ь*	*i*	*ę*	*ǫ̈*

The pronunciation traditionally ascribed to OCS vowels is identical to that of analogous Russian vowels under stress. The approximate English or other European equivalents are provided below.

u	E b<u>oo</u>t	ü	E <u>u</u>se
o	E <u>or</u>	e	E b<u>e</u>t
a	E bl<u>ah</u>	ě	E b<u>a</u>t The OCS vowel ě is called jat' [yaht'].
ъ	E b<u>u</u>t A lax, high-mid, back vowel called back jer [yér].	ь	E b<u>i</u>t A lax, high-mid, front vowel called front jer.
y	R b<u>y</u>t A tense, high, central vowel called jery [yi-rée].	i	E f<u>ee</u>t
		ę	Fr v<u>in</u>, f<u>aim</u>
ǫ	Fr t<u>on</u>, <u>bon</u>	ǫ̈	Fr br<u>un</u>, Verd<u>un</u>

In unblocked position (not preceded by a consonant), front vowels are pronounced with preceding [j], e.g. *estъ* [je], *znaę* [ję], but *se* [e], *sę* [ę].

A CONSONANT (C) is any element that cannot occupy final position in the syllable. The consonants are subdivided into four classes: neutral (labials and dentals), velar, semi-soft (dental affricates), and soft (palatals). They can be arranged according to their combinability in clusters into five rows as follows:

	1	2	3	4	5
Neutral = C^N	s		p t		
	z		b d		
				m n	l r
				v	
Velar = C^V		k x			
		g			
Semi-soft = C^{SS}			c		
			ʒ		
Soft = C^S	š		č ѱ		
	ž		ѫ		
				ń	ľ ŕ

1 = sibilants (dental and palatal)
2 = velar obstruents
3 = nonvelar obstruents (labial, dental, palatal)
4 = nonliquid sonorants (nasal, glide)
5 = liquid sonorants
The vertically paired plosives, sibilants, and affricates are ordered voiceless/ voiced.

The pronunciation traditionally ascribed to OCS consonants is approximately equivalent to that of the analogous consonants in Russian with the following caveats. Before front vowels, neutral consonants are pronounced with moderate palatalization (softening), e.g., *ti* [t'], *bě* [b'] (compare *ta* [t], *by* [b]). Soft and semisoft consonants are pronounced with full palatalization in all environments, e.g., *čisto* [č'], *cělo* [c'], *stьʒa* [ʒ'].

The dental affricates *c* and *ʒ* are pronounced approximately as in E ca<u>ts</u> and a<u>dz</u>e, respectively, but with full palatalization. The soft consonants symbolized as ѱ and ҡ represent the OCS reflexes of Common Slavic sequences **tj* and **dj*, respectively. Originally these were probably palatovelar *k̂* and *ĝ*, but local usage permitted a wide range of variation. Texts of Macedono-Bulgarian origin suggest phonetic sequences [šk̂] or [š't'] and [ž'g'] or [ž'd']. Texts of Moravian-Pannonian origin have reflexes *c* and *z* rather than ѱ and ҡ, respectively.

Syllable types

V	-	any vowel but ъ, ь, y
CV	-	*not* C^N + *ü, ǫ̈*
	-	*not* C^V + V^F
	-	*not* C^{SS} + V^B other than *a*
	-	*not* C^S + V^B (except in composition)
CC(C)V	-	no geminates
	-	obstruents follow only sibilants
	-	sibilant agrees in voice with following obstruent

Ideal OCS syllable types preclude specific combinations as indicated above in three general groupings. The absence of these combinations is predicted from the operation of actualization rules (see below). In type V, the jers and jery are excluded by virtue of their inability to stand alone. In type CV, consequences of syllabic synharmony disallow the realization of particular combinations of consonant and vowel. In such cases, the actualization rules determine that the consonant will effect a change in the vowel or vice-versa. In type CC(C)V, actualization rules limit tolerated sequences. The permitted sequences preserve the order of the five rows above, for example, *sp* (1+3) is possible, *ps* (3+1) is not. Rare exceptions to these rules are found in foreign words.

B. Actualization

$$V \left\{ \begin{array}{llllllll} V^B & u & o & a & ъ & y & & ǫ \\ V^F & ü & e & ě & ь & i & ę & ǫ̈ \end{array} \right.$$

j

$$C \left\{ \begin{array}{llllllllllll} C^N & s & z & t & d & n & l & r & p & b & m & v \\ C^S & š & ž & č & Ψ & ʌʀ & ń & ľ & ŕ & pľ & bľ & mľ & vľ \\ C^V & x & g & k \\ C^{SS} & ʒ & c \end{array} \right.$$

$$\left\{ \begin{array}{llllllllll} C^N & st & zd & sn & zn & sl & tr & dr & str \\ C^S & Ψ & Ψ & ʌʀ & šń & žń & šľ & Ψŕ & ʌʀr & Ψŕ & šv \\ C^V & sk & & & & & & & & & xv \\ C^{SS} & sc & & & & & & & & & sv \end{array} \right.$$

1.	$[C^S\_, C^{SS}\_, j\_, Ci\_, ji\_]$	$V^B \downarrow V^F$; $ě_2 \downarrow i$
	a.	on $C \downarrow$ ǫ̈C
	b.	$y_2 \downarrow i$
	c. $[C^{SS}\_]$	$a \downarrow a$
	d. $[Vj\_, \#j\_]$	ъ, ь $\downarrow i$
2.	$[\_]$	$j \downarrow \varnothing$
3.	$[\_V^F]$	$C^V \downarrow C^S$
	a. $[\_ě_2, \_i_2]$	$C^V \downarrow C^{SS}$; $x \downarrow s$
4.	$[\_e]$	$C^{SS} \downarrow C^S$
5.	$[\_j]$	$C \downarrow C^S$
6.	$[V]$	$Ci \downarrow C^S$; $ji \downarrow \varnothing$
7.	$[\_t]$	x, gs, ks, z, t, st, d $\downarrow$ s; p, b, v $\downarrow \varnothing$
8.	$[\_]$	gtV, ktV $\downarrow$ ΨV^F
9.	$[\_s]$	s, z, t, d, p, b $\downarrow \varnothing$
10.	$[\_V^B]$	gs, ks $\downarrow$ x
11.	$[\_V^F]$	gs, ks $\downarrow$ š
12.	$[\_C]$	or $\downarrow$ ra; ol $\downarrow$ la; er $\downarrow$ rě; el $\downarrow$ lě; ъr $\downarrow$ rъ; ыl $\downarrow$ lъ; ьr $\downarrow$ rь; ыl $\downarrow$ lь; ьm, im, ьn, in $\downarrow$ ę
13.	$[\_m]$	d $\downarrow \varnothing$
	a. $[\_]$	sedm $\downarrow$ sedm
14.	$[C^N\_C, C^V\_C]$	on $\downarrow$ ǫ

Finally, after applying the relevant numbered rules, delete all consonants following the vowel farthest to the right in the resulting form.

The grammar of OCS presented here is based on a linguistic analysis that distinguishes two levels of description: an underlying, abstract level of NORMALIZED representation and a surface, concrete level of ACTUALIZED representation. By distinguishing these two levels, one gains considerable insight into the structure of OCS words, their derivational patterns, and the structural unity obscured by surface-based typology. In the fourteen rules above, the vertical arrow ↓ symbolizes actualization. Elements to the left of ↓ are in normalized representation; those to the right, in actualized representation. The underscore "__" symbolizes "in the environment," "before X" in the case [__X], "after X" in the case [X__], and "everywhere" in the case [__]. Lettered sub-rules are exceptions to the numbered rule under which they are listed.

In the traditional approach to OCS morphology, nouns, pronouns, adjectives, and verbs are each presented in a variety of types and subtypes based on stem-final consonants, stem alternations, and inflectional endings. So-called "hard," "soft," and "mixed" paradigms (see below, p. 192ff.) are shown in isolation without any apparent structural connection among them. The actualization rules provide a systematic means of correlating stems and endings by permitting uniformity at the underlying level of normalization. Actualization rules, like morphophonemic rules and certain phonological rules, serve to relate underlying, abstract representations to the concrete representations found in actual texts. Furthermore, the actualization rules are universally applicable in OCS, equally valid for paradigms of nouns, pronouns, adjectives, and verbs.

In actualization, the elements involved can be arranged in rows that represent correlation by category. In the chart above, for example, the vowels are conveniently viewed in terms of the frontness or backness of articulation with clear correspondences based on this category of tongue position. Thus V^B *y, o, a, u* correspond to V^F *i, e, ě, ü*, respectively. The back nasal *ǫ* corresponds to fronted nasal *ę̇*. Likewise, C^N *s, z, t, d, n, l, r, p, b, m, v* correspond to C^S *š, ž, ψ, ʍ, ń, l', ŕ, pl', bl', ml', vl'*, respectively. The rules are unordered; they are numbered only for ease of reference. Actualization rules may not apply to actualized representations, only to normalized representations. Rule 5, for example, is to be read: In the environment before *j*, any consonant is actualized as its soft consonant counterpart, e.g., $b \downarrow bl'$, s $\downarrow š$, $k \downarrow č$, $z \downarrow ž$.

A review of the morphology of OCS nouns, pronouns, adjectives, and verbs reveals the role of actualization rules in simplifying grammatical description. All OCS inflection is based on the combination of stem (root + affixes) and ending. Noun Declension 1 is presented in the Grammar (above, p. 16), divided into masculine (masc) and neuter (neut) paradigms, (masc-1) and (neut-1), respectively. Unless specified, all neut-1 endings are identical to masc-1 endings. OCS nominal endings vary according to number and case—singular (sg), dual (du), plural (pl) and nominative (N), genitive (G), dative (D), accusative (A), instrumental (I), locative (L), vocative (V).

Four masc-1 nouns traditionally classified into separate paradigms (hard, soft, velar, and mixed) may serve to show distinct levels of unity (normalized representation) and diversity (actualized representation). Grammatically animate masc-1 nouns have the form of the A sg identical to that of G sg; otherwise the form of the A sg in masc-1 and neut-1 nouns is identical to that of N sg.

The noun *gradъ* 'town, city; wall, enclosure' is based on a stem ending in C^N d. Neutral consonants are actualized without change in the environment before any vowel; likewise all vowels are actualized without change in the environment after all neutral consonants. The singular paradigm of gradъ can be shown in normalized and actualized representations as follows (all subscripts and boundaries [-] are deleted in actualization):

	Normalized		Actualized
N	grad-ъ	$\downarrow$	gradъ
G	grad-a	$\downarrow$	grada
D	grad-u	$\downarrow$	gradu
A	grad-ъ (= N)	$\downarrow$	gradъ
I	grad-omь	$\downarrow$	gradomь
L	grad-ě$_2$	$\downarrow$	gradě
V	grad-e	$\downarrow$	grade

The "soft" singular paradigm of *možь* 'man' (grammatically animate) reveals regularities of alternation that can be predicted by rule. The ending of the V sg for masc-1 nouns is -u for stems ending in C^S, otherwise -e.

	Normalized		Actualized
N	mǫž-ь	↓	mǫžь
G	mǫž-a	↓	mǫžě (mǫža)
D	mǫž-u	↓	mǫžü
A	mǫž-a (= G)	↓	mǫžě (mǫža)
I	mǫž-omь	↓	mǫžemь
L	mǫž-ě₂	↓	mǫži
V	mǫžu	↓	mǫžü

The privileges of occurrence of V^B are limited to the environment after actualized C^S. The vowels ъ and ь, for example, may both occur in the environment after C^N, but only ь may occur in the environment after C^S, thus *dъ*, *dь*, but only *žь*, not **žъ*. Likewise we find *do*, *de*, but only *že*, not **žo*. Rule 1 accounts for this distribution.

1. $[C^S\_, C^{SS}\_, j\_, Ci\_, ji\_]$ $V^B \downarrow V^F; ě_2 \downarrow i$
a.   onC $\downarrow$ ǫC
b. $y_2 \downarrow$ ę
c. $[C^{SS}\_]$ a $\downarrow$ a
d. $[Vj\_, \#j\_]$ ъ, ь $\downarrow$ i

Rule 1 states that in the environment after C^S, C^{SS}, *j*, C*i*, or *ji*, V^B are actualized as V^F and *ě₂* as *i*, hence *mǫž-ь* ↓ *mǫžь*, *mǫž-omь* ↓ *mǫžemь*, *mǫž-ě₂* ↓ *mǫži*. Each of these pairs of endings, *-ъ|-ь, -отъ|-emь, -ě₂|-i*, comprises a SYNCRETISM, an abstract unity differentiated by rule at the level of actualization. Thus instead of positing two distinct endings for masc-1 nouns in the N, I, and L cases, one need list only one for each (*-ь, -отъ, -ě₂*, respectively), relying on the operation of Rule 1 to yield the correct actualized endings. The subscript ₂ distinguishes those instances of *ě* actualized as *i* from those that are not.

The lettered subrules are exceptions to the basic, numbered rules. Subrule 1.a states that in the given environments the sequence $onC \downarrow$ $ǫ̈C$ instead of expected $*enC$ (e.g., the Present Active Participle indefinite N sg fem $znaj$-o-ntj-$i \downarrow znaǫ̈ɥi$). Subrule 1.b states that in the given environments $y_2 \downarrow ǫ$, the subscript $_2$ thus distinguishing regular y $\downarrow i$ from the y actualized as the front nasal $ǫ$ (e.g., I pl $mǫž$-$y \downarrow mǫži$, but A pl $mǫž$-$y_2 \downarrow mǫžǫ$). Subrule 1.c states that in a subset of the given environments, namely, the environment after C^{SS}, $a \downarrow a$ rather than expected $ě$ (e.g., $otьc$-$a \downarrow otьca$ instead of expected $*otьcě$; NB: in composition, this exception is often extended to the environment after C^S sibilants and obstruents (e.g., $mǫž$-$a \downarrow mǫža$ instead of expected $mǫžě$). Subrule 1.d states that in the environment after Vj or initial j (# = no element), $ъ$ and $ь$ are actualized as i, (e.g., NA sg $kraj$-$ъ \downarrow krai$, Non-Past 1 sg $jьm$-$ǫ \downarrow imǫ$).

The velar-stem masc-1 noun $bogъ$ reveals a third pattern of actualization:

	Normalized		Actualized
N	bog-ъ	$\downarrow$	bogъ
G	bog-a	$\downarrow$	boga
D	bog-u	$\downarrow$	bogu
A	bog-a (= G)	$\downarrow$	boga
I	bog-omь	$\downarrow$	bogomь
L	bog-ě₂	$\downarrow$	bоʒě
V	bog-e	$\downarrow$	bоže

For those cases in which the velar consonant precedes a back vowel, the normalized representation is preserved at the level of actualization, e.g., G sg bog-$a \downarrow boga$, bog-$omь \downarrow bogomь$. But the underlying, normalized velar cannot be actualized as a velar in the environment before a front vowel. Rule 3 states that in the environment before V^F, C^V is actualized as C^S. Subrule 3.a notes that if the V^F is $ě_2$ or i_2, C^V is actualized as C^{SS} and x as s, instead. In the velar paradigm, V sg bog-e is actualized as $bože$, whereas L sg bog-$ě_2$ is actualized as $boʒě$.

The mixed masc-1 noun *otъcъ* 'father' shows further paradigmatic variation, with some endings like those of the hard stems, others like those of the soft stems. This distribution is predictable by means of the actualization rules.

	Normalized		Actualized	
N	otъc-ъ	↓	otьcь	(=soft)
G	otъc-a	↓	otьca	(=hard)
D	otъc-u	↓	otьcü	(=soft)
A	otъc-a (= G)	↓	otьca	(=hard)
I	otъc-omь	↓	otьcemь	(=soft)
L	otъc-ě₂	↓	otьci	(=soft)
V	otъc-e	↓	otьče	(=hard)

One can demonstrate the underlying unity of the superficially distinct masc-1 paradigm types reviewed above and also account for the substitutions at the level of actualization by using actualization rules that are relevant not only for the nominal system, but for the entire morphological system of OCS.

Examples illustrating the operation of all actualization rules are presented in Appendix B.

APPENDIX B

ACTUALIZATIONS

Examples of actualization rules

Rule 1: Noun (masc-1) N sg *mǫž-ъ* ↓ *mǫž-ь*, G sg *koń-a* ↓ *koń-ě*, D sg *otьc-u* ↓ *otьc-ü*, I sg *kraj-omь* ↓ *kraemь*,Non-Past *nosi-ǫ* ↓ *nošǫ̈, stoj-i-ǫ* ↓ *stoǫ̈.*

Rule 2: Noun (masc-1) G sg *kraj-a* ↓ *kraě*, Non-Past 2 sg *jьm-e-ši* ↓ *imeši.*

Rule 3: Non-Past 3 sg *pek-e-tъ* ↓ *pečetъ*, Aorist 3 sg *mog-e-x-Ø* ↓ *može*, Noun (masc-1) V sg *dux-e* ↓ *duše*

    Subrule 3a: Noun (masc-1) L sg *tok-ě₂* ↓ *tocě*, Noun (masc-1) N pl *bog-i₂* ↓ *boʒi*, Noun (masc-1) L sg *dux-ě₂* ↓ *dusě*).

Rule 4: Noun (masc-1) V sg *otьc-e* ↓ *otьče, kъnęʒ-e* ↓ *kъnęže*

Rule 5: Non-Past 1 sg *pis-j-ǫ* ↓ *pišǫ̈*, Non-Past 2 sg *glagol-j-e-ši* ↓ *glagol'eši.*

Rule 6: Non-Past 1 sg *xod-i-ǫ* ↓ *xoжǫ̈, boj-i-ǫ* ↓ *boǫ̈.*

Rule 7: Prod-Aorist 2 pl *zna-x-te* ↓ *znaste*, Infinitive *ved-ti* ↓ *vesti*, Supine *greb-tъ* ↓ *gretъ*).

Rule 8: Infinitive *mog-ti* ↓ *moψi*, Supine *pek-tъ* ↓ *peψь.*

Rule 9: S-Aorist 1 sg *něs-s-ъ* ↓ *něsъ, grěb-s-ъ* ↓ *grěsъ*).

Rule 10: S-Aorist 1 sg *těk-s-ъ* ↓ *těxъ, žěg-s-ъ* ↓*žěxъ ~ žaxъ.*

Rule 11: S-Aorist 3 pl *těk-s-ę* ↓ *těšę, žěg-s-ę* ↓ *žěšę ~ žašę.*

Rule 12: Infinitive *kol-ti* ↓ *klati, mel-ti* ↓ *mlěti*), Supine *bor-tъ* ↓ *bratъ*, Perfect M sg *umьr-lъ* ↓ *umrělъ*, Infinitive *vъzьm-ti* ↓ *vъzęti.*

Rule 13: Non-Past 1 pl *dad-mъ* ↓ *damъ.*

    Subrule 13a: Numeral N *sedm-ь* ↓ *sedmь*

Rule 14: Non-Past 3 pl *pad-o-ntъ* ↓ *padǫtъ, mog-o-ntъ* ↓ *mogǫtъ.*

Final C deletion: PrAP N sg masc indef *nes-y₂-ntj-Ø* ↓ *nesynɣ* > *nesy;*
cf. PrAP D sg masc indef *nes-o-ntj-u* ↓ *nesǫɣü*

Sample actualizations of verb forms

1. Non-past

1 sg	*nosi-ǫ* ↓ *nošǫ̈*	*glagol-j-ǫ* ↓ *glagol'ǫ̈*
2 sg	*rek-e-ši* ↓ *rečeši*	*usъn-e-ši* ↓ *usъneši*
3 pl	*vidi-ntъ* ↓ *vidętъ*	*cěluj-o-ntъ* ↓ *cěluǫ̈tъ*

2. Imperative

2 sg	*nosi-Ø* ↓ *nosi*	*glagol-j-i₂-Ø* ↓ *glagol'i*
2 pl	*rьk-ě₂-te* ↓ *rьcěte*	*cěl-uj-ě₂-te* ↓ *cěluite*

3. Imperfect

1 sg	*nosi-ě-ax-ъ* ↓ *nošěaxъ*	*glagol-a-ax-ъ* ↓ *glagolaaxъ*
2 sg	*rek-ě-ax-e-Ø* ↓ *rečěaše*	*usъn-ě-ax-e-Ø* ↓ *usъněaše*
2 pl	*umě-ax-e-te* ↓ *uměašete*	*bor-j-ě-ax-e-te* ↓ *boŕěašete*
3 pl	*vid-ě-ax-ǫ* ↓ *viděaxǫ*	*cěl-ova-ax-ǫ* ↓ *cělovaaxǫ*

4. Present Active Participle

N sg masc indef	*nosi-ntj-Ø* ↓ *nosęɣ* > *nosę*
N sg masc def	*nosę + i* > *nosęi*
N sg neut indef	*rek-y₂-ntj-Ø* ↓ *rekynɣ* > *reky*
N sg neut def	*rek-o-ntj-oe* ↓ *rekǫɣee*
G sg fem indef	*rek-o-ntj-y₂* ↓ *rekǫɣę*
D sg neut def	*glagol-j-o-ntj-uemu* ↓ *glagol'ǫ̈ɣüemu*

5. Prod-Aorist

1 sg	*nosi-x-ъ* ↓ *nosixъ*	*glagol-ax-ъ* ↓ *glagolaxъ*
2 pl	*umě-x-te* ↓ *uměste*	*bor-x-te* ↓ *braste*
3 pl	*rek-o-x-ę* ↓ *rekošę*	*vъzьm-x-ъ* ↓ *vъzęšę*

196

6. S-Aorist

1 sg	rěk-s-ъ ↓ rěxъ	grěb-s-ъ ↓ grěsъ
2 pl	rěk-s-te ↓ rěste	vъzъm-s-te ↓ vъzęste
3pl	rěk-s-ę ↓ rěšę	grěb-s-ę ↓ grěsę

7. Simple Aorist

1 sg	usъp-ъ ↓ usъpъ	mog-ъ ↓ mogъ
2 sg	usъp-e-Ø ↓ usъpe	mog-e-Ø ↓ može
3pl	usъp-Q ↓ usъpQ	mog-Q ↓mogQ

8. Infinitive and Supine

rek-ti ↓ reψi	greb-tъ ↓ gretъ
ved-ti ↓ vesti	glagol-a-tъ ↓ glagolatъ
umě-ti ↓ uměti	usъnQ-tъ ↓ usъnQtъ
bor-ti ↓ brati	nosi-tъ ↓ nositъ

9. Perfect Active Participle

N sg masc	nosi-l-ъ ↓ nosilъ	glagol-a-l-ъ ↓ glagolalъ
N sg fem	rek-l-a ↓ rekla	bor-l-a ↓ brala
N pl masc	ved-l-i₂ ↓ veli	cěl-ova-l-i₂ ↓ cělovali

10. Past Active Participle

N sg masc indef	nosi-ъš-Ø ↓ nošь
N sg masc def	nošь + i ↓ nošьi
N sg neut indef	rek-ъš-Ø ↓ rekъ
N sg neut def	rek-ъš-oe ↓ rekъšee
G sg fem indef	rek-ъš-y₂ ↓ rekъšę
D sg neut def	glagol-a-v-ъš-uemu ↓ glagolavъšüemu

11. Past Passive Participle

N sg masc indef	*nosi-e-n-ъ* ↓ *nošenъ*
N sg masc def	*nosi-e-n-yi* ↓ *nošenyi*
N sg neut indef	*rek-e-n-o* ↓ *rečeno*
G sg fem indef	*vъzьm-t-y₂* ↓ *vъzętу*
D sg neut def	*kos-nov-e-n-uemu* ↓ *kosnovenuemu*

12. Verbal Substantive

N sg neut	*nosi-e-nij-o* ↓ *nošenie*
D sg neut	*rek-e-nij-u* ↓ *rečeniü*

APPENDIX C

NOMINAL AND PRONOMINAL PARADIGMS

Nouns: masc-1

	grad-	bog-	otьc-	mǫž-	kraj-	syn-
Nsg	gradъ	bogъ	otьcь	mǫžь	krai	synъ
Gsg	grada	boga	otьca	mǫžě	kraě	synu
Dsg	gradu	bǫgu	otьcü	mǫžü	kraü	synovi
Asg	gradъ	boga	otьca	mǫžь	krai	synъ
Isg	gradomь	bogomь	otьcemь	mǫžemь	kraemь	synъmь
Lsg	gradě	božě	otьci	mǫži	krai	synu
Vsg	grade	bože	otьče	mǫžü	kraü	synu
NAVdu	grada	boga	otьca	mǫžě	kraě	syny
GLdu	gradu	bogu	otьcü	mǫžü	kraü	synu
DIdu	gradoma	bogoma	otьcema	mǫžema	kraema	synъma
NVpl	gradi	bozi	otьci	mǫži	krai	synove
Gpl	gradъ	bogъ	otьcь	mǫžę	krai	synovъ
Dpl	gradomъ	bogomъ	otьcemъ	mǫžemъ	kraemъ	synъmъ
Apl	grady	bogy	otьcę	mǫžę	kraę	syny
Ipl	grady	bogy	otьci	mǫži	krai	synъmi
Lpl	graděxъ	bozěxъ	otьcixъ	mǫžixъ	kraixъ	synъxъ

Nouns: neut-1

	sel-	blag-	moŕ-	zъvanij-
NVsg	selo	blago	moŕe	zъvanie
Gsg	sela	blaga	moŕě	zъvaniě
Dsg	selu	blagu	moŕü	zъvaniü
Asg	selo	blago	moŕe	zъvanie
Isg	selomь	blagomь	moŕemь	zъvaniemь
Lsg	selě	blazě	moŕi	zъvanii
NAVdu	selě	blazě	moŕi	zъvanii
GLdu	selu	blagu	moŕü	zъvaniü
DIdu	seloma	blagoma	moŕema	zъvaniema
NVpl	sela	blaga	moŕě	zъvaniě
Gpl	selъ	blagъ	moŕь	zъvanii
Dpl	selomъ	blagomъ	moŕemъ	zъvaniemъ
Apl	sela	blaga	moŕě	zъvaniě
Ipl	sely	blagy	moŕi	zъvanii
Lpl	selěxъ	blazěxъ	moŕixъ	zъvaniixъ

Nouns: fem-2 and masc-2

	žen-	rǫk-	zemľ-	zmij-	sǫdij- (masc)
Nsg	žena	rǫka	zemľě	zmiě	sǫdii
Gsg	ženy	rǫky	zemľę	zmię	sǫdię
Dsg	ženě	rǫcě	zemľi	zmii	sǫdii
Asg	ženǫ	rǫkǫ	zemľǫ̈	zmiǫ̈	sǫdiǫ̈
Isg	ženoǫ̈	rǫkoǫ̈	zemľeǫ̈	zmieǫ̈	sǫdiemь
Lsg	ženě	rǫcě	zemľi	zmii	sǫdii
Vsg	ženo	rǫko	zemľe	zmie	sǫdie
NAVdu	ženě	rǫcě	zemľi	zmii	sǫdii
GLdu	ženu	rǫku	zemľü	zmiü	sǫdiü
DIdu	ženama	rǫkama	zemľěma	zmiěma	sǫdiěma
NVpl	ženy	rǫky	zemľę	zmię	sǫdię
Gpl	ženъ	rǫkъ	zemľь	zmii	sǫdii
Dpl	ženamъ	rǫkamъ	zemľěmъ	zmiěmъ	sǫdiěmъ
Apl	ženy	rǫky	zemľę	zmię	sǫdię
Ipl	ženami	rǫkami	zemľěmi	zmiěmi	sǫdiěmi
Lpl	ženaxъ	rǫkaxъ	zemľěxъ	zmiixъ	sǫdiěxъ

Nouns: fem-3 and masc-3

	kost-	pǫt- (masc)
Nsg	kostь	pǫtь
Gsg	kosti	pǫti
Dsg	kosti	pǫti
Asg	kostь	pǫtь
Isg	kostьǫ̈	pǫtemь ~ pǫtьmь
Lsg	kosti	pǫti
Vsg	kosti	pǫti
NAVdu	kosti	pǫti
GLdu	kostiü	pǫtiü
DIdu	kostьma	pǫtьma
NVpl	kosti	pǫtie
Gpl	kostii	pǫtii
Dpl	kǫstemъ ~ kostьmъ	pǫtemъ ~ pǫtьmъ
Apl	kosti	pǫti
Ipl	kostьmi	pǫtьmi
Lpl	kostexъ ~ kostьxъ	pǫtexъ ~ pǫtьxъ

200

Nouns: masc-4, neut-4

	dьn-	vrěm-en-	kozьl-ęt-	slov-es-
Nsg	*dьnь*	*vrěmę*	*kozьlę*	*slovo*
Gsg	*dьne*	*vrěmene*	*kozьlęte*	*slovese*
Dsg	*dьni*	*vrěmeni*	*kozьlęti*	*slovesi*
Asg	*dьnь*	*vrěmę*	*kozьlę*	*slovo*
Isg	*dьnьmь*	*vrěmenemь*	*kozьlętemь*	*slovesemь*
		~ *vrěmenьmь*	~ *kozьlętьmь*	~ *slovesьmь*
Lsg	*dьne*	*vrěmene*	*kozьlęte*	*slovese*
Vsg	*dьni*	*vrěmę*	*kozьlę*	*slovo*
NAVdu	*dьni*	*vrěmeně*	*kozьlętě*	*slovesě*
GLdu	*dьnu* ~ *dьniü*	*vrěmenu*	*kozьlętu*	*slovesu*
DIdu	*dьnьma*	*vrěmenьma*	*kozьlętьma*	*slovesьma*
NVpl	*dьne*	*vrěmena*	*kozьlęta*	*slovesa*
Gpl	*dьnъ*	*vrěmenъ*	*kozьlętъ*	*slovesъ*
Dpl	*dьnemъ*	*vrěmenemъ*	*kozьlętemъ*	*slovesemъ*
	~ *dьnьmъ*	~ *vrěmenьmъ*	~ *kozьletьmъ*	~ *slovesьmъ*
Apl	*dьni*	*vrěmena*	*kozьlęta*	*slovesa*
Ipl	*dьnьmi*	*vrěmeny*	*kozьlęty*	*slovesy*
Lpl	*dьnexъ*	*vrěmenexъ* ~	*kozьlętexъ*	*slovesexъ*
	~ *dьnьxъ*	*vrěmenьxъ*	~ *kozьlętьxъ*	~ *slovesьxъ*

Nouns: fem-4

	mat-er-	crьk-ъv-
Nsg	*mati*	*crьky*
Gsg	*matere*	*crьkъve*
Dsg	*materi*	*crьkъvi*
Asg	*materь*	*crьkъvь*
Isg	*materiǫ*	*crьkъviǫ*
Lsg	*matere*	*crьkъve*
Vsg	*mati*	*crьky*
NVpl	*materi*	*crьkъvi*
Gpl	*materъ*	*crьkъvъ*
Dpl	*materemъ* ~ *materьmъ*	*crьkъvamъ*
Apl	*materi*	*crьkъvi*
Ipl	*materьmi*	*crьkъvami*
Lpl	*materexъ* ~ *materьxъ*	*crьkъvaxъ*

Adjectives: indefinite

	masc	neut	fem
		dobr-	
Nsg	dobrъ	dobro	dobra
Gsg	dobra	dobra	dobry
Dsg	dobru	dobru	dobrě
Asg	= N/G	dobro	dobrǫ
Isg	dobromь	dobromь	dobroǫ
Lsg	dobrě	dobrě	dobrě
NAdu	dobra	dobra	dobrě
GLdu	dobru	dobru	dobru
DIdu	dobroma	dobroma	dobrama
Npl	dobri	dobra	dobry
Gpl	dobrъ	dobrъ	dobrъ
Dpl	dobromъ	dobromъ	dobramъ
Apl	dobry	dobra	dobry
Ipl	dobry	dobry	dobrami
Lpl	dobrěxъ	dobrěxъ	dobraxъ

		niẹ-	
Nsg	niẹь	niẹe	niẹě
Gsg	niẹě	niẹě	niẹę
Dsg	niẹü	niẹü	niẹi
Asg	= N/G	niẹe	niẹǫ
Isg	niẹemь	niẹemь	niẹeǫ
Lsg	niẹi	niẹi	niẹi
NAdu	niẹě	niẹi	niẹi
GLdu	niẹü	niẹü	niẹü
DIdu	niẹema	niẹema	niẹěma
Npl	niẹi	niẹě	niẹę
Gpl	niẹь	niẹь	niẹь
Dpl	niẹemъ	niẹemъ	niẹěmъ
Apl	niẹę	niẹě	niẹę
Ipl	niẹi	niẹi	niẹěmi
Lpl	niẹixъ	niẹixъ	niẹěxъ

Adjectives: definite

	masc	neut	fem
		dobr-	
Nsg	dobry(i)	dobroe	dobraě
Gsg	dobraego	dobraego	dobryę
Dsg	dobruemu	dobruemu	dobrěi
Asg	= N/G	dobroe	dobrǫǫ̈
Isg	dobry(i)mь	dobry(i)mь	dobrǫǫ̈
Lsg	dobrěemь	dobrěemь	dobrěi
NAdu	dobraě	dobrěi	dobrěi
GLdu	dobruü	dobruü	dobruü
DIdu	dobryma	dobryma	dobryma
Npl	dobrii	dobrii	dobryę
Gpl	dobry(i)xъ	dobry(i)xъ	dobry(i)xъ
Dpl	dobry(i)mъ	dobry(i)mъ	dobry(i)mъ
Apl	dobryę	dobryę	dobryę
Ipl	dobry(i)mi	dobry(i)mi	dobry(i)mi
Lpl	dobry(i)xъ	dobry(i)xъ	dobry(i)xъ

	masc	neut	fem
		niψ-	
Nsg	niψi(i)	niψee	niψě
Gsg	niψego	niψego	niψeę
Dsg	niψemu	niψemu	niψii
Asg	= N/G	niψee	niψǫǫ̈
Isg	niψi(i)mь	niψi(i)mь	niψǫǫ̈
Lsg	niψiimь	niψiimь	niψii
NAdu	niψěě	niψii	niψii
GLdu	niψüü	niψüü	niψüü
DIdu	niψima	niψima	niψima
Npl	niψii	niψěě	niψeę
Gpl	niψi(i)xъ	niψi(i)xъ	niψi(i)xъ
Dpl	niψi(i)mъ	niψi(i)mъ	niψi(i)mъ
Apl	niψeę	niψě	niψeę
Ipl	niψi(i)mi	niψi(i)mi	niψi(i)mi
Lpl	niψi(i)xъ	niψi(i)xъ	niψi(i)xъ

Pronouns: demonstrative

	masc	neut	fem	masc	neut	fem
	t-			s-/sij-		
Nsg	tъ	to	ta	sь/sii	se	si
Gsg	togo	togo	toę	sego	sego	seę
Dsg	tomu	tomu	toi	semu	semu	sei
Asg	=N/G	to	tǫ	=N/G	se	siǫ
Isg	těmь	těmь	toǫ	simь	simь	seǫ
Lsg	tomь	tomь	toi	semь	semь	sei
NAdu	ta	tě	tě	siě	si	si
GLdu	toü	toü	toü	seü	seü	seü
DIdu	těma	těma	těma	sima	sima	sima
Npl	ti	ta	ty	sii/si	si	się
Gpl	těxь	těxь	těxь	sixь	sixь	sixь
Dpl	těmь	těmь	těmь	simь	simь	simь
Apl	ty	ta	ty	się	si	się
Ipl	těmi	těmi	těmi	simi	simi	simi
Lpl	těxь	těxь	těxь	sixь	sixь	sixь

Pronouns: anaphoric, possessive

	masc	neut	fem	masc	neut	fem
	j-			vaš-		
Nsg	(i)	(e)	(ě)	vašь	vaše	vašě
Gsg	ego	ego	eę	vašego	vašego	vašeę
Dsg	emu	emu	ei	vašemu	vašemu	vašei
Asg	=N/G	e	ǫ	=N/G	vaše	vašǫ
Isg	imь	imь	eǫ	vašimь	vašimь	vašeǫ
Lsg	emь	emь	ei	vašemь	vašemь	vašei
NAdu	(ě)	(i)	(i)	vaša	vaši	vaši
GLdu	eü	eü	eü	vašeü	vašeü	vašeü
DIdu	ima	ima	ima	vašima	vašima	vašima
Npl	(i)	(ě)	(ę)	vaši	vasě	vašę
Gpl	ixь	ixь	ixь	vašixь	vašixь	vašixь
Dpl	imь	imь	imь	vašimь	vašimь	vašimь
Apl	ę	ě	ę	vašę	vašě	vašę
Ipl	imi	imi	imi	vašimi	vašimi	vašimi
Lpl	ixь	ixь	ixь	vašixь	vašixь	vašixь

Pronouns: quantitative, qualitative

	masc	neut	fem	masc	neut	fem
		vьs-			k-/koj-	
Nsg	vьsь	vьse	vьsě ~ vьsa	ky(i)	koe	kaě
Gsg	vьsego	vьsego	vьseę	koego	koego	koeę
Dsg	vьsemu	vьsemu	vьsei	koemu	koemu	koei
Asg	=N/G	vьse	vьsǫ	=N/G	koe	kǫǫ
Isg	vьsěmь	vьsěmь	vьseǫ	ky(i)mь	ky(i)mь	koeǫ
Lsg	vьsemь	vьsemь	vьsei	koemь	koemь	koei
NAdu	oba	obě	obě	kaě	cěi	cěi
GLdu	oboü	oboü	oboü	koeü	koeü	koeü
DIdu	oběma	oběma	oběma	ky(i)ma	ky(i)ma	ky(i)ma
Npl	vьsi	vьsě ~ vьsa	vьsě	cii	kaě	kyę
Gpl	vьsěxь	vьsěxь	vьsěxь	ky(i)xь	ky(i)xь	ky(i)xь
Dpl	vьsěmь	vьsěmь	vьsěmь	ky(i)mь	ky(i)mь	ky(i)mь
Apl	vьsę	vьsě ~ vьsa	vьsę	kyę	kaě	kyę
Ipl	vьsěmi	vьsěmi	vьsěmi	ky(i)mi	ky(i)mi	ky(i)mi
Lpl	vьsěxь	vьsěxь	vьsěxь	ky(i)xь	ky(i)xь	ky(i)xь

Pronouns: personal, reflexive, interrogative-indefinite

	1st pers.	2nd pers.		Reflexive
Nsg	azь	ty	N	——
Gsg	mene	tebe	G	sebe
Dsg	mьně, mi	tebě, ti	D	sebě, si
Asg	mę	tę	A	sę
Isg	mъnoǫ	toboǫ	I	soboǫ
Lsg	mьně	tebě	L	sebě
Ndu	vě	va		
Adu	na	va		
GLdu	naü	vaü		
DIdu	nama	vama		Interrogative-indefinite
Npl	my	vy	N	kъto	čьto
Gpl	nasь	vasь	G	kogo	česo ~ čьso ~ česogo
Dpl	namь	vamь	D	komu	česomu ~ čьsomu ~ čemu
Apl	ny	vy	A	kogo	čьto
Ipl	nami	vami	I	cěmь	čimь
Lpl	nas	vasь	L	komь	čemь ~ česomь

APPENDIX D
VERBAL PARADIGMS

Non-past

	nes-	rek-	klьn-	mьr-
1sg	nesǫ	rekǫ	klьnǫ	mьrǫ
2sg	neseši	rečeši	klьneši	mьreši
3sg	nesetъ	rečetъ	klьnetъ	mьretъ
1du	nesevě	rečevě	klьnevě	mьrevě
2du	neseta	rečeta	klьneta	mьreta
3du	nesete	rečete	klьnete	mьrete
1pl	nesemъ	rečemъ	klьnemъ	mьremъ
2pl	nesete	rečete	klьnete	mьrete
3pl	nesǫtъ	rekǫtъ	klьnǫtъ	mьrǫtъ

	moli-	prosi-	mьn-ě-	slyš-ě-
1sg	mol'ǫ	prošǫ	mьn'ǫ	slyšǫ
2sg	moliši	prosiši	mьniši	slyšiši
3sg	molitъ	prositъ	mьnitъ	slyšitъ
1du	molivě	prosivě	mьnivě	slyšivě
2du	molita	prosita	mьnita	slyšita
3du	molite	prosite	mьnite	slyšite
1pl	molimъ	prosimъ	mьnimъ	slyšimъ
2pl	molite	prosite	mьnite	slyšite
3pl	molętъ	prosętъ	mьnętъ	slyšętъ

	umě-j-	zna-j-	bor-j-	glagol-a-
1sg	uměǫ	znaǫ	boŕǫ	glagol'ǫ
2sg	uměeši	znaeši	boŕeši	glagol'eši
3sg	uměetъ	znaetъ	boŕetъ	glagol'etъ
1du	uměevě	znaevě	boŕevě	glagol'evě
2du	uměeta	znaeta	boŕeta	glagol'eta
3du	uměete	znaete	boŕete	glagol'ete
1pl	uměemъ	znaemъ	boŕemъ	glagol'emъ
2pl	uměete	znaete	boŕete	glagol'ete
3pl	uměǫtъ	znaǫtъ	boŕǫtъ	glagol'ǫtъ

	plak-a-	věr-ova-	dvig-nǫ-	ri-nǫ-
1sg	plačǫ	věruǫ	dvignǫ	rinǫ
2sg	plačeši	věrueši	dvigneši	rineši
3sg	plačetъ	věruetъ	dvignetъ	rinetъ
1du	plačevě	věruevě	dvignevě	rinevě
2du	plačeta	věrueta	dvigneta	rineta
3du	plačete	věruete	dvignete	rinete
1pl	plačemъ	věruemъ	dvignemъ	rinemъ
2pl	plačete	věruete	dvignete	rinete
3pl	plačǫtъ	věruǫtъ	dvignǫtъ	rinǫtъ

Imperative

	nes-	rek-	klьn-	mьr-
2,3sg	nesi	rьci	klьni	mьri
1du	nesěvě	rьcěvě	klьnětě	mьrěvě
2du	nesěta	rьcěta	klьněta	mьrěta
1pl	nesěmъ	rьcěmъ	klьněmъ	mьrěmъ
2pl	nesěte	rьcěte	klьněte	mьrěte

	moli-	prosi-	mьn-ě-	slyš-ě-
2,3sg	moli	prosi	mьni	slyši
1du	molivě	prosivě	mьnivě	slyšivě
2du	molita	prosita	mьnita	slyšita
1pl	molimъ	prosimъ	mьnimъ	slyšimъ
2pl	molite	prosite	mьnite	slyšite

	umě-j-	zna-j-	bor-j-	glagol-a-
2,3sg	uměi	znai	boři	glagol'i
1du	uměivě	znaivě	bořivě	glagol'ivě
2du	uměita	znaita	bořita	glagol'ita
1pl	uměimъ	znaimъ	bořimъ	glagol'imъ
2pl	uměite	znaite	bořite	glagol'ite

	plak-a-	věr-ova-	dvig-nǫ-	ri-nǫ-
2,3sg	plači	věrui	dvigni	rini
1du	plačivě	věruivě	dvigněvě	riněvě
2du	plačita	věruita	dvigněta	riněta
1pl	plačimъ	věruimъ	dvigněmъ	riněmъ
2pl	plačite	věruite	dvigněte	riněte

Imperfect

	nes-	rek-	klьn-	mьr-
1sg	neséaxъ	rečéaxъ	klьněaxъ	mьrěaxъ
2sg	neséaše	rečéaše	klьněaše	mьrěaše
3sg	neséaše	rečéaše	klьněaše	mьrěaše
1du	neséaxově	rečéaxově	klьněaxově	mьrěaxově
2du	neséašeta	rečéašeta	klьněašeta	mьrěašeta
3du	neséašete	rečéašete	klьněašete	mьrěašete
1pl	neséaxomъ	rečéaxomъ	klьněaxomъ	mьrěaxomъ
2pl	neséašete	rečéašete	klьněašete	mьrěašete
3pl	neséaxǫ	rečéaxǫ	klьněaxǫ	mьrěaxǫ

	moli-	prosi-	mьn-ě-	slyš-ě-
1sg	mol'éaxъ	prošéaxъ	mьněaxъ	slyšěaxъ
2sg	mol'éaše	prošéaše	mьněaše	slyšěaše
3sg	mol'éaše	prošéaše	mьněaše	slyšěaše
1du	mol'éaxově	prošéaxově	mьněaxově	slyšěaxově
2du	mol'éašeta	prošéašeta	mьněašeta	slyšěašeta
3du	mol'éašete	prošéašete	mьněašete	slyšěašete
1pl	mol'éaxomъ	prošéaxomъ	mьněaxomъ	slyšěaxomъ
2pl	mol'éašete	prošéašete	mьněašete	slyšěašete
3pl	mol'éaxǫ	prošéaxǫ	mьněaxǫ	slyšěaxǫ

	umě-j-	zna-j-	bor-j-	glagol-a-
1sg	uměaxъ	znaaxъ	boŕěaxъ	glagolaaxъ
2sg	uměaše	znaaše	boŕěaše	glagolaaše
3sg	uměaše	znaaše	boŕěaše	glagolaaše
1du	uměaxově	znaaxově	boŕěaxově	glagolaaxově
2du	uměašeta	znaašeta	boŕěašeta	glagolaašeta
3du	uměašete	znaašete	boŕěašete	glagolaašete
1pl	uměaxomъ	znaaxomъ	boŕěaxomъ	glagolaaxomъ
2pl	uměašete	znaašete	boŕěašete	glagolaašete
3pl	uměaxǫ	znaaxǫ	boŕěaxǫ	glagolaaxǫ

208

	plak-a-	věr-ova-	dvig-nǫ-	ri-nǫ-
1sg	plakaaxъ	věrovaaxъ	dvigněaxъ	riněaxǫ
2sg	plakaaše	věrovaaše	dvigněaše	riněaše
3sg	plakaaše	věrovaaše	dvigněaše	riněaše
1du	plakaaxově	věrovaaxově	dvigněaxově	riněaxově
2du	plakaašeta	věrovaašeta	dvigněašeta	riněašeta
3du	plakaašete	věrovaašete	dvigněašete	riněašete
1pl	plakaaxomъ	věrovaaxomъ	dvigněaxomъ	riněaxomъ
2pl	plakaašete	věrovaašete	dvigněašete	riněašete
3pl	plakaaxǫ	věrovaaxǫ	dvigněaxǫ	riněaxǫ

Present active participle

	masc	neut	fem
nes-, likewise rek-, klьn-, mьr-			
Nsg-indef	nesy	nesy	nesǫųi
Gsg-indef	nesǫųě	nesǫųě	nesǫųę
Asg-indef	nesǫųь	nesǫųe	nesǫųǫ̈
Npl-indef	nesǫųe	nesǫųě	nesǫųę
Nsg-def	nesyi	nesǫųee	nesǫųěě
Gsg-def	nesǫųěego	nesǫųěego	nesǫųęę
Asg-def	nesǫųii	nesǫųee	nesǫųǫ̈ǫ̈
Npl-def	nesǫųei	nesǫųěě	nesǫųęę

moli-, likewise prosi-, mьn-ě-, slyš-ě--			
Nsg-indef	molę	molę	molęųi
Gsg-indef	molęųě	molęųě	molęųę
Asg-indef	molęųь	molęųe	molęųǫ̈
Npl-indef	molęųe	molęųě	molęųę
Nsg-def	molęi	molęųee	molęųěě
Gsg-def	molęųěego	molęųěego	molęųęę
Asg-def	molęųii	molęųee	molęųǫ̈ǫ̈
Npl-def	molęųei	molęųěě	molęųęę

umě-j-, likewise zna-j-, věr-uj-			
Nsg-indef	uměę	uměę	uměǫ̈ųi
Gsg-indef	uměǫ̈ųě	uměǫ̈ųě	uměǫ̈ųę
Asg-indef	uměǫ̈ųь	uměǫ̈ųe	uměǫ̈ųǫ̈
Npl-indef	uměǫ̈ųe	uměǫ̈ųě	uměǫ̈ųę
Nsg-def	uměęi	uměǫ̈ųee	uměǫ̈ųěě
Gsg-def	uměǫ̈ųěego	uměǫ̈ųěego	uměǫ̈ųęę
Asg-def	uměǫ̈ųii	uměǫ̈ųee	uměǫ̈ųǫ̈ǫ̈
Npl-def	uměǫ̈ųei	uměǫ̈ųěě	uměǫ̈ųęę

glagol-a-, likewise bor-j-, plak-a-			
Nsg-indef	*glagol'ę*	*glagol'ę*	*glagol'ǫ̨i*
Gsg-indef	*glagol'ǫ̨ě*	*glagol'ǫ̨ě*	*glagol'ǫ̨ę*
Asg-indef	*glagol'ǫ̨ъ*	*glagol'ǫ̨e*	*glagol'ǫ̨ǫ̨*
Npl-indef	*glagol'ǫ̨e*	*glagol'ǫ̨ě*	*glagol'ǫ̨ę*
Nsg-def	*glagol'ęi*	*glagol'ǫ̨ee*	*glagol'ǫ̨ěě*
Gsg-def	*glagol'ǫ̨ěego*	*glagol'ǫ̨ěego*	*glagol'ǫ̨ęę*
Asg-def	*glagol'ǫ̨ii*	*glagol'ǫ̨ee*	*glagol'ǫ̨ǫ̨ǫ̨*
Npl-def	*glagol'ǫ̨ei*	*glagol'ǫ̨ěě*	*glagol'ǫ̨ęę*

dvig-nǫ-, likewise ri-nǫ-			
Nsg-indef	*dvigny*	*dvigny*	*dvignǫ̨i*
Gsg-indef	*dvignǫ̨ě*	*dvignǫ̨ě*	*dvignǫ̨ę*
Asg-indef	*dvignǫ̨ъ*	*dvignǫ̨e*	*dvignǫ̨ǫ̨*
Npl-indef	*dvignǫ̨e*	*dvignǫ̨ě*	*dvignǫ̨ę*
Nsg-def	*dvignyi*	*dvignǫ̨ee*	*dvignǫ̨ěě*
Gsg-def	*dvignǫ̨ěego*	*dvignǫ̨ěego*	*dvignǫ̨ęę*
Asg-def	*dvignǫ̨ii*	*dvignǫ̨ee*	*dvignǫ̨ǫ̨ǫ̨*
Npl-def	*dvignǫ̨ei*	*dvignǫ̨ěě*	*dvignǫ̨ęę*

Present passive participle

	masc	neut	fem
nes-			
Nsg-indef	*nesomъ*	*nesomo*	*nesoma*
Npl-indef	*nesoma*	*nesoma*	*nesomy*
Nsg-def	*nesomy(i)*	*nesomoe*	*nesomaě*
Npl-def	*nesomii*	*nesomaě*	*nesomyę*
prosi-			
Nsg-indef	*prosimъ*	*prosimo*	*prosima*
Npl-indef	*prosima*	*prosima*	*prosimy*
Nsg-def	*prosimy(i)*	*prosimoe*	*prosimaě*
Npl-def	*prosimii*	*prosimaě*	*prosimyę*
nazyva-j-			
Nsg-indef	*nazyvaemъ*	*nazyvaemo*	*nazyvaema*
Npl-indef	*nazyvaema*	*nazyvaema*	*nazyvaemy*
Nsg-def	*nazyvaemy(i)*	*nazyvaemoe*	*nazyvaemaě*
Npl-def	*nazyvaemii*	*nazyvaemaě*	*nazyvaemyę*

210

Productive aorist

	nes-	rek-	klьn-	mьr-
1sg	nesoxъ	rekoxъ	klęxъ	mrěxъ
2sg	nese	reče	klętъ	mrětъ
3sg	nese	reče	klętъ	mrětъ
1du	nesoxově	rekoxově	klęxově	mrěxově
2du	nesosta	rekosta	klęsta	mrěsta
3du	nesoste	rekoste	klęste	mrěste
1pl	nesoxomъ	rekoxomъ	klęxomъ	mrěxomъ
2pl	nesoste	rekoste	klęste	mrěste
3pl	nesošę	rekošę	klęšę	mrěšę

	moli-	prosi-	mьn-ě-	slyš-ě-
1sg	molixъ	prosixъ	mьněxъ	slyšěxъ
2sg	moli	prosi	mьně	slyšě
3sg	moli	prosi	mьně	slyšě
1du	molixově	prosixově	mьněxově	slyšěxově
2du	molista	prosista	mьněsta	slyšěsta
3du	moliste	prosiste	mьněste	slyšěste
1pl	molixomъ	prosixomъ	mьněxomъ	slyšěxomъ
2pl	moliste	prosiste	mьněste	slyšěste
3pl	molišę	prosišę	mьněšę	slyšěšę

	umě-j-	zna-j-	bor-j-	glagol-a-
1sg	uměxъ	znaxъ	braxъ	glagolaxъ
2sg	umě	zna	brae	glagola
3sg	umě	zna	bra	glagola
1du	uměxově	znaxově	braxově	glagolaxově
2du	umĕsta	znasta	brasta	glagolasta
3du	uměste	znaste	braste	glagolaste
1pl	uměxomъ	znaxomъ	braxomъ	glagolaxomъ
2pl	uměste	znaste	braste	glagolaste
3pl	uměšę	znašę	brašę	glagolašę

	plak-a-	věr-ova-	dvig-nǫ-	ri-nǫ-
1sg	plakaxъ	věrovaxъ	dvigoxъ	rinǫxǫ
2sg	plaka	věrova	dviže	rinǫ
3sg	plaka	věrova	dviže	rinǫ
1du	plakaxově	věrovaxově	dvigoxově	rinǫxově
2du	plakasta	věrovasta	dvigosta	rinǫsta
3du	plakaste	věrovaste	dvigoste	rinǫste
1pl	plakaxomъ	věrovaxomъ	dvigoxomъ	rinǫxomъ
2pl	plakaste	věrovaste	dvigoste	rinǫste
3pl	plakašę	věrovašę	dvigošę	rinošę

S-aorist

	nes-	rek-	greb-	vъzьm-
1sg	něsъ	rěxъ	grěsъ	vъzęsъ
2sg	nese	reče	grebe	vъzętъ
3sg	nese	reče	grebe	vъzętъ
1du	něsově	rěxově	grěsově	vъzęsově
2du	něsta	rěsta	grěsta	vъzęsta
3du	něste	rěste	grěste	vъzęste
1du	něsomъ	rěxomъ	grěsomъ	vъzęsomъ
2du	něste	rěste	grěste	vъzęste
3du	něsę	rěšę	grěsę	vъzęsę

Simple aorist

	id-	sěd-	mog-	dvig-nǫ-
1sg	idъ	sědъ	mogъ	dvigъ
2sg	ide	sěde	može	dviže
3sg	ide	sěde	može	dviže
1du	(idoxově)	(sědoxově)	(mogoxově)	(dvigoxově)
2du	(idosta)	(sědosta)	(mogosta)	(dvigosta)
3du	idete	(sědoste)	možete	(dvigoste)
1pl	idomъ	sědomъ	mogomъ	(dvigoxomъ)
2pl	idete	(sědoste)	(mogoste)	(dvigoste)
3pl	idǫ	sědǫ	mogǫ	dvigǫ

212

Infinitive and supine

	nes-	rek-	greb-	ved-
Inf	*nesti*	*reųi*	*greti*	*vesti*
Sup	*nestь*	*reųtь*	*gretь*	*vestь*

	vъzьm-	sěd-ě-	glagol-a-	kos-nǫ-
Inf	*vъzęti*	*sěděti*	*glagolati*	*kosnǫti*
Sup	*vъzętь*	*sědětь*	*glagolatъ*	*kosnǫtь*

Perfect active participle

	nes-	rek-	sěd-ě-	vrьg-
Nsg-m	*neslъ*	*reklъ*	*sědělъ*	*vrьglъ*
Nsg-f	*nesla*	*rekla*	*sěděla*	*vrьgla*
Nsg-n	*neslo*	*reklo*	*sědělo*	*vrьglo*
Ndu-m	*nesla*	*rekla*	*sěděla*	*vrьgla*
Ndu-f	*neslě*	*reklě*	*sědělě*	*vrьglě*
Ndu-n	*neslě*	*reklě*	*sěděslě*	*vrьglě*
Npl-m	*nesli*	*rekli*	*sědělı*	*vrьgli*
Npl-f	*nesly*	*rekly*	*sěděly*	*vrьgly*
Npl-n	*nesla*	*rekla*	*sěděla*	*vrьgla*

Past active participle

	masc	neut	fem
nes-, likewise rek-, klьn-, mьr-			
Nsg-ndef	*nesъ*	*nesъ*	*nesъši*
Gsg-indef	*nesъšě*	*nesъšě*	*nesъšę*
Asg- indef	*nesъšь*	*nesъše*	*nesъšǫ*
Npl- indef	*nesъše*	*nesъšě*	*nesъšę*
Nsg-def	*nesъi*	*nesъšee*	*nesъšiě*
Gsg-def	*nesъšěego*	*nesъšěego*	*nesъšęę*
Asg- def	*nesъšii*	*nesъšee*	*nesъšǫǫ*
Npl- def	*nesъšei*	*nesъšěě*	*nesъšęę*
moli-, likewise prosi-, xodi-			
Nsg-ndef	*mol'ь*	*mol'ь*	*mol'ьši*
Gsg-indef	*mol'ьšě*	*mol'ьšě*	*mol'ьšę*
Asg- indef	*mol'ьšь*	*mol'ьše*	*mol'ьšǫ*
Npl- indef	*mol'ьše*	*mol'ьšě*	*mol'ьšę*
Nsg-def	*mol'ьi*	*mol'ьšee*	*mol'ьšiě*
Gsg-def	*mol'ьšěego*	*mol'ьšěego*	*mol'ьšęę*
Asg- def	*mol'ьšii*	*mol'ьšee*	*mol'ьšǫǫ*
Npl- def	*mol'ьšei*	*mol'ьšěě*	*mol'ьšęę*

213

umě-j-, likewise zna-j-, věr-ova-, glagol-a-			
Nsg-ndef	uměvъ	uměvъ	uměvъši
Gsg-indef	uměvъšě	uměvъšě	uměvъšę
Asg- indef	uměvъšь	uměvъše	uměvъšǫ
Npl- indef	uměvъše	uměvъšě	uměvъšę
Nsg-def	uměvъi	uměvъšee	uměvъšiě
Gsg-def	uměvъšěego	uměvъšěego	uměvъšęę
Asg- def	uměvъšii	uměvъšee	uměvъšǫǫ
Npl- def	uměvъšei	uměvъšěě	uměvъšęę
bor-j-			
Nsg-ndef	bravъ	bravъ	bravъši
Gsg-indef	bravъšě	bravъšě	bravъšę
Asg- indef	bravъšь	bravъše	bravъšǫ
Npl- indef	bravъše	bravъšě	bravъšę
Nsg-def	bravъi	bravъšee	bravъšiě
Gsg-def	bravъšěego	bravъšěego	bravъšęę
Asg- def	bravъšii	bravъšee	bravъšǫǫ
Npl- def	bravъšei	bravъšěě	bravъšęę
dvig-nǫ-			
Nsg-ndef	dvigъ	dvigъ	dvigъši
Gsg-indef	dvigъšě	dvigъšě	dvigъšę
Asg- indef	dvigъšь	dvigъše	dvigъšǫ
Npl- indef	dvigъše	dvigъšě	dvigъšę
Nsg-def	dvigъi	dvigъšee	dvigъšiě
Gsg-def	dvigъšěego	dvigъšěego	dvigъšęę
Asg- def	dvigъšii	dvigъšee	dvigъšǫǫ
Npl- def	dvigъšei	dvigъšěě	dvigъšęę
ri-nǫ-			
Nsg-ndef	rinǫvъ	rinǫvъ	rinǫvъši
Gsg-indef	rinǫvъšě	rinǫvъšě	rinǫvъšę
Asg- indef	rinǫvъšь	rinǫvъše	rinǫvъšǫ
Npl- indef	rinǫvъše	rinǫvъšě	rinǫvъšę
Nsg-def	rinǫvъi	rinǫvъšee	rinǫvъšiě
Gsg-def	rinǫvъšěego	rinǫvъšěego	rinǫvъšęę
Asg- def	rinǫvъšii	rinǫvъšee	rinǫvъšǫǫ
Npl- def	rinǫvъšei	rinǫvъšěě	rinǫvъšęę

Past passive participle

	masc	neut	fem
nes-			
Nsg-indef	nesenъ	neseno	nesena
Gsg-indef	nesena	nesena	neseny
Asg-indef	nesenъ	neseno	nesenǫ
Npl-indef	neseni	nesena	neseny
Nsg-def	nesenyi	nesenoe	nesenaě
Gsg-def	nesenaego	nesenaego	nesenyę
Asg-def	nesenyi	nesenoe	nesenǫǫ̈
Npl-def	nesenii	nesenaě	nesenyę
rek-			
Nsg-indef	rečenъ	rečeno	rečena
Gsg-indef	rečena	rečena	rečeny
Asg-indef	rečenъ	rečeno	rečenǫ
Npl-indef	rečeni	rečena	rečeny
Nsg-def	rečenyi	rečenoe	rečenaě
Gsg-def	rečenaego	rečenaego	rečenyę
Asg-def	rečenyi	rečenoe	rečenǫǫ̈
Npl-def	rečenii	rečenaě	rečenyę
prosi-			
Nsg-indef	prošenъ	prošeno	prošena
Gsg-indef	prošena	prošena	prošeny
Asg-indef	prošenъ	prošeno	prošenǫ
Npl-indef	prošeni	prošena	prošeny
Nsg-def	prošenyi	prošenoe	prošenaě
Gsg-def	prošenaego	prošenaego	prošenyę
Asg-def	prošenyi	prošenoe	prošenǫǫ̈
Npl-def	prošenii	prošenaě	prošenyę
proklьn-			
Nsg-indef	proklętъ	proklęto	proklęta
Gsg-indef	proklęta	proklęta	proklęty
Asg-indef	proklętъ	proklęto	proklętǫ
Npl-indef	proklęti	proklęta	proklęty
Nsg-def	proklętyi	proklętoe	proklętaě
Gsg-def	proklętaego	proklętaego	proklętyę
Asg-def	proklętyi	proklętoe	proklętǫǫ̈
Npl-def	proklętii	proklętaě	proklętyę

dvig-nǫ-			
Nsg-indef	dviženъ	dviženo	dvižena
Gsg-indef	dvižena	dvižena	dviženy
Asg-indef	dviženъ	dviženo	dviženǫ
Npl-indef	dviženi	dvižena	dviženy
Nsg-def	dviženyi	dviženoe	dviženaě
Gsg-def	dviženaego	dviženaego	dviženyě
Asg-def	dviženyi	dviženoe	dviženǫǫ̌
Npl-def	dviženii	dviženaě	dviženyě
ri-nǫ-			
Nsg-indef	rinovenъ	rinoveno	rinovena
Gsg-indef	rinovena	rinovena	rinoveny
Asg-indef	rinovenъ	rinoveno	rinovenǫ
Npl-indef	rinoveni	rinovena	rinoveny
Nsg-def	rinovenyi	rinovenoe	rinovenaě
Gsg-def	rinovenaego	rinovenaego	rinovenyę
Asg-def	rinovenyi	rinovenoe	rinovenǫǫ̌
Npl-def	rinovenii	rinovenaě	rinovenyę

Verbal substantive

	nes-	rek-	proklьn-	moli-	prosi-
Nsg	nesenie	rečenie	proklętie	mol'enie	prošenie

	umě-j-	plak-a-	dvig-nǫ-	ri-nǫ-
Nsg	uměnie	plakanie	dviženie	rinovenie

216

ATHEMATIC VERBS

Infinitive and supine

	byti	dati	ěsti	věděti	iměti
	bytъ	datъ	ěstъ	vědětъ	imětъ

Non-past

1sg	esmь	damь	ěmь	věmь	imamь
2sg	esi	dasi	ěsi	věsi	imaši
3sg	estъ	dastъ	ěstъ	věstъ	imatъ
1du	esvě	davě	ěvě	věvě	imavě
2du	esta	dasta	ěsta	věsta	imata
3du	este	daste	ěste	věste	imate
1pl	esmъ	damъ	ěsmъ	věmъ	imamъ
2pl	este	daste	ěste	věste	imate
3pl	sǫtъ	dadętъ	ědętъ	vědętъ	imǫtъ ~ iměǫtъ

Imperative

2,3sg	bǫdi	daждь	ěждь	věждь	iměi
1du	bǫděvě	dadivě	ědivě	vědivě	iměivě
2du	bǫděta	dadita	ědita	vědita	iměita
1pl	bǫděmъ	dadimъ	ědimъ	vědimъ	iměimъ
2pl	bǫděte	dadite	ědite	vědite	iměite

Imperfect

1 sg	běaxъ	daděaxъ	ěděaxъ	věděaxъ	iměaxъ
2 sg	běaše	daděaše	ědašě	věděaše	iměaše
3 sg	běaše	daděaše	ědaše	věděaše	iměaše
1 du	běaxově	daděaxově	ědaxově	věděaxově	iměxově
2 du	běašeta	daděašeta	ědažeta	věděašeta	iměašeta
3 du	běašete	daděašete	ědašete	věděašete	iměašete
1 pl	běaxomъ	daděaxomъ	ědaxomъ	věděaxomъ	iměaxomъ
2 pl	běašete	daděašete	ědašete	věděašete	iměašete
3 pl	běaxǫ	daděaxǫ	ědaxǫ	věděaxǫ	iměaxǫ

Productive aorist

1 sg	běxъ	byxъ	daxъ	ěxъ	věděxъ	iměxъ
2 sg	bě	bystъ	dastъ	ěstъ	vědě	imě
3 sg	bě	bystъ	dastъ	ěstъ	vědě	imě
1 du	běxově	byxově	daxově	ěxově	věděxově	iměvě
2 du	běsta	bysta	dasta	ěsta	věděsta	iměsta
3 du	běste	byste	daste	ěste	věděste	iměste
1 pl	běxomъ	byxomъ	daxomъ	ěxomъ	věděxomъ	iměxomъ
2 pl	běste	byste	daste	ěste	věděste	iměste
3 pl	běsę	byšę	dašę	ěšę	věděšę	iměšę

Present active participle

N sg masc indef	sy	dady	ědy	vědy	iměę
N sg masc def	syi	dadyi	ědyi	vědyi	iměi
G sg masc indef	sǫ̌	dadǫ̌	ědǫ̌	vědǫ̌	iměǫ̌
N sg fem indef	sǫ̌i	dadǫ̌i	ědǫ̌i	vědǫ̌i	iměǫ̌i
N pl masc indef	sǫ̌e	dadǫ̌e	ědǫ̌e	vědǫ̌e	imêǫ̌e
N pl masc def	sǫ̌ei	dadǫ̌ei	ědǫ̌ei	vědǫ̌ei	iměǫ̌ei

Present passive participle

N sg masc indef	—	—	ědomъ	vědomъ	—
N sg masc def	—	—	ědomy(i)	vědomy(i)	—
G sg masc indef	—	—	ědoma	vědoma	—
N sg fem indef	—	—	ědoma	vědoma	—
N pl masc indef	—	—	ědomi	vědomi	—
N pl masc def	—	—	ědomii	vědomii	—

Past active participle

N sg masc indef	byvъ	davъ	ědъ	vědъ	iměvъ
N sg masc def	byvyi	dayы	ědyi	vědyi	iměvyi
G sg masc indef	byvъšě	davъšě	ědъšě	vědъšě	iměvъšě
N sg fem indef	byvъši	davъši	ědъši	vědъši	iměvъši
N pl masc indef	byvъše	davъše	ědъše	vědъše	iměvъše
N pl masc def	byvъšei	davъšei	ědъšei	vědъšei	iměvъšei

Perfect active participle

N sg masc	bylъ	dalъ	ělъ	vě-dělъ	imělъ
N sg neut	bylo	dalo	ělo	vědělo	imělo
N sg fem	byla	dala	ěla	věděla	iměla
N pl masc	byli	dali	ěli	věděli	iměli

Past passive participle

N sg masc indef	—	danъ	ědenъ	vědenъ	—
N sg masc def	—	dany(i)	ědeny(i)	vědeny(i)	—
G sg masc indef	—	dana	ědena	vědena	—
N sg fem indef	—	dana	ědena	vědena	—
N pl masc indef	—	dani	ědeni	vědeni	—
N pl masc def	—	danii	ědenii	vědenii	—

Verbal substantive

N sg	-bytie ~-bъvenie	danie	ědenie	vědenie	iměnie

References

See also the literature survey pp. 3–7.

Birnbaum, Henrik and Jos Schaeken. 1997. *Altkirchenslavische Studien, I. Das altkirchenslavische Wort: Bildung – Bedeutung – Herleitung.* Munich: Otto Sagner.

———. 1999. *Altkirchenslavische Studien, II. Die altkirchenslavische Schriftkultur: Geschichte – Laute und Schriftzeichen – Sprachdenkmäler (mit Textproben, Glossar und Flexionsmustern).* Munich: Otto Sagner.

Diels, Paul. 1932. *Altkirchenslavische Grammatik* (2 volumes in 1) Heidelberg: Carl Winter. (Second edition, 1963.)

Dostál, Antonín. 1954. *Studie o vidovém systému v staroslověnštině.* Prague.

Durnovo, Nikolaj S. 1929. "Mysli i predpoloženija o proisxoždenii staroslavjanskogo jazyka i slavjanskix alfavitov", *Byzantinoslavica* 1.48–85.

Meillet, Antoine. 1897. *Recherches sur l'emploi du génitif-accusatif en vieux slave* (Bibliothèque de l'École des Hautes Études publiée sous les auspices du Ministère de l'Instruction Publique. Sciences historiques et philologiques, 115). Paris.

Repp, T. 1954. "Zur Kritik der kirchenslavischen Uebersetzung des St. Emmeraner Gebets im Euchologium Sinaiticum". *Zeitschrift für slavische Philologie* 22.315–32.

Vaillant, André. 1964. *Manuel du vieux slave,* 1–2. (Collection de manuels publiée par l'Institut d'Études slaves, 6.) Paris: Institut d'Études slaves.

Vondrák, W. 1894. "Althochdeutsche Beichtformeln im Altkirchenslavischen und in den Freisinger Denkmälern". *Archiv für slavische Philologie,* 16.118–132.

SAMPLE PAGES
FROM THE MANUSCRIPTS

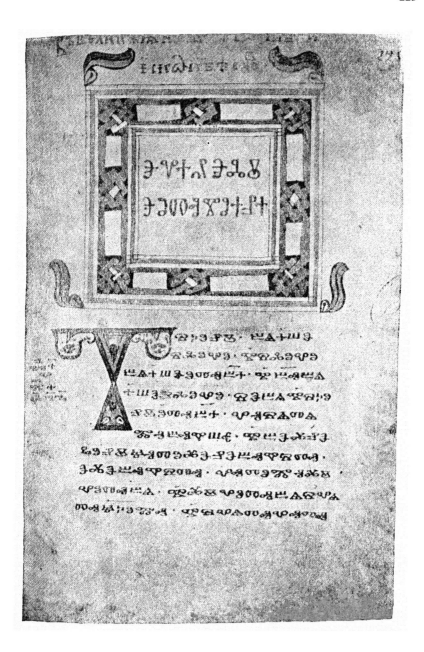

1. From the *Codex Zographensis*.

2. From the *Codex Zographensis.*

3. From the *Codex Marianus.*

4. From the *Codex Assemanianus.*

5. From the *Codex Assemanianus*.

6. From the *Glagolita Clozianus*.

7. From the *Psalterium Sinaiticum.*

8. From the *Psalterium Sinaiticum*.

9. From the *Kiev Missal.*

10. From the *Kiev Missal*

11. From the *Euchologium Sinaiticum*.

12. From the *Euchologium Sinaiticum.*

13. From the *Codex Suprasliensis.*

ВНѢ ІСАНХЪ· ПОТРЕХЪЖЕДЬНЕХЪІАВНША
ΕΑ ЕПНЕІЕІѴПОѴ ГРАДАТОГІ· НМЕНЕМЬПЕТРѴ·
ΗΚΙΕΑ ТЪСЪХРАНЕНЪІКОСТНАШАСЕѪІЬЦ
ЕТѢ· ПРНДНОѴ БОВ ЕНОШТНИІ҂НЕСННЪІН
ΖАРЕКЪІ· НПНМЪ ЕППЪ ΚΛΗΡΗΚЪІНИЦΑ
ЖАВѢРѦНЪІ· НПРНШЕДЬСТАНΑ БРѦ҂ѦРѢ
ΚЪІ· НЕЕПРЕБЪТѣ ШΑЕΑΚΙΕΤΗΕΤЪІНХЪЫ
БІДѢ· ΛΚЪІΗΕБѣТΗΛБΗΗΥΗ· ΗΑШΤΕΚΔΕΕ
ΕΤΛΒЬΗΝΑБЪІБΛΛШЕΚΟΕΤЬΕΒѢΤΕΜЪΙΑΒЬ
ΗΑШΕΑ· ΗТΑΚΟΕЪБЪ ΡΑΒЪШΕΚΟΕΤΗΕΤЪΙΗΧ·
ΜΑ ΥΕΝΗΚЪ ΠΟΛΙΖΗШΑΑΑΒЪΡΑΚΛΧЪ· ΗΕΗ
ΥΕΠΕΤΡΑДΑΒЪШΕБѢΝЪΥΛΗΗѢΙШΑ· ΗΕΗ
ΜΙЖТЪ ΗΑΚΙΗ҂Бѣ ΖΑЪΙБЬБЬΕΕΜЬΜΛΗΡѢ·
ЕІГІѴБѢРΟΒΛΒЪШΕ ΧΕΑΗΕΠΟΚѢΔΑΒЪШΕ·
ΕΤΛΛΓΟДΥΛΗ ΕΟΤЪБΟΡѢΓЪШΕΑ· ΠΡΟΕΛΑΒЪШΕ
ΗΗЪΙΒЪΙШΕΟΥѢ· ΠΑΛΑТЪБѢЖΗ ΤΗΗΕΕΜΖ
ΟΕΤΛΒΗШΑ· ΝΑΕЪΠΛΕΕΗΗΗΒΕΕѢΜЪБѢРΙѴΙΑ
ШТΗΙΜЪ· БЪΟΥЧΗΕΝЪΗΕΤЪΙΗΔΧЪ ѢТΗΧΕ
ΕЪΙШΑΕΤΗΗΜΑΥΕΝΗΥΗΝΑΜΑΥΕΗΗΕΟΥѢ·
ΠΡѢЖΔΕΥΕΤЪΙΡЖΑΛΛΝΔЪΜΑΡΤΑ· ΕΗΡѢΥΙ
БѢΚΕΟΦΕΥΡΙΑΡΑ· ΠΡѢΔΑШΑЖΕΕЪΙΑΔΙѴШΑ
ΓΙΕΠΟДΕΚΗ· ΠΡѢЖΑΙѴΔΛΝΕΑΙΑΡΤΑ·Α ΠΟΗΛΗ
ΚΗΝЬΗΕΑΜΟБΛΑΕΤѢΗΗ ΝΑΛΙΚΕΥΕΕΑ ΡΕΕΤΒѢ
ΗΑШΤΟΥΓΙѴΝΑШΕΜΟΥ ΗΕѴΥΗΕΠΟΥ Η БΛΑ
ДЪΙΥѢ ΝΑШΕΜΟΥ ІС ΧΕΟΥ· ΗΑΙΥΥЖΕΕ ТЪΕΛΑ
БДΗДΡѢХΑБΛΗΥ ΕΕΤѢ· ΝΕΕΝѢ ΗΠΡΗΕΝΟΗΒΕ
БѢΚЪΙБѢΚΟΜЪ· ΛΜΗΝ҂

ΕΤЪΛΓΙБΕΝΛѢΛΥΧΗΕΠΡΑΚΕΕΑΡΗΑΚΑΠΛΔΟΚΑΗΙΕΚΙΑ

14. From the *Codex Suprasliensis.*

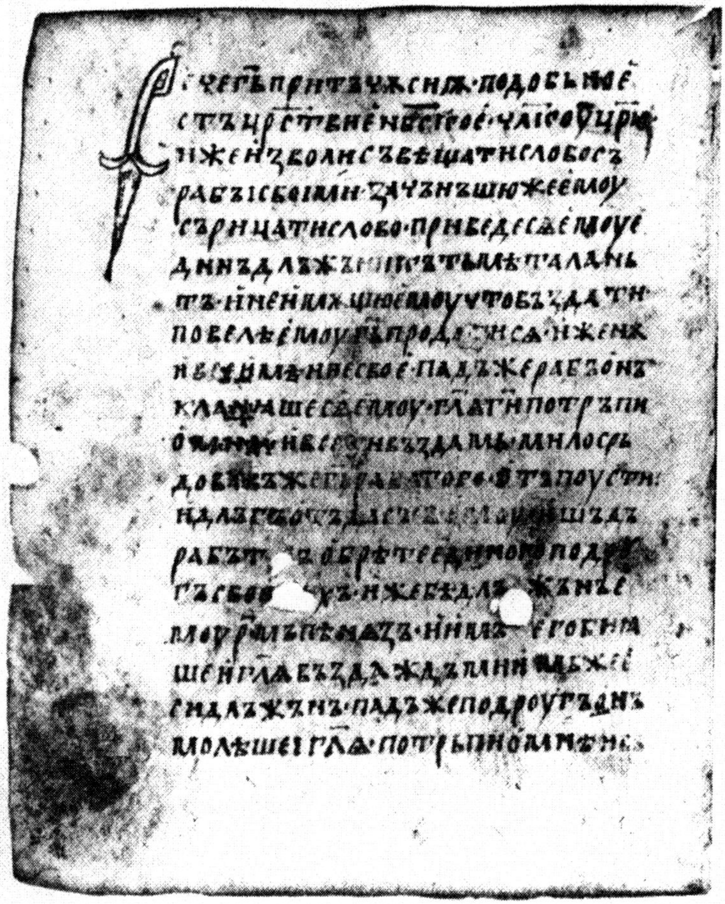

15. From the *Sava Gospel.*

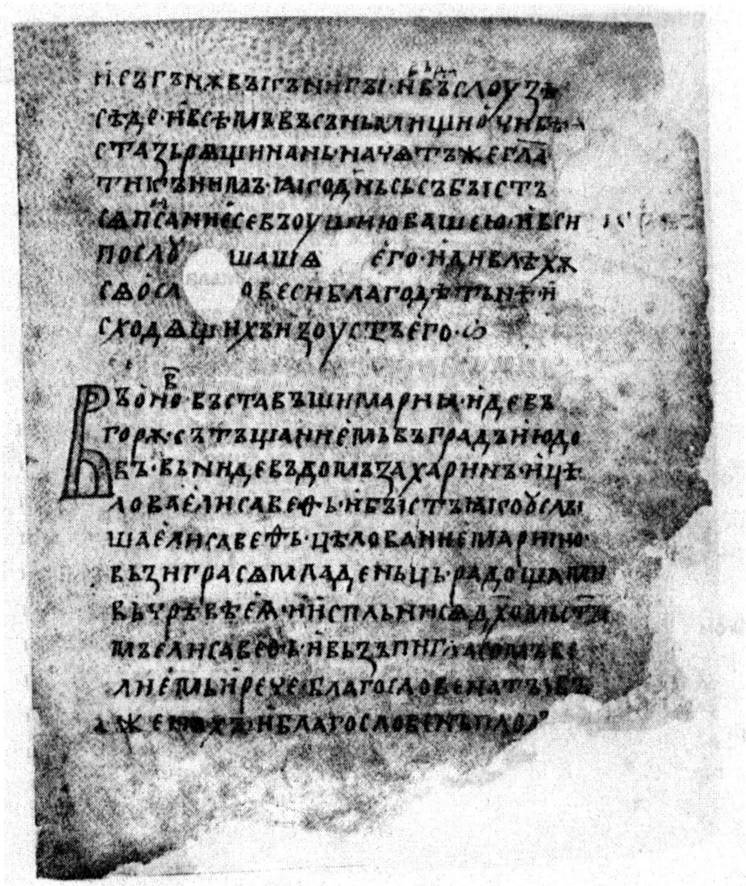

16. From the *Sava Gospel*.

ERRATA

Page	line	For	read:
12	18	N	N
19	25	sьe	sьже
	29	tųe	tuже
	36	kъdo	kъžьdo
22	5	-ml	-mь
86	2	Vs ẽM	VsẽM
92	6	milostъ	milostъ
	7	neposram^len	neposram^lenь
97	10	повелѣ	повелѣ
120	29	yz	из
129	29	aßte	аште
139	2	отлѭ унвъ	отлѭунвъ
191	13	V^B	V^F
201	10	dobra	dobrě
202	13	dobrii	dobrač
	16	dobryę	dobraě
	21	niʍego 2x	niʍěego
	22	niʍemu 2x	niʍüemu
	32	niʍě	niʍěě
203	28	vaša	vašě
204	last	nas	nasь
205	15	mьn´ǫ	mьńǫ
206	14	klьnětě	klьněvě
209	24	nesoma	nesomi
	29	prosima	prosimi
	33	nazyvaema	nazyvaemi
210	23	brae	bra
211	2	rinǫxǫ	rinǫxь
216	21-28	ědaše, ědaxově, ědašeta ědašete, edaxomъ, ědaxǫ	ěděaše, ěděaxově, ěděašeta ěděašete, eděaxomъ, ěděaxǫ
	23	iměxově	imčaxově
217	10	běsę	běšę
	13	iměi	imčęi
	14	dadʍě	dadǫʍě
	16	imêǫʍe	iměǫʍe
	27	dayьi	davyi

R